AERATE

AERATE

TIFFANY M FORSYTH

CONTENTS

MAGICIANS

Vincent sat up. His neck hurt, again. He rolled his head from side to side and turned to look down at his pillow. Flat, again. Vincent vigorously grabbed both sides, squeezing and fluffing until the middle plumped. He eyed the pillow, groaned, and plopped his head down. He didn't like this pillow she made, and the gray feathers inside didn't like him. Often after fluffing attempts, the feathers had faux fainting spells and flattened out just as his head landed. Or they would bunch up and crawl like caterpillars to the sides and corners of the pillowcase. Vincent would feel them moving underneath. When he sat up to confront the feathers, they would rapidly move to the center, fluff themselves up, and freeze. The pillow would remain spitefully still under his scrutiny. On rare occasions, he would fall asleep before they had fully migrated, but he always woke up with an aching, unsupported neck. Vincent had tried to show this trickery to her, and a handful of times they had studied the suddenly welcoming and unmoving pillow together.

Smiling inside, Sylvia would have been instructing the feathers and thanking them with her eyes. After a bit of observation, she would speak to Vincent with faux sympathy, and say, "Dear, perhaps you are imagining things?" or "Maybe it was a dream?" When she turned to leave, the feathers would crawl wildly in all directions.

"Sylvia!" he shrieked.

But she never looked back, her delighted eyes whispering.

He punched the pillow, but the feathers darted out of the way. She closed the door while he stayed in there, wrestling with himself and calling out her name.

"Sylvia!"

The pillow problem had begun one night a couple months before when Vincent decided he needed to go to bed early. He wanted some reprieve from Sylvia's frivolous, nonstop chatter and interrupted her "whiny monologue," as he called it, to suggest she grab her big bowl and go on an adventure. She knew this cue for silence and squinted at him, twitched her nose, and tried not to let her feelings get hurt.

"Fine!" she huffed.

Her giant blue bowl flew off a shelf in the kitchen, right past Vincent's head and into her arms. A sack from the cupboard unfurled, and a string of kernels poured out into the air and floated in a line to her. She didn't break eye contact with Vincent as the kernels suspended themselves above her bowl and systematically dropped into it.

He knew better than to look away because her movements were often dependent on her mood, and although he couldn't tell the degree of her anger, he knew this slow kernel drop was meant to piss him off and hold him captive. As Sylvia summoned each kernel to pop, Vincent's eyes began burning. Sylvia showed off her ability to conduct it all while her eyes remained upon him. Deeply jealous, his own eyes wandered.

Vincent snapped his fingers behind his back, and a bottle of eyedrops from the nearby bathroom scooted off the sink and tumbled across the room. "Up!" he commanded, and the eyedrops hovered near his face and squirted a few drops in each eye while his other eye remained on Sylvia. Relieved, he narrowed his revitalized gaze in an act of intimidation, and yellow and blue butterflies fluttered in his gut at this unexpected and exciting competition. Sylvia blinked at him and shook her head in boredom.

"I'm going to watch!" she yelled, which was her declaration before any television bender. Sylvia saluted Vincent as though embarking on a brave sacrifice and stomped past him to the living room.

And when she had withdrawn, his butterflies folded in defeat. *I was the one who wanted space—why did she leave?*

Although infrequent, when Sylvia binged on TV, it was for seven or eight hours at a time. She watched only the Travel or Discovery channels or escaped into documentaries. She lived vicariously through Anthony Bourdain and Steve Irwin, and when they'd passed, she'd handed the remotes to Vincent and wept and moaned for weeks. Although Vincent saw her grief as melodramatic and told her as much, a hidden sadness filled his heart. Vincent had long envied her admiration for those men; they sought exploration, learning, and growth, and he remained homebound, stagnant, and shrinking. But now he missed them for her too.

When she'd triumphantly asked for the clickers back two months after Bourdain died, he'd handed them back to her, not showing his happiness. She resumed her binging, and a few years passed without the remotes being in his possession. That is until that regretful night he left her square in front of the television with her big blue bowl, entranced by an investigative documentary on commercial animal abuse.

He now remembered glancing at the screen as he went up the stairs and, upon seeing some happy geese flying in the cool morning air, determined it to be just another show on wildlife and looked away. As Vincent drifted off to sleep, he thought about his last assistant and her red rose lips. He ached to cut her in half one more time. He ached to see her mouth open in horror as beautiful confusion spread across her radiant and youthful face. He ached to hear the audience gasp, gaping at him in wonder as he spun the boxes before their astonished eyes. Stunned, the red-lipped assistant also gazed at him in wonder.

His previous assistant, the one before the red-lipped lady, the one with the purple lipstick, had always stolen the show. At first, the crowd's attraction to her charm didn't upset him, and at times he even thought it endearing because he loved her too. But soon the deafening sound of their applause for her rang in his ears, keeping him up at night and torturing him even more than his current pillow predicament. She tried not to react when she saw his lips curled into a grimace and his eyebrows furrowed. Sylvia, cloaked in purple, would smile and lift his hand high into the air to the cheers of the crowd.

"Let's share this! They love us," her eyes pleaded.

"They love *you*," he shot back, gripping her hand tightly.

Although *his* name blinked in neon, *his* hand held the saw, and *his* magic separated her body into eight boxes across the stage, Sylvia only had to smile, and everyone knew she was the star.

Vincent realized he needed to do the only thing that would get her off his stage, and so he got her pregnant. Before he knew it, her bright purple smile stemmed from this new status. Doctors had advised her to stop performing completely. Although painful, she'd nodded in tender understanding at the news. Vincent shook his head and put on a torn and despondent face.

He mumbled about safety being most important, while his insides fluttered with cheer and hope.

Vincent had never thought of having kids. It wasn't so much that he was firmly against it, but more that he'd never considered the possibility that one day he might need to prioritize someone over himself. But Sylvia's palpable excitement as she banged a wobbly shopping cart around Target, her gushing and squealing over baby clothes, her happily gazing at him, were all growing on Vincent.

Oftentimes during shopping trips, other beautiful, younger moms-to-be with perfect skin looked Sylvia up and down. When they heard her giggles in the baby section, their unstrained eyes focused on her gray roots and the dimples and lines on her face. Once, a pregnant woman shot her a nasty look and tsk-tsked in disgust. Sylvia smiled back and said, "Isn't this exciting?!" but her eyes flashed, *Go fuck yourself!* Vincent knew that if this stranger didn't have a baby on the way, Sylvia would have cursed her with an eleven-hour migraine.

When Sylvia's ultrasound detected twins, her joyous shrieks hurt his ears. While his heart also raced at the news, he maintained a cool, indifferent demeanor, trying to ensure she would focus solely on herself and not acquire a new audience. But months later ... everything changed, and Vincent wished he had just asked her to step down and stop smiling, to step out of his limelight and off his stage.

⤳

The rapid stomping up the stairs woke him, and Vincent struggled to hold on to his sleep. Sylvia's mind swung the door open, and she pounced on top of Vincent. She yelled his name once before ripping the pillows out from underneath him. His head fell on the mattress.

"What in the—" But she cut him off.

"Oh, Vincent! These pillows have blood on them! Do you know how these pillows were probably made? Do you? Do you? Do you know what is done to those poor geese and ducks to make these pillows? Oh my goodness! It's awful! I'm so guilty! Blood is on our hands, our heads, our pillows! How could I have been so stupid?!"

Vincent didn't move; he simply watched her. *Sylvia has totally lost it.* He tried to tune her out, but she had begun an animated performance of plucking at herself, pulling on her abdomen and neck. She yelped and howled and cried in pain like a wounded and tortured goose and clung to the blood pillows for comfort. Vincent wanted to laugh but didn't dare; instead, he snapped his fingers, and three sets of chatter teeth began chuckling and chattering on his desk in the office downstairs. He sighed in relief and sat up fully to study her. *She has a lot of energy for sixty-five but never spends it on me.* He waited for her to pause and asked, "Is this about Anthony?"

"No!" She hit him as hard as she could across the face with a pillow, but upon seeing his eyes she realized her error and quickly hugged the pillow. "Oh no, I'm just like a plucker! I'm hurting the down and feathers of those beautiful birds."

"Good grief, Sylvia. No, you aren't. These feathers can't feel anything." He reached his hand out to pat her shoulder as she continued weeping.

"Yes, they can." She looked up at Vincent with her red, tired eyes.

He shook his head while hers fell back down into the pillow. *How you exhaust me, Sylvia.*

"Poor birds," she groaned.

"Oh, Sylvia!" He patted her back again. "I think they would be categorized as waterfowl."

She cried louder.

That night she removed every single pillow from their house. Vincent didn't get up once to help her; instead, he stayed in bed, curious and waiting for his pillow replacement. He watched her fluster about in their bedroom and listened as she stomped down the stairs and rummaged around the living room collecting pillows. He heard her in the kitchen banging around to get out trash bags and heard the back door slam. Beaming, she triumphantly tossed the pillows into the garbage and smiled as she pushed and shoved them down. She dusted off her hands. *I'm blood free.*

Sylvia stomped upstairs to their bedroom, and while she half-hoped Vincent would say something sweet, she knew him and knew better.

"Well?"

Sylvia ignored him—didn't even look at him—but knew his elbows hurt from posturing. She walked to the bathroom.

"Is this about that stupid bird documentary?"

"Don't you mean *waterfowl*, Vincent!" she yelled as a neat stack of towels unfolded and flew towards him. The first one landed on his head and wrapped around his thinning dyed black hair.

"Sylvia, stop!" Vincent screamed, as the towel spun faster, messing up his perfect comb-over and gel application. He caught the others midair with his mind, and they folded up underneath his head. When Vincent finally pulled the towel off him, he knew the combination of the towel swirling and heavy gel had left his crunchy hair sticking out in all directions. He laughed and looked around for her, but she had shut the bathroom door. He wished she would have laughed or at least smiled, but he knew her and knew better.

The towels weren't as uncomfortable as he thought they would be, though once he allowed himself to think about his old, wondrous pillows, his lip twitched. He tried multiple times to fluff them, but every time they fell flat instantly. *Sylvia created this problem, and she needs to take care of it tomorrow.* That thought repeated itself in his mind, and soon he was asleep.

In the morning, Vincent restacked his towels and turned on his side to face her. She had slept undisturbed on her back, but his rustling had woken her wild head of graying brown curls. *Why doesn't she ever move while she sleeps?* He copied his wife's position and sighed. He thought about his saw, *that* ruby red smile, and the betrayal. Did she only like him because she understood he had *true* powers? Would she have even looked at him if he worked in retail, or at a bank? Would she have smiled at him if he wasn't magical? Why did she vanish? Why did she go to Vegas? What's so great about *his* residency? Who cares that he made a casino disappear?! Was *any* of it real?

About seven feet from their bed, the burgundy cloak of curtain wiggled, wrinkled, and pulled itself back a bit. Eager light poured in, and Vincent blinked and rubbed his eyes. He turned on his side as the curtain drew itself back five more inches. Light shone on Sylvia's face, and he looked at her pale skin and her faint pink mouth. The corners of her eyes fanned out into symmetrical crow's feet, with too many toes for his liking. He saw her nose twitch and groaned. It was a habit of hers, or it was a tick. "Sneeze or stop doing that!" he had often yelled at her, to which she always responded, "I can't help it!" One time he told her, "You are no Samantha, you couldn't bewitch anyone!" He knew he had gone too far, but her retort stung just as much. "I'm not trying to bewitch you, Vincent, and I'm not trying to be someone I'm not. That's your magic."

Vincent rolled on his back and reached up to fluff the towels beneath him. As he brought his arms back down, he held his hands in the air and studied them. He hated his wide, silver nails, and hated how his fingertips looked like small moons. He hated his long, delicate fingers and his giant, sloping knuckles.

He needed more bones in his hands and had wished his whole life he could bulk them up to be more masculine. While on stage, Vincent always moved his arms around rapidly. On Sylvia's first day as his assistant, she saw he shared her secret and thought his frantic movements were an attempt to hide his true identity as a wizard. But he was only trying to distract from his soft hands.

Vincent had tried doing hand-strengthening exercises in private, but one day Sylvia came home early and walked in on him sitting in their shared office watching a YouTube video. He was squeezing small orange balls and softly singing a made-up song, "I'm the man with the strong sleight of hand." He stopped and dropped the balls. Sylvia looked at him, looked at the screen, looked back at him, and walked away without saying a word. Vincent flushed in humiliation, and as soon as she was out of sight, he picked the balls up, threw them in the air, and lit them on fire. A few days later, he found them restored in his dresser with a note that said, "Exercise is important." But they hadn't moved since.

After giving up on the strength training, Vincent wondered if outdoorsy hands might give him the rugged manly look he desired. He tried to go a whole afternoon without washing his hands and even bravely went outside and plunged them into Sylvia's pots of soil and plants. This attempt at tough and dirty only lasted a few minutes. Once he went back inside, the dirt under his fingernails prevented him from being able to touch or do anything. He scrubbed his hands until they were red, looked at his orblike fingertips, and tried not to think about it. *At least now I can open the mail without issue.*

A motion distracted him, and he looked at her head. Her hair had risen in the air, separating itself into strands that began intertwining, forming her usual hairstyle, a big loose bun with braids through it. Sylvia's thinning hair moved slowly; the aging gray strands paced themselves as they moved through their job of creating a facade of fullness. *How many times have I witnessed these movements?* As the process became complete, Sylvia's eyelashes fluttered like butterflies. Her hazel eyes opened, and she looked at Vincent without a hint of emotion. She let out a deep sigh, rolled her eyes closed, and turned over to face the other direction.

"What's the matter, Sylvia—expecting someone else?"

"No, Vincent, but a girl can dream."

"You are an old, old lady, Sylvia, not a girl!" His mind moved the covers back, and he got out of bed. If she had been facing him or if he had been looking, he would have seen her tears.

"My neck hurts. I can't sleep. You need to fix this today!" he yelled on his way to the bathroom.

"Vincent, maybe the problem isn't with your neck but with your spine?" she sniffled. But the bathroom door had closed, and her words slammed against it and tumbled down onto the carpet.

At breakfast, Vincent struggled with his daily routine of reading the newspaper. He couldn't ignore his continued frustration at the pillow situation. Sylvia stood at her blender, her purple dress swaying back and forth as she poured in frozen fruit, spinach, green powders, and proteins, and arranged her daily routine of vitamins and supplements. She picked up a wooden muddler and began smashing huge chunks of straw-berries. The pounding startled Vincent, and even though she made this noise every day, his lip started twitching.

"Sylvia! Can you please shut up?"

Sylvia stopped, muddler midair, and looked at him with pained confusion.

"Eating green won't make you green," he huffed and snapped the newspaper page and held it up in front of his face. Sylvia squinted at it, and the letters and pictures slid off the pages and into his coffee.

"Damn it, Sylvia!" Vincent scowled as the hot liquid splashed everywhere.

He blotted his shirt with a napkin and stared at his cup until the words rose in strings and shuffled back onto the pages. She smiled at him and turned the blender on. Vincent watched the images of people, buildings, and war wring themselves out and reorganize on the pages while the machine churned loudly in the background.

"You need to grow up, Sylvia!" he yelled as she turned the blender off.

"Alright, Vincent." She poured the green smoothie into a giant glass. "When I act like a serious, mature adult, you tell me I'm no fun. Do you want me to be seventy or seventeen?"

"Neither. I don't want you at all, Sylvia."

"Then why am I here?"

"Good question." He took a sip of his coffee.

"There is no need to hate me for being better than you, Vincent."

His lip quivered. Her piece of toast, her single breakfast indulgence, hung briefly in the air and fell back to her plate, singed black.

"Vincent, dear, I hate you so much!"

"Oh, that's okay. I hate you too, Sylvia!"

"Oh no, Vincent, I completely forgot. Your vitamins!" The cupboard opened, and Sylvia pulled a handful of bottles down. The lids unscrewed, the protective films pulled themselves back, and pills from each bottle assembled themselves in a tiny bowl that floated over to Vincent.

"I only like gummies," he whined. "I gag on these. You know this."

"I know, Vincent. You despise the chewables and gag on the ones you need to swallow."

"I want the gummies."

"We ran out of the gummies, and there is something strange about a squishy vitamin. I don't trust them. Please just try these."

"What was this one for again?" He pointed his silver nail at a wide pill in disgust.

"Some are multivitamins. Others are vitamins A, B, C, D, E, calcium, CoQ10, magnesium—"

"This is too many."

Sylvia walked over to him and separated the pills into a large and small pile.

"Can you try the ones on the left, Vincent? Please?" She motioned to the small pile.

Vincent looked at her and sighed, picked up some of the pills, and put them in his mouth. He reached for his orange juice and took a gulp but struggled to swallow. His cheeks filled with backed-up orange juice and pills. Panicking, he shook his head at her and spit it everywhere. Vincent wheezed and coughed like he had just been pulled from a turbulent current and barely survived.

"Wow, you are so theatrical!" She picked up the remaining wet pills and walked away from him.

"Is that why you let us run out of gummies? Because you want me to gag?" he yelled between coughs.

"Of course not, Vincent. I don't want you to gag. I want you to choke."

"You know what, Sylvia? You are squishy, and I don't trust you."

"I do hope you choke, Vincent."

"You're just old, and old-fashioned. Gummies are for the new, young, hip generation." He took a big gulp of orange juice and smiled. "You wouldn't know anything about it."

"I hate you, Vincent." She squeezed the vitamins so hard they crumbled, and she let the pieces fall to the floor. "Say, maybe you can pick up gummies next time you buy your hair products."

"I hate you, Sylvia! I don't dye my hair!" He took his last sip of juice and put the cup down.

Silence.

"Sylvia? Sylvia?"

Vincent heard shuffling by the front door and hurried over to see her putting on a coat and shoes.

"Wait, where are you going?"

"I'm getting you pillows, Vincent. I'm solving your problems."

"It's cold outside, Sylvia. Will you be warm enough?"

"Bye, Vincent!" she said as she slammed the door.

Hours later, she came home from the outlet mall with bags on each arm, and over the next few days, Vincent tried every alternative to a down pillow available. But he had to have down—polyester, memory foam, faux down, even cotton didn't work. Polyester felt irritating on his skin, memory foam felt like quicksand (and sinking was his greatest fear), faux down got chunky like clouds huddled together, and cotton never kept its form.

"Sylvia! You need to fix this!" he screamed, throwing his lumpy pillows across their bedroom, but she had already started down the stairs and didn't respond.

Vincent threw the covers back, stomped to the bathroom, and stood in front of the mirror. He leaned in and examined his smooth skin. Vincent didn't have lines, wrinkles, or any sign of aging, and this bothered him greatly because his hair had been turning gray for quite some time, but his face still looked like a very, very young man's. He pined for a strong, distinguished, and weathered look, but instead he looked like a strange baby with gray hair, so he had been secretly dyeing it while he waited for his skin to catch up. For a few minutes, he made faces—smiling and furrowing his brow—actions he thought might bring some wrinkles or imprints and make him look like he had truly lived.

Downstairs, Sylvia was spreading her body out across the dining room—her legs on the floor, her arms on the chairs, her smiling head, of course, floating above the head of the table, and her torso right below it. When Vincent finally made it down, he trotted right past Sylvia's display and didn't acknowledge her reminiscent act at all. Enraged, Sylvia threw one of her legs out to trip him. Her slipper caught him right on the shin, and he tumbled down to the ground.

"Really," he sighed, standing up. "Is this what we have come to?"

"I know how you loved to saw *her* apart!"

"Sylvia, if you want me to cut you, I'll cut you!"

"You have always had a weak blade—I doubt I would feel it," her head snapped.

"You know what, Sylvia," Vincent calmly pulled out a chair, lifted her arm up, put it on the table and sat down, "I realized that two magicians can only live together if they no longer care about each other, each other's secrets. And I don't want to know how you do your magic."

Sylvia's eyes welled with tears, and she couldn't bear to look at him, so she lowered her gaze to the table. "Vincent, when I'm with you, I feel totally alone. This solitude isn't a gift. This ability to be alone above all else, well, it's a curse."

"Hmmm … interesting, Sylvia. Your curses are only mildly uncomfortable."

"I don't know who you are, but you are not who you used to be," she sobbed before spinning her head around to hide. He looked down at her other arm in the chair right next to him, then picked it up. Vincent waved it at her turned-away head.

Nothing.

"Sylvia, I'm going to go get something to eat." He put her arm down next to her torso.

"Loving you has left me in pieces!" she cried out as he walked away.

"Oh, Sylvia." The words brought a halt to his steps, but he didn't look back.

"Shut up, Vincent!" Her head spun around. "You are an irrelevant wizard, and your magic is meaningless!"

Silence.

Sylvia summoned her torso to sit up, called her legs to reconnect, and her arms picked up her head and put it back on her shoulders.

"Fine!" she huffed and scanned for something to distract herself and instantly remembered her cards. Sylvia floated through the living room and passed Vincent in the kitchen before turning the corner to enter the office. She sat down at her purple round table and picked up her stack of homemade tarot cards and began happily shuffling. On the wall above her, the neon light that read "See Your Future with Sylvia" lit up.

Maybe this will be it. Maybe I'll be a famous fortune teller. I'll be a star!

"Welcome! My name is Sylvia. Are you ready to see your future?" She smiled, nodding at her imaginary audience, before going on to explain the card-reading process in elaborate detail.

In the kitchen, Vincent started some hot cereal but promptly forgot about it on the stove while he was rummaging through the cupboards for his vitamins. All the bottles looked the same, and he struggled to read the fine print. His cereal bubbled over and burned. "Sylvia!"

Silence.

Vincent dumped the burning pot in the sink and closed his eyes. In the other room, Sylvia had laid out her card spread, but as she opened her mouth, the tiny creatures on her cards stood up and started running around her table. Angelic and dreamy figures covered in leaves wandered around aimlessly—miniature lions roared in horror at their small stature, snakes hissed at their short length, the hermit hobbled around looking for a place to hide, the cups triumphantly clanked together but dropped like thimbles, the swords fell like toothpicks, and the sun stayed dim.

"You aren't a fortune teller; you are a fool," Vincent said, smiling from the doorway.

"Is this about your hand exercises?" Sylvia looked at Vincent and laid her palm open on the table, and a lion walked onto it. She closed her fingers like a perfect cage and flexed to hold the position. The lion paced and slammed itself against her hand, but she held tight. Vincent's lip twitched, and his venomous gaze hurt them both. She opened her hand, and the lion ran off.

"Vincent, the elephant isn't in the room—the elephant is here." Sylvia unbuttoned her shirt, and Vincent saw a beautiful, tiny gray elephant running across the deep red sand of her heart. "Now tell me please: Am I in second or in very last place in your mind?"

"I don't care about your creatures, Sylvia." But seeing the elephant pained him. He had always wanted one, but she had refused to show him how it was made. Sylvia grabbed her snakes. She threw them at Vincent, but they veered right when they saw his white rabbits sitting in a giant crate on the counter. They dove inside and wrapped around the rabbits' necks, and the rabbits jumped around and cried in panic.

"Release the rabbits!" Sylvia cried out, but the snakes still held on and tightened their grasp. "Vincent! Do something!"

"Release! Release! Release!" Vincent commanded. The snakes fell to the ground and slithered away.

"Sylvia! Do something!" Vincent pointed an orb finger towards his limp rabbits and covered his face to hide his sobs.

Sylvia dashed to the crate. It popped open, and she brought them to her chest.

"Can you save them?" he cried.

"Shhhhh." She nodded and closed her eyes and began singing and swaying and petting them.

Minutes passed, and Vincent peeked between his fingers.

Sylvia's eyes remained closed. "It's okay. They are going to be alright." She lifted her hands a bit to show Vincent that his two beloved rabbits were alert and happy. She lowered them into the crate, latched the door, and took a moment to spread a drop of blood from her finger, painting her lips red.

Sylvia turned around, and upon seeing her red mouth, a tender, pitiful pain clawed at Vincent's heart.

"This is your fault, Vincent! You interrupted my magic, my tarot practice!"

"That wasn't magic; that was just a monologue, Sylvia," he sneered and began levitating to prevent her from looking in his eyes and seeing his confusion and pain. She stomped towards him, grabbed his legs, and quickly pulled him down. He landed with a thud.

"Wow, that was easier than I thought it would be! Hmph! See you later, Vincent."

"Wait, where are you going?" He scrambled to his feet to follow her out.

"Getting feathers! Making sure you sleep. What are you doing?" As she got to the front door, she grabbed her tall, pointy black hat off the top of the coat rack.

"Sylvia, you look like a witch!"

"At least I look like something!" She pulled her hat down and reached for her coat and mittens.

"Your ethical treatment of animals has gone too far!"

"Where's my tote?"

"In this cupboard. I moved the totes so you would have more room, and here is your favorite."

"Thank you!"

"Your coat is too thin, and it's still cold. How are you going to be able to do anything with those floppy mittens?" He motioned with his arms like his hands were helpless hand puppets.

"Well, I'll take them off then." She paused and waited for the floaties in her vision to pass. "I don't mind if my hands get exposed to the elements."

"Just go. Take all the time you need," Vincent shooed her away.

"I will. It's nice when things take time," she smirked. She opened the door and slammed it shut.

Sylvia spent the day at the park with a lake asking ducks and geese for their feathers so she could make him pillows. Her strategy involved sitting on a bench, and when they trotted by, she approached and pleaded her case. Often, they rolled their eyes at the strange lady asking for feathers and instructed their friends and family members to keep walking. But others felt bad for her and donated immediately and let her place her hands near their bodies so that when they shook the downy feathers off, she caught them before they touched the ground and gently placed them in her sack. When she had been gone for five hours, Vincent began peeking through the blinds every five minutes. He wrung his hands and ran his fingertips over his smooth knuckles but then remembered her words and dropped his hands to his sides. Finally, he spotted her a couple blocks away, so he grabbed a book and dove for his recliner. But minutes passed with no sign of Sylvia.

About a block away from home, an idea came to her, so she paused and opened the bag. She lowered her head above the opening and took in the soft, wild smell before whispering to the feathers and breaking out in giggles. Impatient, Vincent rose from his chair and peered out the window. He saw Sylvia at the end of the street, her head hovering over her bag. She looked like she was talking, but then she looked up and directly at the house, so he dove back to his chair. Sylvia opened the door and put her bag down to take off her coat.

"I thought you got lost, or did you not see feathers in your future?" he smirked.

"Your book is upside down, Vincent," she scoffed without looking at him and hung up her hat.

He threw his book at her, but she stopped it midair. He scanned her beloved bookshelves and sent her books tumbling down, knowing that crumpled or bent pages drove her crazy. As items fell, he was careful that her collection of multicolored glass orbs landed gently, and the urns holding their premature twins' ashes remained perfectly safe on the shelf. Sylvia opened her sack, and hundreds of feathers descended on Vincent as she frantically picked up her books.

At first, he laughed at her silly feather attack, but soon they were poking in his eyes, ears, and mouth. They stuck to his skin and clothes, and when he pulled them off, they came back with even more aggression and force.

"Sylvia! Do something!" His irritated skin reddened as he became covered in feathers.

"I'm trying, Vincent. They just don't like you!" She murmured a spell, but they didn't let go.

"Try harder!" He fell back in his chair and curled up like a baby to try and block them.

"I can't!"

"Sylvia!" he whined in tears. "These feathers are dirty! Help me!"

"Come on, Vincent, let's get you in the shower!"

She grabbed his hand lovingly and rushed him to the bathroom. She lifted his sweater, and a flurry of feathers came out. But for some reason he had another thick sweater underneath. As she reached for it, he yelped in defeat. Once this sweater was pulled up, her eyes widened. Shoulder pads drifted to the floor alongside the feathers. Only his undershirt remained, and she fumbled with it as she saw how frail he had become.

"Oh, Vincent!"

"Don't!" he yelled, completely nude. All of his feathers had been plucked.

She pulled the faucet handle, and he hobbled underneath the water as feathers slowly began to slough off his body. Hair dye ran down his neck, and he turned away from her.

"Please," he begged. She nodded and summoned a white steam to fill up the room. Sylvia bent down to pick up a single feather and held it softly in her fingertips.

"Sylvia," he mumbled under the pounding water.

"Yes, Vincent?" she whispered back, examining the fine details.

"Your magic is better than mine, but you were always better than me. You are the star."

"I know, Vincent," she whispered so quietly that only she could hear.

Sylvia blew the gray feather into the air and watched it slowly fall to the tile.

EXECUTIONER

The prisoner smashed his left hand against the wall, and the raw stone tore at his knuckles. As blood rushed to the surface, he tenderly studied his hand one last time. *How much they have touched, how much they haven't touched.* He put his hands behind his back and paced the cold, damp floor of his tiny cell. He sensed handprints and knew that scent of fecal matter suspended in the air. The prisoner shivered and pulled his shoulders up. Patches of cloth and strands of brown string hung on him. *I would give more than my life to be held one last time.*

The food slot in the door groaned, and a pewter tray flew inside, clanking and rattling across the floor. A gray watery mush splattered and hit the prisoner's feet, and a piece of bread ravaged by mold rolled nearby. His thirst and hunger had become unbearable, but he could not bring his peeling lips to the spilled gruel. His heart smashed against his ribcage, and he placed his hands on his chest. The prisoner bent down to study the slight outline of his deer, which had faded in the life-eroding air. He had collected dirt from the corners, scooped it up and spat on it as much as he could, and with his fingertips, spread the thin mixture across the wall in the shape of the creature.

"Be my protector and I'll always remember you," he whispered to the visionless deer.

Near death, he rose, stepped to the window, and wrapped his hands gently around the bars. The prisoner tightened his grip and looked out on the pale blue sky. He had so often ached to see a real bird. Tears fell down his face.

"God, show me grace. Show me, God."

Somewhere, a church bell rang out. The prisoner closed his eyes and listened to the bell. He uttered a petitionary prayer but knew he would not be spared. Today would be the day he died. He ran his hands over his shaved head and wiped his burning eyelids. He scanned the room in desperation. He fell to the floor, screaming, crying, and frantically pounding at the floor.

"No, stop, stop!" he commanded himself.

The prisoner remembered the church bell, and his dignity returned. He stood up, put his hands on his heart, and held still, waiting for the next ringing of the bell.

"I'm going to keep this time for all time. This is mine."

He faintly smiled. A moment passed. Then the iron door creaked.

"It's happening."

He looked to the open doorway. A towering man leered as he walked in, and the prisoner turned to face his executioner. He seemed triple the width of the prisoner, with dark leather bands around his waist and draped over his broad shoulders. His rust-colored shirt billowed over his body, but the prisoner sensed the soldierly form beneath. The executioner's tanned temples and neck were wet with perspiration, his cheekbones held tight, and his wavy black hair curled at the ends.

The prisoner's breath quickened, and without thinking, he leapt and flung himself upon the executioner, pounding his frail arms on the giant chest before him, a move that would have cost him his life if he hadn't already been dead. Blood from the prisoner's wounded hands smeared on the executioner's neck and arms, and when he saw his own blood, he cowered and covered his face.

The executioner did not speak but glanced down at the blood on his body. He grabbed the prisoner by the wrists and shook him. The prisoner looked up to beg for it to stop, but the executioner's eyes stopped him from speaking. Green and soft, open and wide, they held an intensity, a sadness, a tenderness that struck the prisoner and brought him new pain. He blinked, then searched the executioner's eyes again for another glimpse of the heart he had seen. It was gone.

The executioner studied the prisoner and kept his hands firmly around the prisoner's tiny wrists—his arms held the dead man upright. The prisoner peered into his eyes again, seeking deeper. He didn't want to be left alone. But the executioner's warmth had fully withdrawn, and the prisoner lowered his gaze. Veins protruded from the executioner's neck, and he saw the barrel chest of the man who would end his life rise and fall. The prisoner's eyes lingered on the soft moisture forming in the nook of the executioner's collarbone.

"Is it true that I should die for this? Is it true that I deserve it?"

The executioner didn't respond, but they locked eyes. The prisoner peered again into those green fields before him. Nothing. As his body fell, the executioner held him up and leaned in.

"It's time," the executioner commanded.

"Please carry me, I beg of you. My life is down to minutes now."

The executioner bent and lifted him up into his arms, and the prisoner rested his head against his chest, relieved to have heard his executioner's voice. The executioner inhaled suddenly at this closeness but continued down the hall. *I'm free.* The prisoner closed his eyes and closed his thoughts to the cries and blood echoes of the headless souls who had taken these same steps. *I'm free.* No church bell rang, no time was counted, and only the sound of the executioner's footsteps remained. The prisoner felt the muscle, the sweat, and the gentle ways of his executioner. He wrapped his frail arms around the strong neck and shoulders and pulled himself up to whisper in his executioner's ear.

"I say to you, my executioner, we are exactly the same.

Some would think we are worlds apart, but I say, my tongue is as your own.

The object you wield, my executioner, I understand.

For I use my own, it is carried in front.

Oh, my executioner, I feel you close and smell the wine on your breath.

I too drank from that cup. Does it help you as it helped me?

You aren't speaking anymore to me, my executioner, but your eyes have shown me.

Your flesh is my human error.

Oh, my executioner, a great disservice has been done to me.

I am beneath your will and will bow to your blade.

I am timid, tired, and not ready.

How is it possible to prepare for this loss?

You, my newly adored stranger, will lose me forever.

Oh, my executioner, do not fail me, do not leave me flailing!

Make it clean, do it right.

One thing must go correctly for me.

I have done no wrong. No man can accuse me.

Do you believe me, my executioner?

When you end me, will you look away? Or will you keep your gaze on me?

This must be public. There is no other way.

Don't you see, my executioner, you too are waiting for death.

I will bow down, the red river of my life undone.

You, my executioner, have won."

The prisoner nestled himself back in against the body beneath him. He had pictured an ideal death in the arms of his beloved. *But this must do. It will do.* The prisoner pressed his ear to listen to his executioner's heart, and as he did, something baffling and curious transpired in his own. He nodded, and with wide eyes, looked directly at the man holding him.

"I love you, executioner; it must be you. I know I will see you again."

The executioner's body twitched at those words. The prisoner opened his mouth to speak, but as he did, sunlight struck his face. A bell rang. And soon came the plank, the ax, the bending of the knees, the jeering and hollering from the crowd, and the joker with a crown.

"Any last words?" some fool yelled.

The prisoner looked to the sky and saw a single dark bird. He gazed up at his executioner and met his eyes. The prisoner smiled, looked forward again, and yelled, "My executioner's eyes are green!"

Whack!

The long blade came down swiftly and sliced through the stack. Jett eyed and evened up new paper before pulling on the lever once more. Her green eyes narrowed as she assessed the damage. Half of the inventory had been destroyed by her cutting an X through each piece, leaving useless triangles of paper everywhere.

"I have been waiting for you all my life, Quinn. Why did you make me your ex?"

Jett's tears fell on the scattered pieces of paper before her, her black hair flipping on its side with the movement. Quinn had dyed the tips of her hair blue, but they had faded. Well, they had colored it together in the bathroom before a sudden kiss had taken them to the living room.

"I'll keep cutting for you to show you I love you," Jett wailed.

She pulled everything off the shelves and knocked down, kicked, and dumped out paint containers, stencils, cutouts, envelopes, huge sheets of uncreased paper, and boxes of Mylar. Jett paced the one-room shop.

"Oh, my X, my EX
We are each other's executioner.
You are right.
My ex, my Quinn, you have cut me.
And here I am, your ex, cutting you, beheading your dream!
You cut off who we needed to be.
Who you needed to be.
Why couldn't you look at me when you made me your ex?
Oh, thank you, my ex.
For sparing me a lifetime of pain! For ending me now.
It's not you, it's me, you said.
Well, Quinn, you are right, my dear,
It is always you!
Mark me, cut me, and move on, Quinn.
Why couldn't you look at me when you cut my heart?
You were the one, Quinn. You were my beloved.
Why did you let me hold you if you were only going to let me go?"

Jett fell to her knees. She wailed and screamed. Hours passed. When her tears had run out, she looked around at the wreckage. A few feet away from her were the remains of her favorite card, the one with the buck with the too-long antlers on it. She picked the scraps up, held them close to her heart, and closed her eyes. She remembered …

Jett leaned against the counter and looked up at the blackboard. *Christ, I can't afford this coffee.*

"Ummm … you know what, I just want to keep it simple today. Can I get an eight-ounce coffee please?"

"Two-fifty," the barista groaned.

"Keep the rest," Jett said, handing her $3. The barista muttered a thanks and loudly dropped the measly quarters in the tip jar. *Fuck you.*

Jett smiled and picked up her coffee. She headed to the alternative milk counter and grabbed two brown packets of raw sugar. She shook them roughly, and a nearby wannabe tech hippie guru looked up from his laptop. He eyed Jett with disapproval.

"Good morning," Jett waved sarcastically. "You look *super* busy. You *must* be important."

"Bitch," the wannabe tech guru hippie loudly grunted.

"You got it!"

Jett emptied the packets into her coffee and poured in too much almond milk. She lifted her drink and took a tiny sip. *This needs to last.* She meandered to a nearby bulletin board and skimmed advertisements with phone number pull tabs that sought general laborers, movers, and nude models for art classes. *No school listed for nude modeling—that's not suspicious.* But in the top left-hand corner of the board, a neon orange sign caught her attention.

NEED HELP AT CARD AND ART SUPPLY SHOP. START IMMEDIATELY.

MINIMUM WAGE BUT CASH PAY, FLEXIBLE HOURS.

Jett tore the ad off, folded it, and tucked it in her back pocket. She took a big swig of coffee. *I have to act now. Card and art, hmmm. How long was I at that gas station?* She walked to the door and waved goodbye to the wannabe tech guru hippie. He flipped her off. Jett let the door slam and walked behind the building before pulling the paper out and punching the digits into her flip phone. Her fingers ran through her black mohawk. *Ugh. Can't wait to dye this thing.*

Ring!

Ring!

Ring!

Don't sound desperate. Don't sound desperate. Don't sound desperate. Sweat formed on her neck, and she glanced down the alley. Three men were smoking, and one looked like he might be maneuvering to take a piss. *Fucking cigarettes, and what a weird fucking place. Pick up. Pick up. Please pick up.*

"Hello! Quirk by Quinn! How can I help you?"

"Oh, hi, Quinn. I saw your ad, and I'm the person you are looking for, for your card and art supply shop. I can start today, and I won't let you down."

"Hi … umm … thanks for calling. What's your name?"

"Oh yeah. I'm sorry. I'm Jett." She wiped her forehead.

Jett eyed the men again and saw that one guy was peeing and waving his dick around. *Oh my god! That's enough bullshit for one day.* She tucked her coffee in the nook of her arm and reached into her coat pocket for the pack of cigarettes she was trying to save.

"What's your background? And do you have any retail experience?"

"In terms of experience, I really don't have any with cards or art supplies. But I have loads of customer service and can run the cash register, stock, you name it. And before you respond, please know I'm willing to learn, I'm reliable, flexible, and I will do whatever you ask, above and beyond. I'm a clean slate and can be molded however you want."

Silence.

"I'm new to New York, originally from Ohio, and I really, really need this chance," she added and took the pause to light her cigarette. *All my money went to moving here and the hole in the wall apartment. I have $45 left. Help me!*

Silence.

"I can meet you right now. You don't even need to pay me for the whole week. It will be a free trial to make sure I'm the right fit." Jett heard something fuzzy on the other side. "Hello, Quinn?"

"I'm here. Thank you for telling me. You know, I'm really looking for someone with an arts background or experience with cards and crafts."

"I *have* experience and really know how to read people. I can help and point them in the right direction! I can sell anyone anything! I am responsible, loyal, hardworking, and will do whatever it takes."

Fuck! Don't get angry.

"Please?" Jett begged after a few seconds of silence.

"Hmmm … it's about three now. If you can get here at five, I can take an hour to show you things and see if you're interested."

"Yes!"

Jett took off. The frantic trip included two subway rides and a long one-mile run, but Jett found the place. On the store sign was the word Quirk, each letter in a different color, the letters tilted to be quirky. The 'by Quinn' part sat below in a simple black font, no tilting. Jett peered in the window and saw a woman about her age adjusting a rack of cards. She opened the door but waited for an invitation.

"Quinn!" Jett waved. "I'm Jett!" She pointed playfully to herself.

Quinn had a shoulder-length brown bob, vintage eyeglasses, and a clip that held her bangs to the side. Everyone always told her she looked like Thelma from *Scooby Doo*, but she resented being compared to a cartoon. She wore a blue jumper with an open, brown knit sweater over it.

"I like your sign!" Jett pointed, and Quinn glanced over at it like she hadn't seen it before.

"Thanks." Quinn wrinkled her nose.

"Can I come in?"

"Oh gosh! Of course, sorry!" Quinn waved.

Jett stepped inside and glanced around. She opened her mouth in awe and smiled like she had just opened the doors to heaven. Quinn's one-room shop held a handful of rotating racks stocked with cards in the front. There were two wooden block tables in the back for measuring, creasing, and cutting paper. The walls held various art supplies: sketch books, scissors, crayons, colored pencils, rulers, erasers, colored paper. As Jett stepped further inside the store, she turned to take in Quinn more fully. They held eye contact, and Quinn found herself getting nervous as she stared at Jett's soft, green, open-wide eyes.

"Is Jett your real name, or do you call yourself that because you're dressed all in black?" Quinn joked, trying to break up the intensity from Jett's gaze.

Jett looked down at her clothing: tight black jeans, a black long-sleeved shirt, and a black jacket with self-applied patches, most fading and needing to be replaced. *Ugh. I'm sweaty. I hope my mohawk still looks alright.* Her black goth boots were horrible to run in, and while she hoped she didn't stink, she couldn't worry about it, nor could she stress about her clothing. *God, I hate this question.*

"No, I'm called Jett because I can run fast." She winked, putting her arms in motion as though she were running.

Quinn's mouth curved like she wanted to smile but had made a promise not to, so instead wrinkled her nose.

"Okay, okay, my mom named me Jane, but that didn't work for me, so now I'm Jett." She gripped each side of her open jacket flaps and shook them to assert her presence.

Quinn softly nodded but still looked like she was trying to figure something out.

"Do you know who you look like?" Jett asked, eager to change the conversation.

"Don't say it!" Quinn yelled and put up her hands.

Jett's eyes widened.

"Wait, I'm sorry," Quinn mumbled anxiously. "I just hear it all the time."

"No, I'm sorry, I—"

Before Jett could finish, Quinn clapped her hands.

Jett relaxed her shoulders and flashed a toothy smile, hoping to put Quinn at ease.

"Your teeth are very white," said Quinn.

"Yep, born this way." Jett winked again. *Wow, this stranger has no sense of humor. Say something else.* "I have found a great whitening toothpaste to counteract all the coffee I drink." Quinn nodded seriously. *Ummm … I wasn't explaining physics. What's going on?*

Without breaking eye contact, Quinn clapped again awkwardly and leaned against the table behind her. "Okay, Jett," she said with a playful ring in her voice, "tell me about the best card you ever received. What made it so great?" She folded her arms and grinned.

She's flirting with me. Jett smiled back. *Oh fuck. Card. Card. Think of something.*

"Best card, best card, best card, let me think." *Shit. I don't think anyone has ever given me a card. Oh fuck. I can't lie about some Hallmark shit. I've got nothing. Nothing. That's it. Nothing!*

"Oh, Quinn," Jett hung and shook her head, gearing up inside for a sob story. "The truth is," she looked up at Quinn with doe eyes, "I have never received a card. Not one, ever. It weighs on me, you know, never having received a simple, tangible gesture, a sweet kindness, something to let me know I am loved." Jett brought moisture to her eyes and wiped at her eyelids. "That's why I would love nothing more than supporting you here while you create beautiful expressions of love, joy, and gratitude." Jett reached for the closest card on the rack. Her eyes scanned the image, a picture of a forest with the phrase, "Honor Your Nature." Jett read the words out loud, closed her eyes, and nodded. *Oof, this may be overkill.* She opened her eyes and put the card back down. But it had worked.

Quinn removed her square glasses and wiped her eyes with the sleeves of her brown sweater. "Well, I appreciate your words, and now I know what to gift you if we work together." Quinn sniffled and looked up at Jett.

Gosh her eyes are beautiful. I feel sick. I want a cigarette.

"Want some chocolate? I'm always emotional during this time of the month," Quinn sighed and put her glasses back on.

"Sure." Jett shrugged. *God, I hate when women blame emotions on their period. But chocolate means I'll eat today. Win!* Jett smiled and met Quinn's unwavering gaze. *Why is she still staring at me? Weird flirting Quinn. She must not get out much.*

"Want to go through a few things together? To see if this could work?"

"Yes!" Jett smiled.

"Great. Follow me," said Quinn. She waved a 'come with me' motion, as if they were embarking on a long adventure, but within five steps they were at their destination. She scanned left and right and covered her awkwardness by walking around to the farthest corner of a table.

"Have you ever cut card stock before?" Quinn asked. She

lifted and began unwrapping a ream of paper and continued without giving Jett a chance to respond. "Eventually, when we get big enough, I want to be able to work with a printer who can print the designs on the cards, you know? But before that I need a computer and more advanced graphic design training."

"Oh, I can help you with graphics. I'm an expert at that stuff." *Shit, already lying.*

"Really!" Quinn rested the paper on the table and looked at Jett. "Oh my gosh! How exciting! You have made my day. I know tons of people are good with that stuff, but I need to be able to work well with someone, you know? What a relief!" Quinn smiled for the first time.

Oh fuck, what have I done. Oh fuck, look at that smile. I'm OK with computers, I'll figure it out.

"Wow! You were right. I'm going to need you." Quinn smiled again.

"No problem. It will be easy." Jett nodded. *Look up graphic design classes and find money to pay for them.*

"I do everything by hand, so it takes a lot of time. That's why I need you to prep the card stock and man … I mean … *woman* the displays and racks." Quinn winked. "And help customers. I'm really trying to create an interactive experience. So, if a customer can see the artist at work, it might be more meaningful for them. Or maybe even parents could bring their kids in to make holiday cards together. Wouldn't that be so sweet?"

"Yeah, but wouldn't you want them to keep buying your cards? If you teach them how to do it, they might not come back. Right?" Jett asked. *Uh oh, what's that face?*

"Yes, anyone can make cards anytime they want, but they might not have access to me, my encouraging mentorship and experience, and not to mention, the supplies. I have *everything* here to support *everyone* in the process. I'm sure parents don't want to buy all this stuff or clean up the mess. But even if a family buys their own materials because their kid came here, got inspired, and now they want to transform their home into a card company and produce their own, who cares? Maybe when they grow up, they will commit to our art form and help keep the card makers of the world going! Help keep us relevant and respected. We need to do away with e-cards and this mass-produced meaningless shit! It makes me so angry!"

"Okay, okay, you're right, I'm just looking out for you, but I also have no idea what I'm talking about. You are the expert. You know what you are doing, and you are teaching me. I'm sorry," Jett said softly. *Crap, she is still pissed. Do something!* "I'm going to go get a better idea of the types of cards you create. Be right back."

Quinn nodded but didn't say anything. She continued dividing paper into stacks and pulled envelopes out.

Jett wandered over to the display at the front of the store and delicately lifted a handful of cards from the rack. "Your designs are so beautiful, Quinn. Please tell me when you first discovered that you were a creative, an artist? How did it all start?"

"I'll tell you the story! Be right there!" Quinn beamed.

Jett watched her as she hurried over and pulled a chocolate bar out of her jumper. *Wow she looks like a lonely kid who just discovered a fairyland of friends.* Jett looked down and attentively studied each card. While mostly nature scenes, many of them had iterations of owls or other types of birds or animals with antlers, and some were sketches and others watercolor.

"Watercolor is hard, but I love it more."

"Uh-huh." Jett nodded but kept her eyes on the cards. *Quinn needs attention.*

"Your owls are adorable, and I love these antlers." Jett held up a card of a walnut-colored buck with uneven antlers so long they seemed to puncture the sky. The mountainous background and the clear, unending sky drew Jett in. *I know this creature.*

"Oh, this is one of my favorites, for sure, Quinn. Can I ask you a question?" Jett met her eyes.

"Sure." Quinn straightened her back to sit taller.

"When would you give someone a card with a buck on it?"

"When wouldn't you? When you are telling someone to stay strong, or if you see how strong they are, and you want to recognize it. We are all either owls or antler animals, observers or protectors who, deep down, want to keep others safe. People like to remember, or be reminded of, who they are."

Wow. She's smart. That's deep stuff. Jett maintained eye contact until Quinn looked away.

"At least that's what I think. I'm working on an animal series. I want cards for every animal, every motion that animals make, every emotion that animals feel, I want them on a card."

"I love it, and I agree completely. People like to know who they are." Jett smiled with her teeth, and her emerald eyes radiated softness.

Quinn tried to smile back before looking down.

"Who am I—an observer or a protector?" Jett asked.

"I don't know yet." Quinn looked up and met her eyes.

"Well, when you find out, please let me know." Jett winked. "Ready to get back to it?"

"Yep!" Jett smiled. *Damn, why didn't I ask for any chocolate?*

Hours passed at Quirk by Quinn, and Jett learned about measuring, cutting, presentation, stenciling, watercolors, envelopes and Mylar, customer service, card stock, how to open and close, run the cash register, and take inventory. When Quinn ran out of things to teach, her owl watch told her how late it had become.

"Let's go eat," Quinn smiled. "I know the best taco place in the whole city, 24 Hours of Tacos!"

"Shoot, I can't. I left my money at home to be safe. I'm still learning the city." *Be cool.*

"No, no, no, I'll get it! Please! Please!" Quinn stammered.

"Are you sure?"

"Yes! You can get it next time we go out!"

"Will do!" *Next time? Yeah right! I'll have to cook you ramen noodles. Fuck. Don't worry about that right now.*

Thirty minutes later, they stood in front of a brightly colored taco truck.

"What do you want?" Quinn asked, moving a bit closer to Jett.

"Ummm … I'm not sure. What do you usually get?" Jett relaxed her shoulders.

"Everything!" Quinn laughed.

Jett smiled. *She's blushing. Thank God, she has loosened up. Seems like a different person now. Crap, what should I get? I can't get too much. Fuck, I'm hungry.*

"Can you order for us?" Jett asked, gently touching Quinn's back.

"Sure!" Quinn said.

"Thank you so much. I can never decide what I want."

Quinn smiled and nodded and stepped forward to order.

Jett stepped back to give room to the line of people behind them. *Fuck, I hate being broke. I hope I don't look like one of those controlling assholes who makes the woman pay for everything.* Jett felt her pocket for her pack of cigarettes. *Hmmm … probably a bad idea.*

Quinn popped up right next to her. "Hi!"

"Oh, hey, thank you again. I'm sorry about that. I promise it will be my treat next time."

"I'm not worried about it, Jett. By the way, I really do like your name." Quinn looked away and asked, "Where do you want to eat? It's too cold to go sit somewhere."

"Let me give you my jacket. It's a little old and probably smells like cigarettes."

"It does smell like cigarettes, but sure, that would be nice." Quinn smiled.

Wow, she is adorable. Jett removed her coat and gently put it on Quinn's shoulders just as a staff member yelled, "Quinn!"

"I'll get it." Jett hurried to the counter and paused as she grabbed the two bags. *Could I have her over? It's a small, empty space. I don't even have chairs yet. Oh God, she can't come over.* Jett turned around. *Be cool.*

"I'm going to sound like such a jerk, but my place isn't comfortable. You know, I just moved and I have been so busy trying to find work that I haven't really unpacked or decorated yet. But like with the tacos, I will make it up to you, I promise. Why don't we just walk towards your place so I can make sure you get home safely. If you don't mind me nabbing a couple tacos, we can just talk tomorrow, alright?"

Quinn fell silent.

"You still want me to come by at nine for more training, yeah?" *Don't sound desperate. Chill out.* "Mmmm … tacos!" Jett playfully held up the bags. *What's that look?*

"Yes, don't worry, you still have a job," Quinn huffed. "Tonight is simply about me taking my new employee out as a congratulations. Welcome to the team! I wanted to get to know you a bit more, so if you aren't tired, why don't we go to my place to eat?"

"Sounds good." Jett smiled. *She still seems upset.* "Where to?"

"Just back where we came from."

"Alright, like in the direction of Quirk?"

"No, we are going back to Quirk."

"Oh!" Jett exclaimed. *Maybe she lives at the store and is poor like me.*

"I live above Quirk, but don't tell anyone."

"I have no one to tell, and I never would do that."

"I believe you, but I just had to say it. My mom got us the apartment and then a year lease on the store before she passed. She put everything she had left towards looking out for me and helping with my future. I'm so lucky. I love my mom so much. But we had just moved here, and she didn't get to see it, she didn't get to see any of it." Quinn hung her head and exhaled. She had tears in her eyes. "She knew that owls are my favorite and gave me this watch on my birthday, the last birthday I had with her. The eyes glow in the dark, and the watch charges by sunlight." Quinn held up her arm, and Jett saw the face of a light-brown owl with two little plastic ears on top. Close to the two and the ten were dark brown eyes with drops of yellow in the pupils.

"I'm so sorry. Where did you live before you two moved here?" Jett asked.

"I'm from Minnesota. We wanted to try something new. I only had about a year with her here. She knew she was sick, but she didn't tell me. I thought about moving back, but I didn't know how to. I learned about the store in her will while sitting at the lawyer's office. It was the only thing I've ever done without her. She called me Quirk my whole life. It's like she knew what would happen."

"I'm sorry about your mom. It seems like she was a thoughtful lady who loved you a lot. What an amazing gift she gave you." *Wow she is opening up.*

Quinn smiled but looked away.

"Shall we go?" Jett asked.

Quinn nodded. "Are you close with your mom?" Quinn asked as they started walking.

"No. Haven't lived with her for ten years. I have never known who or where my dad is."

Quinn nodded again but didn't say anything.

Oh fuck. Shouldn't have said that. "You sure you want me to come up tonight?"

"Yeah."

When they made it back to Quirk, Quinn guided them past the storefront and around the corner of the building. She stopped at the first heavy iron door on the block and pulled keys out of her knapsack. *Wow, she has more owl keychains than actual keys. That is so cute.* As they hiked single file up three flights of stairs, Jett opened her mouth wide to get as much air as possible so she didn't pant or seem out of breath. *Please don't look back.*

"Here." Quinn turned back to Jett, who quickly closed her mouth and smiled.

Quinn's apartment matched what Jett had imagined it would be—cozy, with a quaint kitchen nook and a tiny table, a narrow bedroom with a queen-size bed covered in brown blankets, and a small living room that doubled as an art studio.

"Want to sit on the couch while I serve?"

"Sure."

"Want something to drink?"

"Water's fine, thanks. Can I help?"

"No." Quinn smiled, grabbing the dinner bags.

Jett sat down on the couch and looked at the TV that sat about five feet in front of her. Alongside and behind the TV stood wooden stands with canvases coated with bright blue rivers, warm, purple mountains, and green and gold forever fields. *Dang, she's good.* Jett noticed she had left her shoes on.

"Jesus Christ." Jett bent over to slip them off.

"Don't worry about it. Only take them off if you would be more comfortable."

"Oh gosh, I didn't see you standing there! You are quiet." Jett leaned back on the couch, trying not to seem startled.

"I'm really sorry. I just totally spaced. I'll take them off right now."

Quinn shrugged and took a couple steps forward. She had two full plates in her hands and sat a foot away from Jett on the couch. "Beef and chicken tacos." She handed Jett a plate. "Are you okay eating here, or do you want to go to the kitchen? I can bring the table over. Whatever you want."

"I'm fine here. Thank you again, Quinn. I really like your home, and your art is beautiful!" Jett picked up a taco and ate half of it in one bite. Wide-eyed, she turned to Quinn and mumbled with a full mouth, "Mmmm … you weren't kidding! So good!"

They ate in silence, smiling at each other on occasion. By the fifth taco, Jett felt warm and full and exhausted. *I could pass out right here. Oh shit, I have no idea how to get home.* She sat up.

"I think it's too late for you to go home. It's already two-thirty. This is my fault, and I'm sorry for keeping you here so long. I would be concerned for your safety if you left now, especially because you're new here. I'd offer to walk you home, but I don't go out this late alone either."

"I wouldn't let you do that anyway," Jett asserted. *Oh thank god I'm staying.*

"See, then we would both be headed back here anyway, so let's just save ourselves the trip and stay." Quinn laughed and blushed.

"I'm cool with it." Jett leaned back on the couch.

"Cool," Quinn repeated. "I'll grab you some blankets. Think you will be comfortable on the couch?"

"I can, and have, slept anywhere. Don't worry about me." *Shit. Why is she looking at me like that? I shouldn't have said that.*

"Want me to let you sleep, or do you want to watch some TV? Ugh! I never got you your water. Hold on."

"You are so sweet, Quinn. But I can get it." *I'm so tired. Shit, she wants to stay up.*

"No, no, I'll be right back. Think about what you want to watch. I have Netflix."

Well, I still have a flip phone.

Jett took the opportunity to shake her head and gently slap herself awake while Quinn got them water.

"Hey, thank you for the water," Jett said when Quinn returned. "We can definitely watch a movie or something, but I'm going to ask you to pick it out. I'm a bit out of the loop with Netflix. I mean, I know the whole 'Netflix and chill' thing. Oh God, I shouldn't have said that. I guess I am tired."

"No, I know what you meant. We've had a long day. Maybe we just watch for a little while, let our food settle?" Quinn turned on the TV. She scrolled rapidly once she hit the home screen and kept scrolling without looking at the options. *She seems tense. Is she alright?*

"That looks good." Jett sat up and leaned forward, hoping she could wake herself up.

Right as Quinn clicked play, she turned and kissed Jett on the cheek. Shocked, Jett kept her eyes on the screen for a moment and felt Quinn's breath. *Oh no, but I didn't start this, so …* Jett turned to passionately kiss Quinn. Their mouths met, and Jett reached to wrap her arms around her, but Quinn pulled back and away from Jett, abruptly stood up, and stepped away from the couch.

"Oh my God, I'm sorry!" Jett hid her head in her hands.

"It's alright," Quinn uttered slowly.

"I don't understand. I'm sorry, I thought you wanted … oh, I'm so tired … I just thought … oh fuck."

"It's fine," Quinn stammered, on the verge of tears.

"I think I need to sleep. I can leave if you want me to. I don't want to upset you. I can grab a taxi," Jett said, knowing full well she couldn't afford it.

"I'm not upset."

"What? Then why … look, I have no idea what's going on right now, Quinn, but we just met today, and it's been a big, wonderful, and long day. It's been wonderful but weird. I'm sorry for tonight—I misunderstood and I ruined everything," Jett groaned, rubbing her eyes. *I'm going to be sick.*

"You didn't do anything wrong. I'm just … I'm not …"

"Not what?"

"You know."

"No, I don't know, Quinn," Jett snapped.

"You know …" Quinn made that motion across her neck, like she had lost her head.

"What?"

"You know." Quinn repeated the motion.

"No, I don't know, Quinn. I don't know what that means! You lost your head? You're firing me? You kissed me first!"

"Shut up!" Quinn cried. "I'm not gay, you asshole!"

"Oh, I see. You're one of those. What am I even doing here, Quinn?" Jett stood up. "I gotta go."

"No, please stay!" Quinn yelled. "I'm sorry. I'm so sorry." She ran to Jett and grabbed her hands. "You aren't an asshole. I'm an asshole. I don't know what's wrong with me. I'm sorry. Please, Jett."

"No, I'm sorry. I didn't know you weren't out yet," Jett said softly and squeezed Quinn's hands.

"Out where?" Quinn asked, looking like a lost and wounded owl.

"Oh gosh." Jett pulled her hands away and sat down again. "Out of the closet, Quinn," she mumbled slowly. "Like out as a gay or lesbian person, or bisexual, or whatever you are."

"Oh." Quinn nodded and sat down next to Jett.

Jett felt bad for her, but worse about the whole night. *Don't fuck with your boss, I know better. I just had to fuck this up.*

"Let's go back in time, to right after tacos, and just go to bed. Deal?" Jett held out her hand for a shake.

Quinn's eyes widened, and she took Jett's hand in her own. "I'll get you your blankets."

"Thank you."

Within a minute, Quinn came back, owl-patterned blankets and pillow in hand. She put them on the couch and turned to Jett and said, "I'm sorry again. Please forgive me. Goodnight."

"I'm sorry too, Quinn."

Jett fell asleep instantly. When she woke up, her mouth was unbearably dry and she reached for her water and looked around. The couch had been comfortable enough, but she hated not having been able to brush her teeth. The apartment was silent. She stood, stretched, and walked quietly to the kitchen.

"Quinn? Quinn? Quinn, are you here?"

No reply.

Jett looked at the table and saw a plate of toast, scrambled eggs, and apple slices. A big cup of coffee sat beside it, with a letter leaning on it. Jett picked up the lukewarm coffee and let the letter fall. She drank the whole thing. She sat down to pick up the card, saw her name on the front, and looked around one more time even though she knew Quinn was already downstairs in the shop. *What have I done?* She tore the envelope open. The buck with too long antlers looked up at her, and Jett smiled and shook her head. Inside, it read:

Hi Jett,

Please forgive me and please still work with me. I'm the asshole, and I'll work on my closet.

Quinn

P.S. – Come down whenever you are ready. You can take a shower if you want.

For four years, Jett labored by Quinn's side. Four years of measuring, four years of cutting, four years of dealing with the bank, four years of begging for rent extensions, four years of ordering and stocking supplies, four years of trudging through the snow, four years of dealing with indecisive and irritable customers, four years of staying in the shop with no air conditioning during the unbearable heat of summer, and four years with periods of unending slowness and stress during down time. Four years of helping Quinn think about the bigger picture, four years of convincing everyone she met to buy a card. Four years of work, six or seven days a week, supporting Quinn's dream, which had also become her own. Jett waited and waited … and waited and was patient with Quinn, patient with their relationship, patient with herself. But she felt deep down in her heart that all she heard from Quinn were excuses and lies. Jett loved Quinn and for years told herself that eventually she would be ready, be brave, that she had been working on her closet and would soon come out. Jett got used to distance, to dinners in, to holding hands in hiding, to solitary holidays at the shop while Quinn flew to visit her dad and other family.

One Sunday night, Jett and Quinn sat in bed together. Earlier that day, they had gotten into a fight at the park when Jett had tried to hold Quinn's hand. Quinn had bluntly rejected it and glanced around to see if anyone had seen. Jett lost her patience and said, "Why don't you hold my hand? Are you still embarrassed, still ashamed, still want to be hiding? You don't know anyone else in this city! You're worried about what your mom would think? Well, news flash, she's dead. I don't think she would have cared anyway. You believe she is in heaven? Well, look up and tell her who you are! Come out, Quinn!" Jett looked to the sky and shouted, "Hey, Beth, your daughter is a lesbian! Deal with it!"

People glanced over.

"Everything's fine!" Jett yelled at them. She shook her head at Quinn.

"That's not how you talk to people in heaven. Don't talk to my mom that way," Quinn sobbed and fell to her knees. "You don't even believe in heaven, Jett!"

"What the fuck is wrong with you?"

"We do go out together!" Quinn wailed.

"No, come out! You know exactly what I mean! I'm so sick of this. I have waited so long!"

"I am out with you," Quinn yelled hysterically, covering her face with her arms.

"No, that's not true. Please come out to yourself! I'm living this lie, and you can't live your truth! You don't want somebody special; you want anyone who will hide with you! I can't be your prisoner!" Jett yelled and stormed away from Quinn.

Quinn stumbled to a nearby bench, collapsed on it, and curled up in a ball. Jett went to a taco truck, came back, and wrapped her arms around a still-sobbing Quinn.

"You're going to be the death of me, aren't you, Quinn?" Jett sat down and handed her a taco.

"What?" Quinn sat up and reached for her food. "No way. You're my executioner, with those green eyes."

Jett furrowed her brow and looked away from Quinn.

Ashamed, Quinn tried to lighten the mood and said, "Maybe we don't kill each other but just live happily ever after?" She reached to put a hand on Jett's back.

"Do you have a card for that, Quinn? Couple decides not to end each other and live happily together forever?"

"Not yet," Quinn sighed. "It's a good idea though."

"I'm trying to decide which of us is the prisoner," said Jett. "You can't come out and live your real life in the world, and the way I love you means that I can never leave you. I'm trapped, and it isn't all heavenly."

Quinn rose to her feet. "Let's walk," she said.

Jett stood, and they walked quietly together around the park. Quinn sobbed occasionally as they passed through the night-quieted park, and when she did Jett looked intently at her face. Jett felt her lover's presence intensely and wanted to fall into her. *This is my time, and no one can take it from me.* Then something in Quinn steeled, which Jett could feel as well.

"You don't even know that we are the same, Quinn," said Jett.

A church bell rang in the distance. *A little late for a church bell.*

"There are things I might have to do. I might have no choice," said Quinn. "No two people are exactly the same. My story is my story, even if I love your part in it."

"I've never wronged you, Quinn. Nobody can speak against how I've been with you," said Jett.

"And I never will," said Quinn.

They turned and walked back to Quinn's apartment. Instead of coming in, Jett decided that she should sleep at her own place.

"I'll give you some space to feel through things. I trust you. I love you," said Jett.

"I only want good for you," said Quinn.

A week later, Jett was still staying at her own place. She had decided to come to work an hour early so she could watch Quinn draw. When she arrived at the shop, she saw Quinn inside with a paper delivery guy who had given Jett a bad feeling. Quinn had repeatedly brushed off what she called "Jett's jealousy" and explained how necessary it is to be friendly with business partners. But now, Quinn had her hand on his arm and laughed, and he had his hand on her back while they looked at her drawings together. Jett punched the brick wall with her left hand and let out a scream. Quinn and the guy looked up, but Jett was gone. Jett's skin had been torn at the knuckles, and bright blood had rushed to the surface.

As Jett walked swiftly home, her phone rang in her pocket. She didn't answer. She thought it could only be Quinn. Jett spent the day pacing, everything feeling distant and unreal. She tried to eat but found she couldn't. In the evening, in a moment of quivering strength, she dialed her voicemail. The only message was from Quinn. Quinn explained how she saw Jett as her ex now, but that they could still work together and be friends.

Jett stumbled out into the street. She felt like she hadn't eaten for weeks, and that she would never eat again. *It's all just gruel, anyway. Who could want it. I can no longer bend down to suck at it.* Jett felt a beast of emptiness envelop her, and then that beast, utterly devoid of hope, entered her through her breathing. Jett moved through the night according to the will of the beast, a terrible creature working according to the rules of love, her executioner. She arrived at Quinn's store. It was no longer their store; it was only Quinn's store now, so that it had become an alien place, an inexplicable misplacement. She used her key to enter. There was a stack of deer cards sitting on a bookcase, the ones with the beautiful, mystery antlers. She paused for a moment to tear several of them into pieces. Jett wanted Quinn to hear her, she wanted Quinn to come down the stairs and see her there. At this thought, Jett felt her love for Quinn rise up, like hope, like a spasm of life, but this quickly passed. She went to the paper cutter, lifted the blade and positioned one arm underneath the blade. She thought about Quinn's tiny wrists.

"I'll see you again, my Executioner," Jett whispered and pulled the blade down.

WHACK!

PIT

1“ , 2, 3, 4, 5, 6, 7, 8, 9, 10, 11, 12, 13, 14, 15, 16, 17, 18, 19, 20.” “Henry, my love, you don't need to be counting.” She kept pushing the cart.

"1, 2, 3, 4, 5, 6, 7, 8, 9, 10, 11, 12, 13, 14, 15, 16, 17, 18, 19, 20." Henry counted in sync with the black, dusty rubber wheels as they went round and round across the linoleum. He kept his eyes fixated on their movement and listened for the soothing sounds that came with each completed rotation. He trotted behind his mama, Julie, and as he completed this second round of counting, the wheels slowed down, and a panic set in. He dared to briefly look up and realized they were approaching the end of the aisle. *Count slower.* Julie paused to turn the corner, and the view of the wheels was briefly blocked by her blue pumps.

"1, 2, 3, 4, 5, 6, 7, 8, 9, 10, 11, 12," he whispered, hoping she didn't hear. *Keep moving, keep moving.* He stopped breathing and waited for the wheels to roll.

"13, 14, 15, 16, 17, 18, 19…" As they turned a corner, she stopped and glanced at a discounted soup display arranged neatly at the end of the aisle. She tapped her long fingernails on the handlebar. He whimpered and knew she could hear him, but she tapped her fingernails even harder before reaching for a can, studying it, and letting out a "hmmm."

Push the cart, push the cart, push the cart, you can't stop at 19. He whined again, but she didn't move. A few seconds later, she tossed the can in the cart and pushed the cart forward. Henry whispered, "20" and exhaled in relief.

"Henry." Julie stopped, turned around, and looked at him. She shrugged her shoulders and sighed as they gazed at each other.

"What, Mama?" he asked softly. He didn't want to start apologizing. Henry grabbed his left wrist tightly with his right hand and tried to stop thinking about numbers.

"Nothing, Henry." She pushed the cart against the side of the aisle and took two steps towards him and crouched down. She covered his hands with hers and tried to gently loosen his grip.

"Henry," she whispered. But he couldn't let go and didn't know why. Julie began pulling fingers back and off his wrist, one at a time. When she had all of them, she slid his thumb out from underneath. As soon as his right hand had been freed, she took it with her left and grabbed his left hand with her right so they were holding hands.

He couldn't look at her. "I'm sorry, Mama," he mumbled in shame.

"It's alright, Henry. I know this is stressful. I know you hate grocery stores. I'm sorry."

Henry nodded, but his hands were getting sweaty, and he tried to pull them away from her.

"Henry, stop. Here, put your palms on mine." She opened her hands and held her palms up and released him from her grasp.

He knew what she was doing, and even though he kept

looking at her eyes, he wondered about how the wheels were doing.

"Henry. Hey, Henry, put your hands on my hands."

He timidly put his hands against hers.

"Close your eyes and take some deep breaths, Henry. You are safe, and I'm here to protect you."

He closed his eyes and tried to breathe. His fingers wanted to curl up in a ball. He wanted to grab his wrist, and his right hand started to move towards it. Julie pressed against his hands, so the pressure would keep his fingers in place. Henry opened his eyes and began crying.

"Hey, lady, move your cart. I'm trying to get in there!" boomed an angry man.

Julie didn't look up, but Henry stared at the man and stared at his cart and thought about their own cart and the wheels. Those wheels, sitting there. Tears streamed down his face.

"Lady, move your cart and your kid!"

"One second, Henry." Julie bit her lip and inhaled.

"Lady, move your cart!"

"You … move … the … cart." Her stern and commanding voice caught Henry off guard.

"Bitch." He shoved her cart forward. Luckily, it didn't swerve but continued halfway down the aisle before stopping.

Henry's concern for the wheels grew, and he wanted to run to them.

"Ignore him. That man needs a bottle and a nap. Stay with me, Henry," she smiled. She slowly pulled back her hands from his but remained in the same position, so they were perfect reflections of each other. "Be my mirror, Henry."

She made fists, and then Henry made fists. She opened up her hands wide and waved them in the air, and he did the same. She balled her hands up again and made a *whooshing* sound as she burst them open, and they gently moved through the air like shooting stars. Her eyes grew wide, and she opened her mouth in awe, as though real stars had magically appeared in the supermarket. Henry smiled, pretending to be amazed by her shooting star hands. He didn't notice the stranger right next to them, loudly toppling corn and green bean cans into his cart.

"Henry, your turn."

He opened his palms and fingers wide and made a *whooss-hhhhhh* sound as his stars moved through the air. When his hands had completed their motion, Julie balled up her fists again and sent even more stars into the air. He did the same, trying to keep up. They burst out laughing, and Julie took his hands in hers.

"Are you alright?" she asked.

Henry didn't want to be done playing the game, but he nodded.

"Let's keep shopping." Julie stood and looked down the now-empty aisle for the cart.

Henry hadn't moved, and she reached her hand down for him. He eagerly grabbed onto it.

"How big is your stress now, Henry?" Julie lovingly glanced down at him.

"It's about as big as a sneeze."

Confused, she nodded but didn't say anything. When they got to the cart, Henry locked eyes on the wheels. Her hands gripped the handlebar, and she began pushing.

The wheels in Henry's mind told him to start counting. "1, 2, 3, 4, 5, 6, 7, 8, 9, 10."

"Henry," she smiled, but exhaustion welled up inside. "Please let me see your star hands."

He winced but stopped to ball up his hands and shoot stars through the air.

"Wow, Henry! That was amazing, even better than last time!"

Henry clapped his star hands.

"Do you want to hold onto the cart or do star hands as we walk?"

He reached for the cart. His joy momentarily distracted him from the counting, but soon the sound of the wheels told him to count. "1, 2, 3, 4, 5, 6, 7, 8, 9, 10, 11, 12, 13, 14, 15 …"

Julie ignored the counting and pulled out her list, a handful of items remaining. She eyed her cart, counted, and added it up the best she could, but already she knew it was going to be too much. *Those other items will have to wait. I can't keep up with how much he needs.* Stress over her inevitable bad check set in.

"Henry, we are leaving now. Do you want to practice star hands until we get to the checkout line?" She felt tears behind her eyes.

As they walked all the way down the bread aisle, Henry alternated between counting and star hands.

When they approached the checkout line, she asked, "How are you going to help Mama get through this final step?"

"I'll help you, Mama." Henry nodded.

"I'm counting on you." She laughed, rubbed the top of his head, and recited a silent prayer that it would go well. *Please no screaming numbers, please no meltdowns, please no lying on the floor to touch the wheels. Please, please, please, let's get through this with ease and grace. Amen.*

Henry smiled. She guided them to the closest cashier, and a bright orange paper sign hanging down from the counter caught her eye. NO CHECKS. Julie flushed, and her hands felt clammy. She gripped the handlebar, swallowed, and moved her shoulders so her tan blouse loosened on her perspiring body.

"Good afternoon." She smiled at the cashier, a young woman with a bob of curly dark blonde hair. Julie saw her name tag read "Emma." "Henry, I'm going to go talk with Emma. Can you hold our cart?"

He nodded while Julie walked in front of the cart to the cash register. She pulled the front of the cart up with her hand, while Henry held the handlebar, hung his head, and looked at the wheels. He needed to start counting, so he pulled the cart back a few inches in preparation.

"Henry, please stop. Scoot the cart forward before you hurt someone."

"I'm sorry, Mama." Embarrassment flushed his cheeks, and he forcefully pushed the cart forward.

"Ouch! Henry!" Julie shrieked as it ran right into her side.

"Oh, Mama, I'm sorry." He whimpered and squeezed his eyes shut. He couldn't believe he had hurt his mama.

"Henry, I'm fine. Please just stay still." Julie turned to Emma and sighed. "I'm sorry. Thank you for your patience, Emma. I hope your day isn't too busy! Would it be possible to write a check?" Julie leaned over the counter and smiled, a hint of desperation in her voice.

"I'm sorry, ma'am, no checks." Emma pointed down to the sign that Julie was now leaning against.

"Gosh, silly me. I didn't even see that." She backed up and tried to look at the sign like she had never seen it before and then shook her brown hair and rolled her hazel eyes.

"Yeah, I'm sorry, ma'am. Just too many bad checks lately."

"Not a problem at all. I must be tired!" Julie smiled at her own silliness and fumbled through the black purse that hung over her shoulder. "Oh, oh, I almost forgot." She pulled out a giant handful of wadded-up coupons and casually put them on the counter. Usually, she was able to check if she had coupons for any of the products in the cart, or she was able to shop by using the coupons as a guide, but not today. Emma's eyes widened. Julie's shame was unbearable. She reached down for her card and held it out to Emma.

"Perfect. I just need a minute to go through these and ring

you up, and then I will need that." Emma smiled.

"Wow, Mama needs a nap today. Good grief!" Julie flushed.

"You are doing great." Emma nodded as she started unfolding the irrelevant coupons. Julie believed she meant it. Tears came, so she blinked them back and noticed the cart moving in the corner of her eye.

Henry had put one foot on the bottom shelf of the cart and was moving it back and forth to help the wheels do a complete rotation. "1, 2, 3, 4, 5, 6, 7, 8, 9, 10, 11, 12 …"

"Henry!"

"Henry!"

"Henry!"

But he couldn't look up and couldn't look at his mama. He needed to get to 20, but it was getting too loud. The wheels told him they wanted to go faster to get more rotations done before he left.

"Hey, Henry, look at me. Show me your star hands!"

Henry briefly held his hands up in the air with open palms, but his head still hung down. "Henry! Stop!" she yelled, but he grabbed the cart and pushed it back and forth even faster. He needed to get to 20. *Why is Mama stopping me? Why is Mama stopping me?*

"Mama, don't stop me!" he shouted, almost out of breath. Henry pulled the cart back as hard as he could. He didn't see the old woman's cart a few feet behind him. His body crashed into the front of her cart.

"Henry!"

"Ouch, Mama!" He looked up at her and touched the back of his head.

"Henry, are you hurt? What has gotten into you today?"

The old lady, who remained hunched over her cart, tsk-tsked and examined her diet soda, boxed macaroni and cheese, and crackers to make sure they were not damaged.

"I'm sorry," Julie started and squeezed her body alongside the cart towards her son. "Everything in your cart looks fine." She smiled timidly and pretended to briefly look at the stranger's cart before reaching for Henry's head to check it.

"Control your child, or else he will grow up to be a brat! Kids these days! I can't believe it. We didn't tolerate that in my day. Kids *and* their moms have gone soft. Disrespectful." The old lady pointed her wrinkly finger as she spoke. Henry thought he could smell her breath and wondered if the wheels could smell it too.

"I am so sorry. He is not a brat; he is just having a hard time. Have you ever had a bad day before?" Julie had raised her voice, and Henry felt her hand shaking in his.

The old woman shook her head. "Just hurry up. We all have places to be."

"I'm sure you do." Julie smiled and let go of Henry's hand to start loading the items on the conveyor belt. She frantically unloaded the lettuce, dressing, cereal, milk, spaghetti, sauce, canned soup and canned veggies, bread, peanut butter, jam, bananas, sliced deli meat, butter, cookies, and two small sacks of fruit.

"Henry, I'm going to push the cart forward now. Please take my hand again."

He reached up and took his mama's right hand while she pushed the cart forward with her left. She paused at the counter and apologized to Emma and watched her run each item across the scanner. Julie didn't want to see the red number total increasing with each beep, so she looked at Henry and smiled.

"Paper or plastic?" Emma asked calmly.

"Doesn't matter. Here is my card. I don't want to know the total." She looked back at her son and said, "Please go wait up by the bagger."

He slumped his shoulders and took the five steps forward towards the teenage boy who was sorting the groceries as they slid down. The boy popped open some paper bags and pulled the cart around next to him.

"No!" Henry yelled.

"What's with your kid?" the boy hollered at Julie without acknowledging Henry.

"Zack, stop!" Emma yelled at him.

"Henry, one second. I'm sorry." Julie held a star hand up.

"Here's your card, receipt, and your coupons, ma'am." Emma handed them to her and smiled.

"Everything's okay?" Julie asked.

"Yeah, everything's just fine," Emma winked. "I found just the coupons you were looking for."

"I want my cart!" Henry yelled.

"Thank you, Emma! See you next time!" Julie hurried to her son who stood glaring at Zack.

"Your kid is crazy," he huffed.

"Yeah, I am too." She glared at him and grabbed Henry's hand.

"Zack, enough!" said Emma.

"Whatever." He shrugged and continued bagging. Julie nodded and smiled at Emma but knew she needed to think of something to distract her son. She scanned the small pile of items waiting to be bagged and saw a clear, crinkled sack of apricots. With her free hand, she ripped the sack open and pulled the closest apricot out.

"Here, Henry, this is really important to me, and I want you to take care of it." She released his hand and gently put the apricot in his palms like she had just gifted him the whole world. "Can I trust you with this?"

His eyes grew wide at the beautiful, soft, yellow and orange ball in his hands. He looked up at his mama and nodded, but suddenly he didn't feel safe and needed to give his apricot his full attention.

"Thank you, Henry. That means a lot to me."

Henry remained motionless, studying his apricot.

"What do you want me to do with that?" Zack demanded, pointing down to the ripped sack.

"Are you kidding me? Well, you can tie the plastic bag shut and put it in my paper bag, or just throw the fruit straight in there. If you want, I can get my child to show you how to tie the bag closed. Do you want me to get him to help? Or you got it?"

Zack tied the sack so tight that the remaining apricots smashed together. "Here you, go" he said, and stepped back from the cart.

"Thank you, Emma!" Julie waved and asked Henry to wave, but neither he nor the apricot had moved. "Let's go, Henry."

He started walking but didn't look up and just followed his mama's steps.

As Julie pushed the cart past Zack, she loudly said, "Henry, that's what happens to boys who don't listen to their mamas. They turn into punks." She looked down at Henry who was still smiling and admiring his apricot. "You got a hold of that thing? You are taking such good care of it until we can get home to enjoy it, Henry!" Julie reached down and grabbed his shoulder. "We are stopping right now to look both ways before crossing. Always watch the road, or you could get hit by a car. Do you understand how serious that is? I never want you to get hurt. Please, please pay attention."

Henry nodded and held perfectly still while she loaded the car. She told him to stay in eyesight while she pushed the cart to the cart return. He stayed still, continuing to stare at his apricot.

In the car, Henry sat forward so that he wouldn't jerk around.

"Henry, have we never had fresh apricots before? I know I fed them to you as a baby, but that was baby food in a jar. Do you remember that? Eating apricots as a baby?" she playfully asked, briefly glancing at him.

He nodded furiously without looking up from his apricot.

"Just never eat the pits, Henry. They will make you sick, and too many are dangerous, like poison. Always give them to me. Understood?"

He nodded again, but his mind had become stuck on the word pit. *Is there something in there?*

Their tiny, two-bedroom house sat on a corner, and as they pulled into the driveway, she asked him, "Can you please help me unload?"

He didn't say anything. He didn't want to be separated from his apricot companion.

"Don't worry. We will find a safe place for it," she sighed, reading his mind.

Henry nodded but didn't want to put it down.

Julie looked at her son. She had never seen Henry so enthralled with anything before. *What a strange and wonderful boy*, she thought. But behind her adoration lived a deep worry about him, about his future. Teachers had told her that he didn't socialize well or have any friends. They recommended testing, doctors, or even a "special school," but she hadn't taken any steps towards any of that yet. She didn't know what to do but didn't want him to feel different or like an outsider. Julie reached out her hand and began stroking his hair.

"Mama, what can we name it?" he asked without looking at her.

Julie took a deep breath, smiled, and said, "Honey, you can name it whatever you want, but Henry, look at me."

The boy slowly turned and looked up at his mama.

"Honey, you know it's not a pet, right? Apricots are food.

We can have it for dessert tonight. And I will get you more if that punk kid doesn't destroy them all. Now, Henry, tell me you know it's not a pet," she gently begged.

"I know, Mama. It's food, and we will have it for dessert, and you will get me more if that punk kid doesn't destroy them all." He looked at his mama steadily, as shame settled in the pit of his stomach.

She lovingly searched his eyes and sensed his growing discomfort. "Okay, let's go." Julie unbuckled her belt.

A fascination with apricots consumed Henry's life. Julie made sure they were always in the house, and every time he gave her a pit, he could get a new one. In preparation for colder months, she cut and froze apricots, so she didn't have to drive in bad weather. Three apricot-filled years passed.

One spring morning, Julie realized she had somehow lost track and they were completely out of apricots. The car was in the shop, and she had been walking to her work at the nearby laundromat. Henry begged and pleaded and cried for apricots. She hesitated, but she got on her bike and left for the store. Through the window, Henry watched her wheels as she rode away. When he could no longer see her, he sat at the table and watched the door.

The car didn't see her as it sped across the intersection without slowing down.

When the door finally opened, it wasn't his mama but a man who called himself "Dad."

A man he didn't remember, a man he didn't want to remember, a man he didn't like came in, dropped his bags, nodded at Henry, and smiled as he looked around. Dad yelled, had mean women over, and drank a lot. Dad stumbled to work late, spent evenings crashed out on the couch, and never helped with homework. Dad didn't know what kids ate, and Dad laughed at apricots. Dad didn't care about apricots. Dad stayed at the house until Henry turned eighteen, and on his birthday, he asked his dad to leave. Dad made a phone call, picked up his bags, and left.

For decades, Henry sat at the table and ate apricots and watched and waited for his mama to come back. He even got a job at her laundromat so he could be close to home when she returned. Pits collected in bowls throughout the house.

"I guess you aren't coming home, Mama," Henry cried at the door. He had waited long enough. He gathered all the pits, put them on the table, and took a mallet to them.

Henry filled a pitcher of water and picked up his first piece of the soon to be poisonous pit, put it in his mouth, and swallowed it. "1." He reached for another. "2." That one hurt to swallow. "3." A bit easier. "20." He paused, feeling sick. "I'm counting past 20, Mama. I'm coming to see you. Please wait for me, Mama." Within minutes, 21 became 54, and soon, he lost count.

Then he heard the wheels. He saw his mama on her bike, looking back and smiling at him. She had apricots. He saw the shopping cart, the tiny wheels, and his mama reaching for his hand. The wheels turned and turned and turned and blurred into a pit. He swallowed some more.

"I'm counting, Mama."

She made stars with her hands.

"I'm coming to see you, Mama. Please wait for me."

"Mama."

BUTTONS

"Have I told you my button story? Do you know what she did?"

Fred sighed and reached for the water pitcher, gingerly filling up the glass to his right. His hands wobbled, but because of his guests he refused to grip it with both hands, so he carefully put it back down before continuing. He smiled and refolded the cloth napkin on his lap.

"We were on the very same bus. I had a job interview that morning, and she had her shift. You know she worked as a legal secretary for some hoity-toity lawyer? She kept that place running! She was the real lawyer and advocate for those people. He couldn't even remember their names half the time! He showed up late, took long lunches, and came back smelling of bourbon! He often took the paralegal with him! Two peas in an idiot pod if you ask me. Anyway, she sobered him up, coached and supported him! Both of them sometimes!"

Fred put his elbow on the table and shook his head.

"You'll have to forgive me." He adjusted the napkin in his lap and cleared his throat. "Where was I? Oh, that's right, we were on the bus together. Two strangers! Can you believe it? Iris had noticed me, but I was so anxious for my interview that I was lost in my own head answering questions I thought they might ask. She sat right next to me! Can you believe it? Just got up from her seat while the bus was in motion and sat down! That woman, the courage never left her! You know what she did next? Please excuse me if I have told this story before, but I'm still amazed! She said, 'Hi, I'm Iris! I just love buttons, and I couldn't help but notice the one on your collar. Mind if I take a closer look?' And I, well, I didn't know what to think or what to do, so I simply nodded without saying a word. She stunned me, stunned me! Her delicate fingers reached up and touched the top button on my blue shirt. She got so close to me! I felt her breath and worried about my own. I didn't know where to look. Iris had on a yellow dress, and her soft dark hair was pulled back into a ponytail. I remember her red lipstick and how she peered at the button. I'm ashamed to say, but if she hadn't been so beautiful, I would have felt differently about the whole thing. I was a young man—what could I do? Iris had a right to be impressed. It was my favorite, lucky shirt. Those buttons were a very rich brown earthy tone, and they just complemented the blue shirt so nicely. And you won't believe what happened next! Oh, I know you have heard this before! As the button moved ever so slightly in her hand, it popped right off! The look on her face, sheer embarrassment! Buses don't stop for buttons! Nope, that bus did not stop so we could find that button. But you know what she did? She stayed on the bus, even when I had to get off, and she found that button. By then she had gotten my name and telephone number. She was quite adamant that she had to return it to me. I had waved it off. It was no big deal, even though it was my lucky shirt."

Fred put his head in his hand.

"You know she put her job on the line by staying on the

bus to find the button? I don't know what excuse she told those goofballs, but they bought it! You know what, they owed her!" Fred pounded his fist but remembered his company and softened. "Iris kept a secret from me. Twenty-five years after we had been married, she confessed that she popped the button off with her nail. One button, and I got fifty years of love. I was gifted love." Fred pointed to his chest. "And no, I did not get that job, but you know what? I met up with Iris a few days later, and she fixed the button, and I got the very next job I interviewed for. She was good luck and she was hopeful. That shirt was lucky too." He blinked back tears. "Please excuse me."

Fred wiped his eyes, scooted his chair back, and put his napkin on the table.

"The rolls must be done. I'll bring us some."

He stood and kept talking as he walked to the kitchen.

"Iris taught me how to make bread ... when, you know ... when it all started. You know what she said to me one time? She said, 'Fred, our love is everything you can do with dough! Roll it, squeeze it, flatten it out, ball it up, knead it, toss it in the air. Pound it! You can bake it, savor it, sweeten it, share it! I didn't get it until she taught me how to bake. That's just who we were together, that's just who we were. We tried for kids, but it was alright. Our shared life became my identity. We had each other."

Fred pulled six rolls from the baking sheet and arranged them on a white plate exactly how she used to.

"Fifty years. The world is full of all different types of buttons, but no one talks about them anymore. All types of buttons out there. But the conversation around them is quiet, just like it is here."

Crying, he leaned over the rolls and gripped the counter.

"I'm making my rolls salty," Fred chuckled. "Iris rhymes with virus. That's about all I can take. Six feet apart and six feet underground. We had to be that far from each other. What was that thing preparing us for? Six feet is not a goodbye. I would fuss and complain about everything, everything around me, the day-to-day duties. She would say, 'Fred, why do you need to make the facts of life hot potatoes?' And all these people, making the facts of science hot potatoes. I don't get them. The stress is growing. It's too much for me. Too many rubber bands around a watermelon. I have lost so much, and I still don't go out of my way to hurt those people. I leave them alone. I'm not making anyone's life hell. Why are they trying to hurt me? But it can't get worse than this. They say it wasn't real. But it was real, it is real. It is still real. She was right here, and now she is gone. Her only underlying conditions were a heart full of love and a happy life. Iris rhymes with virus. There is nothing left to say … buttons … buttons … buttons …"

He wiped his eyes and picked up a roll.

"I'll never get over it, but I'll get through it. I'll be strong for her. But why her? Why not me? The doctor told me to 'expect that survivor's guilt could feel like a daily catastrophe.' He's right!"

Fred bit into a roll.

"Have you ever loved someone so much that even saying their name hurts your heart? There was nobody like you Iris. There was nothing like us. Well, have you, have you loved like that?"

The chairs sat empty.

Nobody said a word.

LOCKER

Josie reached up and discreetly pulled the plastic blue string and heard the familiar bell chime. As she lowered her hand, she rolled her eyes at her fake nails. *Why do people like these?* "Stop requested," a voice over the intercom announced.

She adjusted her glasses, sat forward, and casually looked back to see who else was standing up to exit, or if anyone was eyeing her. The bus slowly veered to the side of the street and stopped. Josie headed to the back door and waved thanks at the driver. Her feet hit the sidewalk, and she stayed close to the curb, letting people pass her as she walked the two blocks. Josie adjusted the straps on her backpack and glanced back. The nearest group of people had stopped in front of a pizza place and were looking at the menu illuminated by neon lights. There were some other men visible too, but they were a block back. One was facing the street, while the other was on his phone. *Go now.* Josie darted across the sidewalk and smiled at the bouncer, Max, who had uncrossed his tattooed arms to pull the door open.

Josie stepped into the dark club and cringed at the heavy bass, the erotic thumping emanating from all directions. She scanned the floor and quickly took in each table as she made her way to the dressing room, looking for regulars, any bachelor parties, and newbies. *A bit busier than last Friday. Who's on right now?* She glanced at a stage and saw Elle. *She is such a bitch.* Josie looked to the other stage. *Oh, Bianca is on.* Josie paused and watched. Red lights strobed across Bianca's body, and her sparkly silver eyeshadow popped against her silver bikini and silver stiletto heels. She rolled her curvaceous body and grabbed the pole and was soon upside down. Her chest squeezed together beautifully as her strong legs extended and moved seductively in the air. Her long, dark curls hung dreamily, and her perfectly shaped mouth hinted at a sly smile as she twisted and turned around the pole. Josie stared. *How do you do that? Jesus Christ, Bianca. That's why you're the favorite.*

She continued to the dressing room and opened the door to loud chatter, a dozen different sweet body spray scents, as well as the residue of cigarettes, sweat, alcohol, makeup, and slightly burning hair. About a dozen or so women were in front of their lockers taking selfies, or were in front of mirrors doing their makeup, adjusting their wigs, tucking their tits in or pulling them out, looking at their ass and tan, or texting. Josie crept past everyone without anyone acknowledging her. She adjusted her glasses, unlocked her locker, and tossed her backpack on top of a small pile of shoes and clothes.

"Fuck, I'm tired. What am I going to wear tonight? Hmmm … black and red, I guess."

She pulled out her black heels, black fishnets, and her red top and red thong. Josie headed to the bathroom to change, and she paused or dodged as dancers cut in front of her. Right then the dressing room door opened, and a graceful and powerful looking Bianca strode in. A few dancers turned and eyed her or glanced at her through her reflection in the mirror. Bianca met everyone's eyes with a kind, warm smile as she walked to her locker. The air grew quiet. Josie looked around. *Why did everyone stop talking? Why are they whispering? Why is everybody standing still? What jealous bitches!*

Josie opened the bathroom door.

"Who did this!" a voice yelled.

Silence.

What's going on?

Josie tucked her clothes in her arm and turned around. She weaved her way between a half dozen dancers to find out who had yelled. It was Bianca. She saw Bianca standing in front of her locker, her body tense. Josie squeezed in a bit closer to see what was happening. On Bianca's locker, someone had written in lipstick: "Bianca was a Boy."

"Oh my god," Josie whispered and looked at Bianca.

Bianca still hadn't moved. But her eyes had filled with tears, her jaw had clenched, and her chest rapidly rose and fell.

"Who did this!" Bianca yelled again and blinked back tears. She turned around. "Angel! I know you did this! How fucking dare you! Is this some kind of joke! You destroyed my locker and are trying to humiliate me, just because your regulars left you? I can't help it if they chose me over you. Welcome to the fucking industry! Clean this shit up, now!"

The women shuffled around and snickered as Angel strolled forward in her pink bra, see-through booty shorts, pink thong, and heels. Two dancers held up their phones, and one started laughing. Angel tossed her bleached blonde hair in her fingers and tilted her head.

"What's wrong, Bianca? Should we change the 'was a boy' to 'is a boy?' Or should I call you Brandon?" Angel began whispering, "Bianca is a boy, Bianca is a boy. Are you in drag, Bianca?"

Bianca's hands balled up, and she shook her head. "Stop it, Angel! Stop right now!"

Angel stepped forward and continued to taunt her. Bianca looked away. Josie saw her tears.

"Hey, cut it out, Angel!" Josie leaped in between Bianca and Angel, and they both looked down at her, completely stunned. Josie pointed a finger up at Angel, who towered over her. Josie gulped and panicked. Angel smiled and tilted her head.

"Ummm … ummm … don't you talk to my girlfriend that way!" Josie stammered.

Angel's face fell.

"Yeah, you heard me right, Angel! Bianca is my girlfriend. We've been together for three weeks. I'm a lesbian, but nobody here knows that or gives a shit about me! Look at the stickers on my locker, look at my clothes. Hello! Well, Bianca and I are dating. And I can tell you for a fact, Bianca is not a boy. Isn't that right, honey?" Josie turned to face a completely shocked and terrified Bianca. Josie flashed her eyes at her and gave the tiniest hint of a nod.

Bianca studied Josie for a few seconds before grabbing her hand, leaning forward, and kissing her passionately. When Bianca backed up from the kiss, she smiled and wiped a tiny smudge of lipstick from Josie's bottom lip. Josie's eyes went wide in shock, and Bianca looked up at Angel and shrugged. Josie turned around and faced Angel, who was shaking her head in disgust.

"Bianca is not a boy. Bianca is my girlfriend! See! So, fuck off!"

"Whatever you two are, it's absolutely disgusting!" Angel shouted and stormed off.

Josie spun around to face Bianca, but Bianca was pulling her things from her locker and shoving them in her bag. *What should I do?* Josie waited a minute, but a visibly upset Bianca still hadn't turned around. Josie gave up and walked to the bathroom and changed. She went back to her locker, put her clothes away, and pulled out the black wig, the one with the little red ribbon on it. She walked to a counter and looked in the mirror as she put her short, thin hair in a low ponytail. She began to put the wig on her head, but something didn't feel right with her hair, so she took off her glasses and put them on the counter before re-tucking her ponytail.

"Josie! Oh my god! Don't move. There is something on you!" a dancer named Cinnamon yelled from a distance.

Josie froze and closed her eyes. "What is it! What is it! Get it!" She held her hands up and scrunched her shoulders.

"Just don't move, Josie. I think it's a tick or a small spider or something. I don't want it to bite you. It might have come from your locker. Just don't move."

"Please get it off!" Josie shrieked.

Cinnamon came up and lightly touched the top of Josie's back before winking at Angel, who walked up to the counter.

"I think it's burrowing, Josie! Just hold still. You don't want to see this!"

"Oh no! What the fuck? Get it please!"

Cinnamon scratched the same spot. "Oh wait. Never mind. Nothing there! Bye!"

"Oh my gosh, you scared me! Thank you! That is so weird! Are you sure it's gone?" Josie reached around and felt her neck and back. "Hello? Was that you, Cinnamon? Hello?"

Josie opened her eyes and touched the counter. "Where are my glasses? Hello? Can somebody help me?" Josie ran her hands across the counter. "Goddamnit!" she yelled. Tears came to her eyes, and she ripped her wig off. "I can't see. Somebody please help me!" Josie sat down on the floor and buried her head in her hands.

Other dancers walked past, flushed toilets, giggled, slammed their lockers shut, or quietly went about their business. They didn't want Angel after them.

"Hey Josie, Josie, it's Bianca. I'm here. What can I do?" Bianca touched her shoulder.

"I can't see. Please help me. I can't see without my glasses. I think Cinnamon or Angel took them."

"Fuck," Bianca sighed, looking around the dressing room.

"Here, Josie. Let's get you up." Bianca stood and grabbed her hands and helped her up. She guided a dizzy Josie to a busted-up plastic chair and sat her down.

"Stay right here, no matter how long it takes. I will find your glasses. Don't move until I get back. I don't want you to trip or get hurt. And I don't trust anyone in this room right now."

Josie nodded. She wiped her eyes, but tears kept coming. Bianca touched her shoulder and left.

What felt like twenty minutes passed. Josie heard the door open and close several times. She heard a loud commotion out in the club and banging on the lockers. She wiped her eyes and covered her face with her hands.

"Josie, hey, I found them. Here." Bianca put the glasses in Josie's hand. Josie put them on and blinked. "But they were in the trash. Luckily, that bitch didn't break them. I washed them in the sink with soap multiple times. I'm sorry, but I have to leave now."

"What? No, wait, please. Hold on. I can see. Thank you so much. Don't go. I have to thank you somehow."

Bianca looks exhausted. Her eyes are red.

"No, you don't understand, Josie. I think I'm out of a job. I just yelled at the boss, and it didn't go well."

"What the fuck?" Josie stood up. "What the fuck?"

"Yeah, Cinnamon and three other girls told Jimmy that I

threatened Angel in the dressing room. And then he saw me confront her about your glasses."

"What? Oh my god! I'm going to talk to him right now!" Josie took a step, but Bianca grabbed her arm.

"No, you aren't! It's not worth it. I'm not ever coming back here. It isn't safe. And I know Angel has been fucking Jimmy for a while now, so it's a lost cause."

"What? Ewwww! Fuck that! This place isn't safe for me either then," Josie groaned.

"What? Why?" Bianca raised her eyebrows. "Don't lose a job because of me. Angel has it out for me, not you."

"Not true. Well, not anymore. I think Cinnamon lied to me and said there was a bug on me so Angel could take my glasses. Angel is a bigot, and if she is with Jimmy, that's bad for me. He's a bully. Bianca, I am a lesbian. They will beat me up. I'm only five feet tall. I can't stay here."

"Oh fuck. I really don't want you to lose a job over this." Bianca crossed her arms. "I'm sorry."

"Well, Bianca, I don't want you to lose your job over this. You're the best dancer here! By far!"

"I know that I am, Josie, but I'm not fucking the manager, so it doesn't matter. There are other clubs out there."

"Bianca, do you want to go grab a drink with me, if you drink? I think we both could use it."

Bianca exhaled and rocked her head from side to side in thought. "Ummm ... sure."

"Great!" Josie smiled. *Who am I right now? I'm getting a drink with Bianca. I don't have a job.*

"Just give me two minutes to pull my stuff together, and I'll be ready. I want to get out of here," said Bianca.

"Yeah. Me too." Josie eyed each dancer as the dressing room door opened. "I want to leave before Angel and Cinnamon come back in here. I'm not afraid of them, but I don't want—"

"I know. Let's go." Bianca nodded.

Josie pulled the door open and peeked out. She spotted Angel on stage and scanned each table for Cinnamon. *Oh, there she is!* Cinnamon sat next to a man in a booth and had her legs draped over his lap. She looked up mid-fake laugh, and her eyes narrowed in a venomous glare at Josie. *Cinnamon is stuck. She can't do anything. Someone else will sit in his lap.*

"Bianca, let's go," Josie whispered. Bianca nodded, and they hustled through the club. No one noticed Josie, but heads turned as they saw Bianca.

"Jimmy just came out of the office. Run, Josie!"

Josie pushed the front door open and started running, with Bianca close behind. They ran down the long block and turned the corner before Josie stopped.

"We made it!" Josie held up her hands.

"You are funny! I haven't high-fived in probably ten years." Bianca smiled and raised her hands.

"I'm weird. Today is weird. I'm just glad we got out of there," Josie said quickly. "I see a bar."

The women walked in silence. Every couple of feet, Josie looked up at Bianca to see if she was alright. *I have never seen Bianca with clothes on. She has tennis shoes. She still seems nine inches taller than me. Fuck. I hate being short.*

"Is this alright?" Josie pointed at a small dive bar.

Bianca nodded, and Josie opened the door and motioned for Bianca to go ahead. They sat down at a booth and didn't speak. Josie rolled her neck and took her backpack off. Bianca tucked her own bag away and eyed everyone at the bar.

"Can I see your ID?" the bartender asked Josie as he came up to the booth.

"Of course." Josie smiled at Bianca and pulled her ID out. The man nodded and brought beer.

"What would you do if you didn't dance?" Bianca asked.

"Hmmm … good question. I like health stuff. I got a degree in nutritional science. Saving for next steps, but I'm unsure what those are. Grad school, certification, who knows? I just know I'll need money for it, and regular jobs aren't enough. I tried, but all my money went to rent."

"Yeah, I hear you."

"This work is strange for me. That's why I never go on stage. I'm not confident like you. I'm so short and like a hundred and ten pounds, and everybody thinks I'm super young even though I'm twenty-four. I hate it. I'm just small everywhere. And it's like … the men at that club wanted me to be a 'little girl,' so I just played it up, even if I hated it. I'm good at it, and I guess being good at it makes me more okay with it. It's a muscle I can flex to pay bills, even if it creeps me the fuck out sometimes."

"I understand." Bianca nodded and took a drink.

"Bianca, it's not my business, and you don't have to tell me, but why would those bitches write that on your locker? Do you know them from other places? You don't have to tell me, but please know you can trust me. Ugh, okay, let me start over. I'm here if you want to talk about it."

Bianca looked around and exhaled. "Honestly, I don't know them. But Angel could have known someone, or knows someone who knows someone, who knew me from somewhere … high school, college, I don't know. I wasn't me then. I was hiding, suffering, inside of someone else. How can L.A. be so fucking big and so fucking small at the same time?"

"Yeah." Josie nodded. "So … you mean?"

"Yeah." Bianca nodded back and then looked down at her drink.

"Oh … I see." Josie smiled softly and looked around. "Thank you for telling me."

Bianca nodded.

"Can I ask if your family supports you? Again, you don't have to tell me."

"Ha. Yeah, I trust you. Ummm … so my mom is becoming more okay with it. She always wanted a daughter but never thought it would be me. It's a lot for her to process. I'm alright with her missing her son. I get it the best I can. She can see how much happier I am now, and I know she believes me when I told her I would have died if I didn't transition. It's funny, but like the second or third talk we had about it, she asked about grandchildren. It was like, I was already killing the dream of her son, and she wanted to know if she needed to grieve the dream of grandchildren. Good grief. When I told her I froze sperm beforehand, it was like I told her that she had won five million dollars." Bianca shook her head and took a drink. "My dad doesn't say anything about it, but he's respectful enough. My mom corrects him when he fucks up with pronouns or dead names me. I know he's grieving his son too. It's harder for him. I don't know."

"Oh, Bianca." Josie wiped her eyes and cleared her throat. "Thank you for telling me."

"What about you, Josie?"

"Oh. Uhhhh …" *Oh god. Fuck.* Josie took a drink. "No dad, only child. I grew up in northern Idaho. Awful red state. Blech. So when I came out, my mom kicked me out. I will never go back or see those people again. I lived on campus and got through school. And then I hitchhiked down here two years ago, which I would *never* do again. I just didn't think about it. I was only used to Idaho, and nobody was there to say, 'Hey, Chloe, hitchhiking is dangerous as shit. Buy a plane ticket or take a bus. Somehow, I didn't get murdered. That's me."

"Chloe," Bianca whispered. "I like your name, Chloe."

"It's strange to hear you say it. I mean, after stage names and all."

"Yeah." Bianca smiled.

"Life's a fucking drag, isn't it? Oh fuck, sorry. I'm just. I'm sorry, Bianca. I'm going to get us another round. That okay?" Josie asked as her face reddened.

"No apology necessary. I love drag, and yes, life is a fucking drag. Another round is great."

Josie came back and placed a beer in front of Bianca as she sat down.

"I'd trade with you, you know. I would do it in a heartbeat." Chloe took a drink.

"Trade what?"

"You know ... our ... our bodies."

Bianca sighed and reached to put her hands on Chloe's. "You are very, very sweet. But that's not really ... it's bigger than that. Much bigger than that. Imagine spending decades in the wrong body. Not only wrong, but there's like a deficit, you know? I wasn't seen and known as a cis girl as a child. I didn't go through the rites of passage into womanhood. You know?" Bianca inhaled tightly. "I know I am a woman. I know that deep in my heart and in my soul. But it's been a hard journey to love myself, and Josie, I mean Chloe, it will never be the same. It will never be what you experienced. That's what I missed. I'm grieving it." Bianca blinked back tears.

"Oh fuck, I'm sorry. I shouldn't have said that. I'm so sorry."

"Hey, hey, it's okay." Bianca squeezed her hand.

"No, don't comfort me. This is about you. I messed up. I'm sorry. I need to work on my language. I just have this feeling, or maybe it's the alcohol talking, but right now I feel like I would do anything for you. That's what I was trying to say. Oh my god, I must be drunk. I'm such a lightweight." She put her head in her hands.

"Chloe, stop apologizing. I can feel your intentions and your good heart. You came to the rescue in the dressing room.

Thank you." Bianca reached to pull Chloe's hands down.

"Well." Chloe adjusted her glasses. "I would still be crawling around the floor in the dressing room, but you rescued me." Chloe felt her face flush and looked away. "Bianca," Chloe started, eager to change the topic, "how long have you been dancing?"

"A couple years. As soon as I transitioned, I started pole classes." Bianca took a drink.

"And you enjoy it? It seems like you do. Much more than me at least." Chloe searched her eyes.

"Yeah. It's affirming as shit. I love it. And I'm good at it, if you haven't noticed." Bianca winked.

"Yeah, everyone notices." Chloe took a big drink. "Bianca, you are the most beautiful woman I have ever seen. You are not what they said. You are the brilliant, beautiful, and brave Bianca! I wonder what will happen now."

〜

Two years later, "Poker Face" by Lady Gaga was blaring on speakers. The volume lowered a bit as a voice came over the microphone. Pride flags and rainbow-colored streamers adorned every corner of the club.

"Alright, beautiful people, please put your hands together for the woman we've all been waiting for! Our shining star! Our divine diva! The one, the only—Bianca!"

The lights dimmed, and within seconds, "Born This Way" began. The strobes flashed as the audience whooped and squealed. Bianca emerged on the stage in a short, fringe gold dress. She had on six-inch gold heels, her gold jewelry sparkled, and gold glitter covered her chest and arms and twinkled in her hair.

"Let's go!" She raised her arms and smiled. Everyone

cheered.

Across town, a woman cheerfully tapped her short nails on the counter and smiled at the customer who was placing bottles of vitamins, supplements, and bags of protein on the counter.

"Find everything alright?" Chloe asked as she reached for the items to ring them up.

"I always do. You know my kids will only eat the vitamins from this store? This place has a special energy, good vibes or something. Either way, I'm thankful!" The woman laughed.

"Yeah, it is really special here." Chloe smiled. "Oh ouch." She reached for her belly.

"You alright?" the woman asked and leaned forward. Her eyes went wide.

"Oh yeah, the baby is just kicking along."

"Awww … I remember those days! Congratulations! I hope it's okay to say, but you look radiant."

"Thank you." Chloe rubbed her belly again. "I'm so unbelievably happy."

DISDAIN

I can taste his disdain in this new day's sweat.

I feel it in my mouth when I look at him. It's more like chalk than anything else.

A thing, unsettled, creeps across his face.

It tastes like steel now, inside my head. Train tracks. Those damn train tracks.

Dusty suitcases and dry crops. We lived out there, but now our bodies are here.

I move a comb through my hair.

Grit.

The dog barks in the backyard. He wants to be let in. I only want to be let out.

Any field will do.

My tongue slides to speak, and he crosses his arms.

My teeth are little machines, just winding and grinding at his sense of freedom.

He says, "You can use your mind, as long as those thoughts don't leave that mouth. Let me control these things." Well, he took control and almost killed us.

Every morning he goes out to the field to talk to God.

Why doesn't he stay in here and talk to me?

Too busy doing God's good works to do something good for me.

Goodness doesn't trickle down, not when you are like that.

Good deeds don't spread like sickness does.

I don't want to die, just disappear. I sit here and cry, and he tells me to read the Bible.

When we met, he never said grace. Prayers, that's what I noticed first.

I thought we would get better when he started going to church.

But then I told that man he couldn't walk on water, so now he is walking away from me, or walking all over me. I have been a battered everything. Every possible boundary has been crossed.

I can deal with anything as long as I know where I stand.

Everything can't be God's will, right?

These bills are more present than anything in the sky above.

He's out in the front with God, but this devil is still standing at the back door.

He strokes me like he is swatting at an annoying summer fly.

And then he grins and says, "You're real ripe, aren't you?"

When it's done, my belly is swollen, but I work to keep my other parts thin.

Unwashed rags and stained walls.

All these ashtrays look like me.

It all tastes like copper in my mouth. There are no more seams to split.

I had so many dreams, but these children keep coming.

I can't find anyone in this town who is the same as me. If I had someone, maybe I could leave.

I have been in this field long enough. But all I have are full hands and empty pockets.

There's so much bad blood between us, and I don't even know whose body is bleeding.

I keep trying to take it all with salt or take it with some grace.

He says I talk too much, but I haven't said a word in fifteen years.

He wants me to just follow him around and love him no matter what. Well, I ain't no dog.

Pray the smoke won't hurt this baby.

GARAGE

"Sam." Louise's right hand extended from her long, purple sleeve and tapped on the driver's side window. Sam didn't move.

"Sam." Louise tapped again. "Sam, I need money."

"Sam, why is the music getting louder? Sam, look at me!"

"Sam, look at me!"

"Sam, look at me!"

Sam kept his eyes straight ahead and lit a cigarette before reaching for the radio again.

Louise grabbed her head with both hands and pulled on her thin, sandy hair. *Why is he doing this?*

"Sam!" she wailed.

"Sam!" Louise balled up her fists and lifted them to pound on the window.

In his peripheral vision, Sam saw her and clicked the round radio button off. Louise dropped her arms and looked back across the street. Four people had stopped shopping. One woman with an open mouth clung to a yellow vase, a man shaking his head held a giant wooden picture frame, and two teenagers watched through their phones. Louise scanned the yard but couldn't see the homeowner. She looked at the dimly lit garage. Nothing. *Where is she?* Something seemed to move.

Is that a shadow? What's going on? Is someone in there laughing at me? What did I miss? Louise turned to see Sam staring up at her with smiling eyes. *Why is he mocking me?* He reached for the handle, and the window gradually rolled down. *He's taking forever on purpose. All these people are looking at me. He's ashing in the car!*

"What is it, Louise?" he groaned and ran his hand across his forehead, wiping underneath his dingy, red beanie. A few brown, greasy curls poked out the back of his cap. "Well?" Sam uttered and took a big drag.

Louise bent and gripped the car door right where the window disappears, so he would have to close it on her fingers. "Sam, you heard me! Why did you ignore me?"

"Why are you yelling at me? Do you know how to whisper?"

"I am whispering, Sam!"

Louise glanced back at the people standing around staring. She gave a thumbs up and then a wave while her other hand stayed on the door.

"I need money, Sam." Louise met his eyes again.

"For … what?"

"Why are you talking so slowly, Sam?"

"Why are you talking at all, Louise?"

"Sam, you make me so angry. It's my money! Give it to me, or I'll start screaming!" Louise grabbed her hair and began rocking back and forth. Her feet rose and fell on the pavement.

"Stop! Jesus fucking Christ, Louise. Stop! You are going to make yourself pass out again. Stop breathing so hard. Here, here is your goddamned money."

Sam flicked his cigarette butt right past her as he leaned back in his seat and reached into his pockets. He stuck a flattened wad of small bills out the window. "What new, not needed thing do you *need* now?"

"It's my money, Sam."

"Whatever it is, I don't think it's what Uncle Sam has in mind when you get your 'crazy' check every month." He chuckled and shook his head before reaching for a cigarette.

"You know what, Sam—my 'crazy' money bought your cigarettes. My 'crazy' money kept the heat on and the water running in our home. The home *I* inherited, the home you didn't have to work for or pay for. Where's your money? Why don't you ever have any money, crazy or not?"

"Okay. That's enough!" Sam slammed down on the dashboard.

Louise glanced back across the street. *Oh no, strangers are staring again.* She scanned the yard and spotted the homeowner, who had shielded her eyes with her hand but looked on as well. *I'm going to be sick. Now she isn't going to give them to me.* Louise ran across the street. *I didn't look both ways. Stupid, stupid. Focus, Louise, focus.* She trudged up the driveway with her head down, eyeing the ground, moving around table legs and zigzagging past feet. *Where is she? Where did she go? I'm sweating. I'm sweating.* Louise rolled the damp money in her hand.

"Hello!" a voice in front of her called out.

Look up, Louise. Look up, Louise.

"Oh hi! I was looking for you!" Louise met her eyes and tried to smile.

"Are you alright?" asked the homeowner delicately. She looked to be in her mid-60s, with a white-blonde bob and kind, tired blue eyes, hunched shoulders, and tightly crossed arms.

"Yeah, I'm fine. I like your sweater." *She is just cold because it's chilly out. She isn't judging you, Louise.*

"Oh, oh, yeah, thanks." The woman briefly glanced down and rubbed her fuzzy black sweater.

"My name is Ann. Are you sure you're okay?"

"Hi, Ann. Yes, I'm fine and I have money."

"Wonderful … ?" Ann paused and raised her eyebrows for Louise to say her name, but Louise remained silent. "Well, what would you like to buy?" Ann uncrossed her arms and put them on her hips.

Why is she being so nice to me? Why is she talking to me like I'm two?

"In there, ummm …" Louise pointed to the garage. "The VCRs in there—do you still have them?"

"Oh yes! I'm so glad. You will give them a good home!"

Louise nodded in relief and turned to hold up a just-one-minute finger to Sam, but he wasn't looking. *Please don't drive off and leave me here. Please don't drive off and leave me here.*

"Your ride okay?"

"Yeah, why?" Louise looked back at Ann. *Oh no, I'm turning red, I can feel it. Louise, say something.* "He's grumpy, didn't sleep good. He thinks he is funny when he messes with me, but he's not."

"Ahhhh …" Ann softly crossed her arms again. "I gotcha. I have one of those myself." She winked and smiled. "Husbands, right?"

"What? Oh yeah, right." Louise tried to smile back. *Why is she looking at me like that?*

"Well, let's get you those VCRs." Ann waved to her with a come-this-way motion as she walked towards the garage. Louise followed. *Don't look. Don't look. Only buy VCRs. Only buy VCRs.*

"You know, I am just so glad you can give these a good home," Ann repeated as they entered. They approached the corner of the garage where four old VCRs sat double-stacked on a shelf. Louise glanced in all directions. *No one's here. Maybe no one was laughing at me?*

"Gosh, I didn't do a very good job of cleaning these off." Ann ran her hands across the top VCRs, and a light layer of dust brushed into the air.

"Yeah, you made the decision to use a dry paper towel, not a slightly damp one. It's alright."

Ann's eyes widened in curiosity, as though she had asked a question without speaking, but her bewilderment broke out into a smile.

"Wow! You *are* attentive! Gosh, if my teens had kept these half as tidy as I have a feeling you will, they would be in much better condition. I can't believe each of my kids demanded their own VCR. Oh well, it kept them off my back. Those were the days, right?"

"Yes, right."

"Hmmm … those days," Ann sighed wistfully. She wiped her hands across the gray plastic again.

Louise frowned. *What's happening? Is she going to give them to me?* She reached for her hair but stopped herself and took a step forward.

"How much do you want for them? They just have green stickers, and I don't know what the green sticker means." She opened her hand and unfolded a five and three crinkled ones. *Should have looked before, Louise.* She didn't notice Ann reading her eyes and then her hand.

"Green sticker, green sticker, green sticker. Oh yeah, a green sticker is a dollar fifty."

"Humph … are you sure?"

"Oh, heavens yes!" Ann waved her hands. "Honestly, I just want them out of here. If you want all four, that's six dollars even."

"Yes, I do. No tax?"

"No tax. This is a garage sale, not a gas station."

Louise pulled the five and a dollar and folded them together as nicely as she could before handing them to Ann. She tucked the two extra dollars in her pocket. *Not going to tell Sam.*

"Thank you very much. Now, I'll help carry them to your car."

"No, that's alright I—"

"Don't be silly." Ann lifted two VCRs off the shelf. "If you grab those other two, we will be good as gold." She smiled as she passed Louise.

Oh no. Not good as gold. Not good as gold. What's happening?

Louise grabbed the other two and dashed towards Ann, but not before a mustard-colored blender and two blue ice trays on a card table called her name. *These are perfect. I don't have a blender like that … I wonder if I just … No wait, no wait … Don't look at those things. Don't look!*

"Ann! Ann! Ann! Please stop!"

Ann had stepped onto the street but paused as Louise shuffled past and stood in front of her.

Those people are looking at me again. Don't look at them, Louise. Focus, Louise, focus.

"I got them. Please, please let me take them!" Louise nodded.

"Oh, well … alright. I really just wanted to help." Ann discreetly glanced past Louise and at the car. Louise turned too and scanned for anything this stranger might see and interpret as strange. *Just Sam sitting in the dirty car smoking. Nothing to see.* Louise turned back and saw Ann smiling but knew those eyes still looked past her.

"I know Sam's just gonna wanna get out of here. Husbands, right? Please, please, just put those on top of my stack right here."

"Oh … Sam. Fine, I don't want to intrude. Just seemed like a lot to carry and I wanted to help. Can't kick those mothering ways." Ann shrugged and lifted the VCRs on top of Louise's, and Louise tried to block her view of the car.

"Thanks again!"

HONK!

Sam slammed on the horn, then held it down. The VCRs shook in Louise's grip as she jumped, but she quickly recovered.

"Ahhhh!" Ann plugged her ears and shook her head while the horn blared. "Oh my goodness! That scared me! What on earth is going on?" Ann lowered her hands and put one on her heart. She shook her head and looked directly at Sam.

Louise mouthed to Sam, "What the fuck?" but he had his eyes straight ahead. His fingers tapped the wheel, and Louise could see his smile. Louise tried to chuckle as she looked back towards Ann. "Sleep deprived and hungry is a bad combination for husbands, right?"

"Yeah … right." Ann stammered.

"Well, thanks again, Ann. I should go." Louise nodded, checked for cars, and hurried across the street. *She is staring at me. Why is she still staring at me?* Louise eyed the handle on the trunk of the car. *Everything's too heavy. I can't open it. I can't put these on the ground.*

"Want me to get that?" Ann yelled.

"No, I got it. I'll just ask him to pop it." Louise adjusted her arms underneath the VCRs and trudged to the front of the car. "Hey! Pop the trunk, or I will get her to help me! The joke's over. This isn't funny anymore."

Louise side-eyed Ann to see if she was buying it. Sam bit his cheek and gripped the steering wheel. *Why is he doing this to me? My hands are sweating. I'm going to drop them.*

"Sam!" Louise yelled.

Sam didn't move, his eyes drilled straight ahead. Ann stepped into the street.

He's leaving me no choice. Louise opened her mouth to scream right as she heard the cha-chunk of the trunk opening.

"He's got it, thank you, Ann! Sam, open it for me or else I'll get her to help."

Sam shook his head and leaned forward. He looked past Louise and Ann standing there across the street. "Fine, back up!" he grunted.

Louise walked to the trunk. When he pushed his door open, a stale, smoky stench came out with him. His brown sneakers hit the pavement, and he scooted himself out and stood up. He adjusted his faded red windbreaker and pulled his jeans up before waddling to the back of the car without acknowledging Louise. He placed his right pinky underneath the slightly ajar trunk, winked at Ann, and lifted it up. He trotted back to the driver's seat and saluted Ann before getting back into the car. Louise lowered the VCRs into the trunk and pulled the door down. She hurried to the passenger side without looking at Ann.

I have to say something. Say something, Louise.

"Thanks again. I'm so sorry." Louise waved and shrugged to communicate her shared disbelief, but a man had come up behind Ann and had placed his hand on her shoulder. His mouth was moving.

We gotta go! Louise sat down and slammed the door.

"What's going on, Ann?" the man asked.

Ann didn't reply but watched Louise get in the car and avoid eye contact.

"Let's go, Sam!"

"Alright, we're going." Sam checked himself in the mirror and revved the engine. As their car pulled out, he lifted his hand and did a toodles wave towards Ann, then burst out laughing. "Got everything you *need*, Louise?" Sam reached for another cigarette.

"You are going too fast. I don't want them to get hurt or crash into each other."

"What? The VCRs? Crash into each other? You know where these things are going? Gimme a break, Louise. Hey, VCRs! Do you want to get broken now or broken later?"

"You are *so* dramatic, Sam!"

He grunted.

Louise grabbed the ends of her sleeves and balled them up in her hands. *I have forgotten something. I know I have forgotten something.* She scanned the streets for garage sale signs.

"No, Louise. We are going home!"

Louise blinked but couldn't stop from crying. She wiped her reddening eyes.

Fourteen minutes later, they pulled into their driveway. Sam reached to the middle compartment and pulled out a faded black and white remote. He pushed it, and the left garage door churned open.

Louise glanced at the floor of the garage. *Please let it be clear. Please let it be clear. Please let it be clear.* She softly rocked back and forth and squeezed on her sleeves.

"Goddamnit, Louise! Get all your shit on your side of the garage. I'm trying to park here!"

"Fine!" Louise undid her seatbelt, pressed the unlock button, and swung the door open. She heaved her body forward and planted her worn, black winter boots on the ground. She slammed the door shut and marched in front of the car. *He could run me over right now. Would he do that to me? No wait, he needs my money. He can't kill me. He would get caught.* Her head whipped back, and she squinted at Sam.

He read her mind and rolled down the window. "If I wanted to, I would have run you over already. I just want to park my car. Now, will you hurry up and move your shit."

Louise didn't reply but bent down and picked up a silver toaster lying on its side. It had tumbled down and crossed the thick line of blue tape that divided their sides of the garage.

Three portable CD players lay scattered a few feet in front of her, and two hair dryers had fallen down too. They had all crossed the line. *What happened? I stacked everything so well. Where can this go?* Her feet rose and fell as she searched for the perfect spot. *Oh no. Oh no. Oh no.* Louise placed the toaster on the corner of a pile, but it rolled down.

HONK!

Louise jumped.

"Everything is slipping, Sam!" She grabbed and pulled on her hair.

"Nobody cares, Louise!"

Oh no. Oh no. Oh no. Where can it go? Oh wait, there! Louise picked the toaster up again and moved it to the right a few inches so that it would be anchored above a small microwave. Louise slowly removed her hands. *Perfect.* Afraid of disturbing her stacks, she moved gently towards the CD players and lifted them up. *Where can these go? Where can these go?* Louise gently laid them on top of a pile containing curling irons, hot water kettles, and broken-down coffee makers. She took a step back and ran her eyes over her piles, but only the top layer had been visible for some time.

"Louise! I'm pulling in! Look out!"

"Wait, wait, wait! It's not ready. I'm not done. I don't know if it will stay!" Louise pulled on her sleeves until balls of fabric formed tightly in her palms, and she hurried out of the garage.

Sam drove past her and parked. He popped the trunk, pushed the car door open, stood, lit a cigarette, and slammed the door behind him.

"Get your VCRs out of the back! I'm heading inside. Lock the car and close the garage."

"When can we switch sides so that my stuff can be by the door?"

"I need to be able to get in my own house after I park. I can't go crawling all over your piles of shit. Some of that garbage is up to my waist. You expect me to navigate that?"

"Well, I hate having to squeeze around the car every time I just want to look at my stuff. I'm the one who spends time out here. When I want to be in the garage, I should only have to open the door to be right with my things."

"I've had it!" Sam stomped to the trunk of the car and opened it, grabbed two VCRs, and held them above his head.

"I'll do it, Louise! I'm so sick of it!"

"No, Sam. No. No. No." Louise cried and pulled her hair and ran at him. Her fists pummeled his stomach, but he didn't flinch.

"I'm showing great restraint with these VCRs, I'm showing great restraint with these VCRs, I'm showing great restraint with these VCRs." He waved them in the air.

"I hate you, Sam. I hate you, Sam."

"You can keep beating me up. Been beating me up for years, Louise! But you don't hate me. You just hate being crazy! Here!"

Sam lowered the VCRs, and Louise grabbed them and darted to her side of the garage and crouched down near a pile. She placed the VCRs on a broken-down TV covered in cords.

Sam wiped his hands and mumbled, "I'm going in."

When she heard the door close, Louise tiptoed back to the car. She pulled out the remaining VCRs. *Where will they go? Where will they go? This might work!* Louise balanced them against an air conditioner and scooted a dusty mixer over to hold them in place. She smiled. *There, everything is here.* After closing the trunk of the car, Louise gazed at her piles once more. She closed the garage door and walked into her house. Louise admired the shelving along the narrow hallway behind the door. *These lines are looking good.* Her finger tapped the orange tip of the first glue bottle, and as she went down the line, she smiled at her precision, exactly four inches between each bottle. When Louise had touched all seventeen tips, she walked back to the first one. Three inches behind it sat a small container of Vaseline. She reached to touch the lid, holding up her sleeve to prevent knocking down the glue bottle in front of it. Louise pressed a finger to each lid of Vaseline until she had reached the number seventeen. She slid her shoes off and walked into the living room and sat on a tan couch wrapped in plastic. A few feet away, Sam lay all the way back in a faded, black recliner, punching the remote.

"What's on TV? Anything good?" Louise asked, trying to sound cheerful.

"Do you want to watch the war channels or the sex channels?"

"Which war is on?"

"I think they all are," replied Sam.

"Pick one we haven't seen before."

"I think we have seen these wars. But I can't tell. They all look the same." Sam shrugged.

"Whatever is fine." Louise leaned back on the couch and ran her hands across the plastic in wide circles. *What is that?* Her left hand had stuck to something, a thin, dry yet still sticky layer of something. She picked at it without looking at it. Tiny pieces flicked off, but a residue remained. *What is that? It's not coming off. Sam eats candy. Why did he do that?*

"Sam, did you eat candy on my couch?"

"Humph?" he groaned. His eyes remained locked in on the shiny square of violence.

"Did you spill on my couch?"

"Really, Louise? There is shit everywhere, and you are worrying about a spot on the couch? Speaking of eating, what am I going to eat today?"

"What you mean is, what am I going to make you?"

Sam grunted.

Louise flinched and picked harder at the couch. *Don't lose it, Louise.* She balled up her sleeves in her fists and walked to the kitchen without looking at Sam. Louise pulled and pulled on the freezer. The door begrudgingly opened. Stacks of food encased in ice squares and a frozen stench greeted her. *These meals are bacteria boxes. They have got to be talking to each other at this point.* She picked at the ice to try and dislodge a box, but the cold burned her fingers. Louise covered her hand with her sleeve and tried to grip one, but it refused to come loose. *I can't get to it.*

"Soup it is!" Louise opened the cupboard and pulled out three old cans of tomato soup. She grabbed a can opener out of a junk drawer and slowly twisted the lids off. Louise bent down and pulled her giant pot from a cupboard and plunked it down on the stove and turned the burner on. The soup came out in thick chunks, and she lined the cans up on the counter. *Those are perfect for storage.* Louise grabbed them and walked to the other side of the kitchen. She pulled on the dingy iron handle of another cupboard until it popped open. Louise eyed the two rows of broken mugs and looked at their injuries as if they were her own. *These ones are chipped, these four have broken handles, these ones are broken in two. So much to do. I'll just put these up here for now.* Louise placed the cans next to the mugs. *Maybe I can fix just one.* She grabbed a white mug, careful to avoid seeing the blue label she had mostly picked off. Louise removed the handle from the inside. *Where is my glue? Gotta go get my glue.* She headed to the hallway for glue and saw Sam standing right behind her.

"Louise. What are you doing?"

"I'm just trying to fix these mugs. How does that hurt you?"

"I thought you were making me lunch!"

Oh shit. Louise rushed past him and to the stove, where angry red bubbles popped through the top layer of the soup.

She picked up a used ladle and plunged it into the pot. Her hands stirred and stirred. Minutes passed. *Don't remember those things. Don't remember those things.*

"Louise! Louise! I'm hungry, Louise!" Sam called as he leaned against the counter, watching her.

"Shut up, Sam!" *I can't stop stirring this pot. I can't stop stirring this pot. I can't stop stirring this pot.*

"Louise!"

"Have something else if you can't wait. It's not ready yet."

"Jesus Christ, Louise." Sam trudged to the freezer, pulled out a frozen meal, grabbed a knife from a drawer, and began scraping the ice off right onto the floor. He threw the frostbitten meal in the microwave and punched some buttons.

"I don't like you putting things in the microwave like that without looking. It's scary."

"Louise, there is nothing scary in this house except for you." *Ring. Ring. Ring.*

Louise jumped at the phone but kept stirring, so he had to answer. Sam picked up and yelled hello. He eyed Louise before stepping around the corner, pulling the coiled cord behind him. He cupped his hand and attempted to whisper into the receiver.

"She's a tornado! How is a tornado ever doing? What is a tornado truly concerned with?"

Louise heard Sam's muffled words and stomped over, the giant spoon dripping in her hand. "Who are you talking to?"

"I gotta go." Sam hung up and turned to face her. "I put up with so much of your shit, Louise."

"Sure, you tolerate me, but you wouldn't save me if I was drowning."

"If you were drowning? All you are doing is drowning. All this shit! All this shit! All this shit! You create shit and clutter wherever you go!"

"Maybe I just happen to be where clutter is already forming."

"I'm going. I'm going far, far away from you. I'm going to be off the grid! You won't find me. None of your shit will follow me. Simple, simple, simple. No stuff!"

"You aren't going off the grid. You aren't going to go live somewhere else. We know you couldn't hack it!"

"If I left, who would take care of you, Louise? Your stuff gonna be looking out for you? Can your stuff handle how crazy you are? You belong permanently strapped to a couch, tied to a gurney, or dead in a coffin. But instead, you are collecting, collecting, collecting, breaking, breaking, breaking, counting, counting, counting! You know *you* broke those mugs, right, Louise? Those mugs you are trying to fix, the ones that be-longed to—"

"Don't you dare say it," Louise trembled. "It could be worse. I could be collecting piss bottles and puke buckets. And well … well, you know what, Sam? All you do is watch trash and eat trash! You are becoming trash!"

"Fuck you, Louise."

"Fuck you, Sam-you-hell." The ladle fell to the floor.

Louise stormed off, and he followed her to the living room.

"Where are your medications?" Sam put his hands on his hips.

"I don't know. I'll just go to church."

"The church is not a hospital, Louise."

"You're nuts too, Sam!"

"I might be nutty, but at least I know what reality is. I wish I could appeal to your higher senses, but they do not exist. Even when you are safe, you are not sound." He tapped his head.

"I'm doing my best to keep it together," Louise cried. "I have to suck it up and suck it up and then I have to keep sucking and then I'm sucking up other people's behaviors and sadness and patterns and bullshit."

"Is that what all this shit is, Louise—other people's bullshit?"

"A lot of what I feel is other people's bullshit."

"So, you think this is all me," he asked, waving his hands around. "Is this why you beat me up, Louise?"

"Even Jesus beat a dude in a temple!"

"I don't think you are remembering that correctly."

"Really?"

"You know what, Louise? The worst people need Jesus the most."

"Fuck you, Sam! Unless you are God, leave me the fuck alone. You don't have a right to judge me. You don't have a right to control me. You don't have a right to shit. Your crazy-making is killing me!"

"No, your actual craziness is killing you. You are making this yourself!"

"Oh, you make me so angry I want to punch a cactus!"

"You don't need a cactus in here. All you need are some padded walls."

"You are soap scum, Sam! You are *so* dramatic!"

"No, you know what's dramatic? Your dad hanging himself in this garage for his family to find, for you to find. *That's dramatic.* You just opened the door and boom, there he was! Hanging there like an idiot! Damn, Dave! That's dramatic!" Sam broke out in laughter.

"Don't say that!" Louise pulled on her sleeves and shook her head. "You know what, Sam? Sanity is a privilege you don't even know you have."

Louise ran past him and down the hallway and pushed the door to the garage open. She slammed it as hard as she could, hurried past the car, crossed the blue tape, and dropped to her knees in front of a pile of cords. *Just braid some cords. Just braid some cords.* Her hands shook as she tried to weave them together. *What's wrong with these cords?* She flung them, and they disappeared in a pile. Louise looked around. *There it is!* She scrambled up and grabbed a baseball bat leaning in the corner.

WHACK!

WHACK!

WHACK!

The bat came down with loud, heavy thuds, and black chunks of plastic and metal flew.

Sam stepped into the garage and pushed the button to open the garage door. He jiggled his keys and unlocked the car. As he sat down and started the car, he yelled, "Just don't hit your door. I can't keep replacing it. You know the looks that repair guy gives me." He closed the garage as he pulled out.

Louise kept smashing in the dark, smashing until she couldn't see it anymore.

Thirty minutes later, the door churned open, but instead of pulling in, Sam parked in the driveway. He got out of the car and walked onto his clean, clutter-free side.

"Hey, Louise, Louise. Why are you lying on those piles? Get up. How do you do that without breaking your back?" He stood near her and shook his head at her contorted body.

"I'm already broken." She wiped her red eyes.

"Come over to my side. I got you something."

"What is it?" Louise moaned without moving.

"Something you need." He held out a matte, silver-colored cassette player, and Louise sat up. "Your cassette players are all broken, yeah?"

She nodded, and he held out his hand to help her up. The piles shuffled underneath her as she stood, and broken household items tumbled down. They stepped onto his side, and he helped her as she sat down and then laid down. She stretched out on the cool cement. He laid next to her as she held the cassette tape in the air and examined it.

"When did the eggshells between us become ice, Sam?"

"When your disease took over our garage. But you know

what, Louise. I know you can't help how you are."

A minute passed.

"Good morning!" Sam said, squeezing her hand.

No response. He squeezed again. She lowered the cassette player and stared at the ceiling.

"Good morning!" He nudged again.

She closed her eyes. "Good morning! Welcome to Dave's Done Right Appliance and Electronics." Tears rolled down her cheeks, but she continued. "We have a wide range of appliances and electronics to meet your home and business needs. Everything from stoves, fridges, and freezers, to washing machines! In need of an air conditioner? Look no further! We have what you need to keep you cool this summer! Want to make your wife happy? Get her a brand-new blow dryer and curling iron set! Or maybe she has her heart set on some new kitchenware? A new mixer, blender, or both? Need to amaze and distract your children? Plop them down in front of one of our brand-new televisions! We even have VCRs so you can watch in style! You'll be the most popular dad on the block! Time to spruce up your office? Check out our affordable fax machines and phone sets! Never be unreachable with our brand-new car phones! Need music? We have a wide variety of record players and even cassette players …"

CONSTELLATIONS

"Billy, you here?" Kip hollered through the porch screen. Billy groaned from the dinner table. He had left the door open to coax the cool evening air in, but this meant light from the dining room could be seen.

"Should have locked the door," Billy whispered. He put his head in his hands and looked down at his plate, hoping that if he sat perfectly still, Kip might go away.

"Billy!" Kip yelled.

Billy jumped and then focused harder on his plate; his blue eyes peered down onto his old potato. He had tried to salvage it by slathering butter on its discolored and dry shell, but it was long on the other side of edible. Billy kept his head in his hands, pushed his box-framed glasses back, and plugged his ears with his thumbs.

"Billy!" Kip hollered again.

Billy's thumbs weren't strong enough to block it out, and he smashed his fists down on the table. His plate, potato, and utensils jumped. *Walk away, walk away, walk away.* Billy looked at the buttery streaks from where his potato had slid. *I shouldn't eat this thing.*

"Billy!"

"Fuck!" He smashed his fists on the table again and pushed his chair out. He wanted to throw the potato against the wall but didn't want the mess. Sweat had pooled in the pits of his dark brown, striped, button-up shirt. He wiped his brow with his arm and trudged to the door.

Kip opened the door and half-entered, pausing in the doorway. He was holding the screen door open, waiting for permission to take another step.

"Good to see you," Kip lied. He shoved his hands in his pockets as the screen door closed. He wiped his feet hard on the floor where the welcome mat had once been. Billy had hidden it away for preservation. He and his mom had bought it together when they'd first moved into the house, and he didn't want Kip stomping on it ever again. Kip looked sheepishly around and scrunched up his shoulders.

"Good to see you too, Kip," Billy lied.

Kip didn't acknowledge any of Billy's words but instead removed his baseball hat and looked around for somewhere to put it. Billy didn't motion to help this man he had known for far too long. Kip looked perplexed. *Wow, look at you, pretending to be courteous to the dead. But you're used to just throwing things on the floor, huh? What are you going to do? She isn't here to pick up after you. This fumbling is so pathetic. How do you not know how to handle your fucking hat?*

Billy saw the idea spread across Kip's face, that he could hand the hat to Billy. Billy shook his head. Kip frowned as though that was the last thing he would ever do. He lowered his hat and held it reverently against his chest. His eyes still looked frantic and lost, as though it was time for him to sing the national anthem at a baseball game, but he didn't know the words. Billy knew Kip was waiting for approval to talk. He needed Billy to speak first. *I have never seen you squirm, but I'm too tired to enjoy this.*

"Come on in, Kip. Do you want some coffee?"

"Sure, sure," Kip nodded.

Billy motioned for Kip to follow him into the kitchen.

"Billy, there have never been any meteorites around here. You need to stop telling people that."

Billy froze and closed his eyes. His glasses pinched the bridge of his nose, and he lifted them to rub his eyes. *Oh fuck, my head hurts.* Kip hadn't moved, and Billy didn't look back.

A moment passed. Billy sighed and kept walking, while Kip's dirty shoes shuffled behind him. Once in the kitchen, Kip hurried past Billy and lunged for the fridge. He pulled out a package of lunch meat, white bread, and a jar of mayonnaise. Billy leaned against the kitchen counter and studied Kip. His common-law stepdad was falling apart. Only half of Kip's faded blue denim shirt had been tucked in, and his gut poked through. His jeans had patches of dirt, and his shoes looked like they hadn't been taken off in weeks. His round, puffy face beamed as bright red as ever, and yellow cigarette stains clung to his graying beard. Billy's mom had kept him fed, kept his laundry clean, his boots scrubbed, and his beard trimmed. Billy squinted at his appalling guest. I *want to wrap my fingers around your neck.* Billy clenched his jaw and shoved his hands in his pockets and sat down at the small breakfast table.

Kip twisted open the canister too roughly, and flecks of ground coffee flew everywhere. He put the coffee pot in the sink, turned the water on way too hard, and rummaged through the cupboards until he found coffee filters. The water overflowed, and he rushed back to it and slammed the faucet off. He poured it into the coffeemaker and paused before turn-ing to meet Billy's eyes. *He doesn't know how many scoops to use.* Billy shrugged. Kip haphazardly dumped eight spoonfuls into the filter. He pushed the START button with a dirty finger and resumed making a sandwich directly on the counter. Kip turned to face him and took a big sideways bite before leaning against the counter and nodding in gratification, breathing heavily through his nose. *He probably hasn't eaten for days.*

"Meteorites don't come to the country. Meteorites don't come anywhere around here. Why do you think anyone would believe you?" Kip yelled while he waved his sandwich around.

Billy stared at Kip. He saw remnants of meat and flecks of bread mush fly out of Kip's mouth.

"Why can't you tell everyone what happened? A meteor didn't kill your mom—a car accident did. You brainiacs are so stupid!" Kip yanked the coffee pot out so hard it hit the top of the coffee maker. "Jesus Christ!"

Billy shook his pounding head.

Kip poured his coffee so fast it overflowed and spilled on the counter. He grabbed milk from the fridge and plunged his hand into a small bowl of sugar cubes, grabbing two while touching all the rest. He yanked a drawer open for a spoon.

"I mean it, Billy. You have got to stop telling people that. Your mom died from a car accident, not from a goddamn space object." He banged his spoon against the inside of his cup.

"Don't say that. Don't say that," Billy whispered. His hands gripped the table. Something formed. It got stuck, and he couldn't swallow it. It traveled through his neck. That meteorite in his throat. "Get out, Kip," Billy said as he stood and met Kip's eyes.

Kip's spoon clinked loudly against his cup. He pulled it out and put it down on the white counter. Drips of coffee splattered, and Billy knew the spoon would leave a small brown ring. His mom hated those rings on her countertops, the way they stayed. Kip never listened to her.

"What?" Kip asked with his mouth full before putting his

coffee cup directly on the counter. He folded his arms and puffed up his chest.

Billy didn't acknowledge the posturing but walked over to Kip and picked up the cup. It had already been sitting on the counter for far too long. Rings were there. Residue of rings. Rings. Rings. Saturn. Rings. Neptune. Rings. Mom. Billy picked up the spoon, which left a tiny ring. He took his sleeve and wiped away the ring residue.

Kip shook his head as he looked down at Billy.

When Billy saw the counter was stain-free, he turned to Kip. "You never listened to her. Now listen to me—I want you to get out."

"No," Kip grunted. He grabbed the coffee cup from Billy's hand, and coffee splashed onto the floor. The hot coffee stung his hand, but Kip didn't react to it. He took a big gulp and put it back down on the counter.

Billy picked the cup back up instantly. Another ring. More rings. Fucking Jupiter.

"Listen, Billy. I've raised you since you were a little boy. You're a smart kid. You know better than this shit. Your mom is buried out back. Don't you remember? We had a funeral. She died in a car wreck!"

"Get out!" Billy yelled as he threw the coffee cup across the room. It hit the wall above the kitchen table with a loud crack, and ceramic slices of meteorite flew everywhere.

"You're crazy!" Kip jumped.

"Get your stupid hat and get the fuck out of my house!"

"I'm fucking leaving! I've had enough of you. Your mom is turning in her grave. At least she is spared your weak-ass behavior now. You'll never be a man. I bet she crashed on purpose!"

"I always thought you would be the thing that killed her, Kipling. You threatened as much."

Kip swallowed and paused. He picked up his dirty hat and stormed out of the kitchen.

"Who are you now without a woman to hurt, Kip?" Billy yelled after him.

The front door slammed shut. He grabbed a rag, ran it under water, and wiped down the counter. He wandered out into the living room and opened the front door, letting a breeze come through. He looked out onto the darkening field.

Billy and his mom had moved into the house when he was five. His father had died and left just enough money for a down payment. The white, two-story house was surrounded by lush fields and silence. They could always see the stars. He'd had a whole year with his mom before Kip came around.

When Billy turned eighteen, he took out loans and left the state to go to college. While he mostly stayed away, he did come home during the summer to visit. For three years, his mom would call him drunk, crying about Kip. Billy would freak out and call the cops. If he didn't answer because he was in class, she would call over and over and yell at him for not answering. On several occasions, he would get up in the middle of a lecture, walk out, and drive home to her. But she would always change her mind when she sobered up. She would say everything was fine, express deep love for Kip, and would yell at Billy for getting the police involved. Kip and his mom would get along for a few days, but then they would drink too much, and it would start again. Billy watched his mom grow more and more erratic. He knew she had been drinking herself away and that she couldn't stop. To show his love, he once sent her a telescope, but she never even mentioned it.

Billy opened the screen door and walked out into the field. The stars were emerging in the slowly turning sky. It was quiet except for the soft hum of crickets that had tucked themselves down against the earth. He took a deep breath and exhaled.

As a child, he and his mom would come out and look at the stars. Kip had no interest in the stars. At night, Kip watched TV. At first, Billy was afraid when they walked out in the dark fields together. He would follow the swooshing sound of his mom's footsteps, anxious until they arrived at their viewing spot. His mom would point out the different constellations and Jupiter, Saturn, Mars, and Venus. She knew the phases of the moon and always pointed to the North Star.

"Jupiter is the king of planets, but Saturn carries the rings," she whispered to her son one night. She would say, "Billy, when you grow up, I'm going to study the stars. I'm going to become an astronomer."

"Don't wait for me, Mom," he cried.

"No, Billy, I'm sorry. I didn't mean to hurt your feelings. You are my star. You are my sky. You are my everything. I have all that I need right now."

She wrapped her arms around him, and Billy hugged his mom tight.

"I promise you, Billy, I'm going to learn. You are going to be so proud of me."

"I'm proud of you now, Mom."

As Billy got older, he sensed his mother's shame of not graduating from high school. He had never asked his mother for help with his homework. He came to understand she would never become an astronomer, and his heart broke and he loved her more.

The man in the field cried out. He ached for his mom and begged the sky to bring her back. Looking at the stars brought fear to his heart, so he cast his eyes down and moved carefully so that he wouldn't see her stone as he trekked back to the house. He stretched out so his fingertips could feel the tops of the cool grass.

The next morning, Billy got into his blue truck. He drove to the winding road on the hill where his mom had lost control on a turn and gone right over the edge. She had been drunk at the time and had sped off from home. Billy assumed she had fought with Kip and fled. He reached the point at the top of the hill and got out of his truck.

Billy moved slowly. He wanted to honor where those last moments had been lived. When he finally reached the ditch, he stared down into it. Black and black and black, an ominous galaxy. Was she down there? While he couldn't see to the end, a meteorite was coming. He knew what he needed to do. Billy ran back up the hill and got in his truck. He was going to meet his mom, and they were going to learn together. The engine roared, and Billy spun the truck around.

"It's just a turn, it's just a turn, it's just a turn, and you let go, you let go, you let go! How did you let go like that? Why did you let go like that?" Billy begged. He dug his fingers into the steering wheel. His body tensed. He swallowed. "It's just a meteor, it's just a meteor. It's just a turn, it's just a turn, it's just a turn. Let go, NOW!"

Billy let go of the wheel at the same turn his mother had.

All went dim.

The orbit was dark and unending.

It was where people went to become constellations.

It was where memory went to become rings of dust.

A figure undefined wrapped a warm cloak of sky across his heart.

An echo inside of him whispered, "I'm learning."

When Billy woke a couple hours later, he felt blades of cold, damp grass in his fingers. He was lying down flat in the field, right where the ground curved into the dark ditch. Billy sat upright, squinted, and looked up. He saw his blue truck parked safely at the top of the hill.

He felt for a meteorite.
Nothing.
It was time to go.

PRE-DEATH PARTY

"I'm nervous, Riley. I'm sweating through my clothes." Ben lifted one arm in front of the full-length mirror and groaned at the spreading wetness in his pit. "Ugh. This is my favorite one, my favorite one! What am I going to do? And my hair—what is going on?" He ran his fingers through his sandy blond hair; it was shoulder length and thick and it looked windblown when he removed his hand. "This wild look isn't working. Riley, what am I going to do?" Ben eyed Riley through the reflection in the mirror and held his hair back off his forehead with his palms. "Riley, is this more controlled look better? I'm sweating so much!"

"You are adorable, Ben. So cute." Riley chuckled from the bed. He rhythmically shook his green juice to stir up the sediment before taking a drink.

"Riley!" Ben pouted. "You are not helping. I love this shirt, but I can't wear it now."

"Yes, you can. Deodorize. Just keep your arms down. There will be absolutely no reason for you to lift them." Riley took a big gulp of his juice while keeping his eyes on Ben's reflection.

He put the glass down on a nightstand and walked up to Ben.

"Here, I'll show you." Riley smiled and kissed him on the cheek. "My gosh, you are nervous. I can feel your cold sweat. Oh sweetheart."

"Stop," said Ben.

"I'm sorry," Riley said before leaning in to kiss his other cheek. He then rotated Ben's body so that he was standing sideways in front of the mirror. Riley stood closely behind him and reached forward. He took Ben's left arm and swung it up and down so that Ben could see from the side that his pit stains weren't showing.

"Look at that motion, and no pit visibility. Wow, look at those arms! You have the body of a surfer—ruggedly handsome with that blond hair and blue eyes. But are you a golf bro? Can we see your swing?" Riley used an exaggerated coach voice.

"Why yes, bro, I do golf!" Ben lowered his voice to a deep tenor. "I got golf gains!" Ben grinned and flexed both arms. His pit stains showed.

"You gonna teach me?" Riley taunted playfully.

"I hope to forever," Ben replied, avoiding eye contact. He turned and positioned himself behind Riley and wrapped his arms around him. "I'll give you a private lesson. But you're too tall! Bend over!" Ben pushed on Riley's back to bend him over a bit.

"Am I truly too tall?" Riley looked up in the mirror.

"You know what you do when you look at me like that with your deep, dark eyes? I feel like a girl at senior prom. Bright and giddy and nauseous," Ben sassed. He lowered his eyes and focused on their intertwined arms and hands, as though an eternity rested on how they teed up.

"This is how you swing—" Ben began, but Riley spun around and grabbed Ben's face with both hands and kissed him. He picked Ben up and carried him to the bed.

"Do you want to take your shirt off first?" Riley winked. "I'll hang it up. It can air dry."

∽

Ben laid in Riley's nook, playing softly with his dark chest hair.

"What if he doesn't like me?" Ben asked.

"Not possible. It's me he doesn't like." Riley sighed.

"And why is your dad so horrible with you? I mean, I have some ideas, but we should talk more about it."

"Yeah, well, you understand all people, so of course you will understand," said Riley. He kissed Ben's head.

Ben reached up and scratched Riley's thick brown beard. "You are very cute, but we should still talk about the way he is so distant towards you. I mean, you've told me the story before, but, especially tonight, I want to feel like I know this territory well. His childhood, the way his family didn't support his creative abilities, the way his parents thought he was soft and different, how he was thwarted and stuck. How he conformed. That he put his creative ideas away and married a woman. I mean, getting married is a lot for anyone, but to marry a woman when you're in the closet. My god. It all makes me so sad to think about it. But I wonder why he is still so awful today?" Ben asked.

"Yeah, my grandparents really wanted to 'straighten' him out," Riley quipped.

"Ughhh, poor guy." Ben looked up at Riley before resting his head again.

"Yeah, my heart breaks for him around that. And for my mom. But a shitty situation doesn't mean you can just be a narcissistic asshole for the rest of your life. Anyway, shitty marriage, shitty jobs. My mom demanded a child. I think he panicked, and ta-da, here I am, lover!" Riley shimmied his torso to make Ben laugh, but Ben didn't laugh, so Riley continued. "A kid is a convenient distraction. I think the sex probably traumatized him. They might never have done it again. So, it is just me." Riley kissed Ben's head.

"What else?" Ben squeezed Riley.

"Fine." Riley looked up to the ceiling. A moment passed. "You know he stayed around to raise me, but he was miserable. When I got older, I knew what was up with him because I was going through it too. Don't know if I ever told you that. I recognized that struggle. But, of course, we didn't talk about it. How could anyone say to their parent, 'Gee, I think you might be gay? Does Mom know?' When I hit eighteen, he left her, and me. Well, I was okay with it—I thought maybe he would die if he stayed. The Midwest at that time … oof. So, he moved here and went wild. He had never partied, never been out, never been with anyone else, or so I assume. I think the insanity of those L.A. free-for-all days released his genius and inspired him more than anything else. But he burned out quickly and almost didn't make it. He was out here, all alone, totally naive, saying yes to everything and everyone. We were both coming out at the same time, but across the country from each other. We had no contact. But the creation that had been in the closet with him began to flow out. It took him years, but he finally got a movie made, *The Inbetween.* A middle-aged gay man in a Hollywood that wasn't tolerating the public gay. But he always tried to write in queer undertones. I have a lot of respect for that. It was revolutionary and brave and vulnerable. I think Robert has had eleven screenplays made into movies, but who knows how many he has written."

"You know, a lot of that stuff I knew from you and the internet, but I didn't know about the ultimatum to your mom. People do monstrous things to get their needs met, and yet out of those monstrous times comes you. And here we are. Life is so strange. I have always wanted to ask you why you call your dad by his first name?"

"Hmmm … I guess it's to lighten the reminder that I'm his son, that I come from a time in his life that he can't deal with, except maybe through his art. I understand. He's a writer and an artist, and that means more to him than being a dad. I don't want to remind him of a painful time in his life. My feelings aren't hurt by it. A couple times I called him Dad as an adult, and he just flat out told me that his name is Robert."

"For some reason, that makes me impossibly angry, Riley, but I'm not going to start. At this point, he's made it, he's an icon, a *gay* icon. His movies of real queer love and romance, gay romance, I mean, they kind of saved me growing up. I'm going to try and not fangirl when I see him—in my forties!— but we'll see what happens. I guess I just didn't think that the writer of these courageous stories could be so bitter. I mean, I just thought … I don't know what I thought. His endings are triumphant, and there is happiness after suffering. I just as- sumed he had found his own happiness, too. And it's so weird and mind-boggling to learn how sad he remained, through all these years."

"Yeah, it's been confusing for me, at times, too. Robert told every love story he didn't live. Now he just thinks everyone wants him for his money. He was traumatized in the constant struggle to be seen, even if sideways; and there is some in- ternalized homophobia, too, as well, even though he is such an icon, like you say. He never loved himself. He retreated to his mansion. He still believes that discrimination is the only reason he never won an Oscar. He thinks they are bigots with pretty words for the gay community. It's not in the realm of possibility that other people could have written better screen- plays and that it's simply the nature of competition. It has to be that people hate who he is. Truth is, he just hates himself. It's not that he doesn't care what you think, or that he won't adore your praise. I mean, gosh, his diet right now is probably mojitos, praise from his staff, and pills, but he never got that award that he wanted, so nothing and nobody else matters. He's a self-loathing narcissist who feels cheated."

"I do feel so bad for him about his Oscar loss though. I remember seeing his face so many times in the little box on the TV, alongside those other huge names. And they never called his. The look he had, the disappointment. Over and over, so sad," Ben said.

"At the same time, he is truly doing just fine compared to almost everyone on earth. He strides the Earth like a colossus. Poor him. Anyway, it's just strange to me that you saw his face at those shows, and … years later, here we are." Riley kissed Ben's head again.

"Yeah, I haven't missed an award show, and I don't think you've ever seen one," said Ben.

Riley shrugged.

"Maybe he will like me since I've been a lifelong admirer?" Ben chuckled. "Oh shit! Riley, what time is it? We are going to be late! He won't like me at all! I'm always on time. This is your fault! Oh shit! We are going to be late! Oh my god! Riley, get up!" Ben jumped up and scrambled for his clothes.

"It's alright, Ben. We'll leave in a couple minutes," Riley chuckled. He sat up and reached for his green juice. He vigorously shook the cup until the sediment rose and swallowed the whole thing down.

In the elevator, Ben studied their reflection in the doors. "What's the plan again, Riley?"

"Well, my love, the plan is to hang out for a bit, have a drink, maybe eat. Remember you can leave whenever you want if it gets weird or he gets mean. It's a pain, but we are driving separately so that you can leave. And then I'll have a wonderful time talking with Robert about his health."

"If I start to fangirl too hard, please let me know and I will leave sooner," Ben pleaded.

"Admire him all you want. He loves praise. But he is surly and disinterested in anyone except for himself. I just don't want your feelings to be hurt by him."

"I'll be fine. If it helps, I'll just see him as another grumpy elderly client, stuck in his ways."

As they drove, Riley kept checking his mirror and slowed down at times to ensure Ben never was more than three cars behind. The extensive estates along the top of Hollywood Hills were mostly invisible behind hills and landscaping, and Robert's mansion was no different. You couldn't see the house from the security gate, where they paused while the security guard briefly chatted with Riley, and then waved them through.

What the fuck is this place, thought Ben. *Be an adult, Ben. This is no big deal. Stop trembling and stop sweating!*

Riley turned right and drove along a long, wide road that eventually circled up a hill until it came to the gargantuan gray mansion. Ben pulled his red Nissan up to Riley's Jeep and turned his car off. He looked at Riley, who smiled and waved and got out of his car. Ben felt his knees wobble as his feet hit the pavement. He looked up.

The expansive, gray stone mansion stood, multiple stories high, with striking turrets throughout, and elegant white trim around the multitude of windows. In front of the house, beautiful, clear water poured from an elaborate white fountain accented with a bright ring of red and gold flowers and a perfectly manicured hedge.

"I guess I don't need to lock my car, for the first time in my life."

"Isn't it obnoxious?" asked Riley.

"I … I don't have any words right now, Riley. My stomach keeps flipping. It's very grand, like a big alien ship."

"Hey, it's okay. I'm here." Riley held out his hand and waited until Ben took it. "If Robert says anything out of line, we'll just leave. I can always discuss it with him later."

"That's not what I'm … never mind. I'm alright. Sorry my hand is clamming up."

"Not at all." Riley squeezed his hand lovingly as they approached the entrance.

The front door was meticulously carved into a maze of delicate flowers and stems. Riley reached up and lifted the black iron knocker. He pulled it down three times and leaned to whisper in Ben's ear, "Everything here is fake except for you. Don't believe what you see."

"Wait, Riley. I know this work. You carved this door, didn't you?"

Riley squeezed Ben's hand again just as the door opened, and a short, curvaceous middle-aged lady with shoulder-length red hair stood in front of them. She wore a black turtleneck and black slacks, and giant pearls hung around her neck and from her ears. She looked irritated. Her eyes were glued to the tablet in her hand. But as she looked up, all signs of annoyance vanished.

"Oh darling, you are here!" She flung her arm around Riley and smiled at Ben, who had taken a step back.

"Hi, Charlie!" Riley exclaimed, hugging her back.

"*Who* is this?" she asked emphatically, staring intently at Ben. Charlie handed her iPad to Riley without even looking at him and soon had Ben in a tight embrace.

Baffled, he wrapped his arms around her too. Ben raised his eyebrows at Riley, who laughed.

"Charlie, this is my boyfriend, Ben. And Ben, this is

Charlene, also known as Charlie. She has been Robert's, well, our family's saving grace, and source of love and sanity for years. She has kept Robert, this property, all of it, going, and has for as long as I can remember."

"Yes, yes, all of that," Charlie said as she released Ben but kept one arm woven into his. "But, more officially, I am Robert's personal assistant and am the house and staff manager."

"Oh, okay. It's very nice to meet you. I'm sorry if I smell bad. I'm nervous," said Ben.

"Aww … Riley. What a catch! Ben, you are so handsome, you are making me nervous. My god, you are gorgeous! And so kind. Wherever did you find him, Riley?" Charlie smiled.

"I know. I am very, very lucky."

"Well, now that I'm all worked up, please give me back my iPad. Oh, Riley, what's this? Thank you, sweetie!" She lifted an envelope from the top of her iPad and tucked it in her back pocket before continuing. "Come inside, boys, so I can give you an update. I need to update the guest list. We had a last-minute cancellation and a request to bring friends. A-list assholes if you ask me. The pre-death party dinner starts in four hours!"

"Ahh!" Ben let out suddenly.

"What's wrong, dear? You look sick, honey. Are you alright?" Charlie peered at him.

"I just … I ummm … I wasn't expecting anything about death."

"Oh, Riley! You didn't tell him about the party tonight? I ought to slug you!" Charlie squeezed Ben's arm assuringly. "I know it's a lot to take in. Meeting Robert the same day a huge party is scheduled. But I promise, you'll be fine, sweetie. Everyone is going to love you, and if he doesn't right away, I'll slug him too! My goodness, I love your shirt. Your eyes are popping, Ben! You look like a supermodel. You will fit right in! It seems you two have some chatting to do, but before I leave you to it, can I please run my seating chart by you both?" She positioned herself in between them without waiting for a reply and held her iPad up.

Riley feigned interest and nodded, and Ben intently read over the names. "What? Are you serious? I'm going to faint! *They* are coming? He's going to be here? *Here*, in this *house*, I mean, in this *palace*! Olivia Shaden is showing up? What? She is going to be *here*? Are you kidding me? I have loved her forever. Oh my god, I'm going to be sick. What am I doing here?" Ben took a step back, put his hand over eyes, and let his jaw come wide open.

Riley took a step towards him and calmly put a hand on his back.

"I think I'm just going to keep the arrangement as is," Charlie said. "I don't know why Robert wants everyone to sit down. Everybody just gets up and wanders around until they find the person they *really* want to be talking to anyway. And Ben, it's no big deal. These people are just like any of us. Even messier, which can be weird. Just a bunch of human monkeys. And just between us, I'll never understand these celebrity parties. Half the people talk too much, and the other half don't say a word. Everyone just wants everybody else to shut up or speak up! See you tonight! Call me if you need anything."

"Sounds good, Charlie. Thank you. Where's he at?" Riley asked.

"Clubhou—" she started but then cut herself off. "As of today, he wants us to call it the Garden House. I think that's entirely your doing, Riley." She dramatically raised an eyebrow at Riley.

"How's he doing, really?" Riley asked, ignoring her words.

"I don't know. Death is a bummer, so I guess the only choice is to party, right? But under no circumstances is anyone allowed to mention death or the fact he is dying. Got it?" She studied both of them seriously. Once they nodded, she perked up and smiled. "Okay! Bye, boys! Ben, make yourself at home." She turned, looked at her iPad, and took off.

"I'm sorry," Riley sighed as soon as Ben met his eyes.

"I can't believe this, Riley. What in the hell is going on here? You didn't tell me this was a party. What is a pre-death? Pre-death? Dinner? Party?" Ben was exasperated.

"No, Ben, nothing weird is going on, outside of the obvious. I wouldn't lead you into anything you couldn't handle."

A tall, thin, aging man with thinning brown hair, immaculately dressed in a narrowing, black suit, approached them. He held a tray of drinks.

"Oh, I'm sorry. Hugh's here." Riley raised one arm to welcome him and grinned.

"Hi, Hugh. How are you today? I have missed you."

"Just fine, sir. Good to see you. I have your green juice prepared. Any other beverages for you both?"

"As always, thank you! Ben, this is Hugh. Hugh is the most incredible chef. I can't express how grateful I am for him. He has kept Robert nourished and healthy for decades and has orchestrated every meal and event that has ever taken place here. Hugh, this is my boyfriend, Ben," Riley said before lifting his tall glass of juice from the tray.

"You are very kind. It's great to meet you, Ben," Hugh smiled, his brown eyes twinkling.

"It's so wonderful to meet you too." Ben nodded.

"What would you like, Ben?" Riley asked.

"You know, I don't know right now."

"No worries. It's okay. I'll grab you some bubbly water." Riley reached for a glass and handed it to Ben.

"You are very kind. It's good to see you, Riley, and welcome, Ben. Now, if you will excuse me, gentlemen, I have to return to the kitchen." Hugh nodded, turned, and left.

"Riley, why didn't you tell me it was like this? I don't even know what's going on right now. I didn't even see that man, Hugh, come up. He just appeared with drinks! I need some air."

"You're right, I'm sorry. Let's go sit down for a minute and talk."

Riley held out his hand, and Ben took it. They passed by coveted paintings and walked through a regal and solemn library. It was a museum-like space, filled with sculptures and antiques. They meandered through an elegant dining area decorated with bouquets of red and white roses. Ben took in as much as he could without staring as Riley guided them out one of the glass doors and onto a broad patio. The air was fresh and cool, and from the patio, they looked over an extravagant landscape and then out over the Los Angeles Basin to the sea. There were shining, white gazebos, multiple pools and hot tubs, and two cobblestone paths that led down to a cottage tucked within a small grove of eucalyptus trees.

"Are you kidding me?" Ben whimpered. "This is too much."

"Ben, I hear you. It's a lot. But remember what I said—this isn't real. Charlie and Hugh are real, but living like this, this property, this luxury, it's delusional. It's stuff, it's imposing. It's all made up. Two and two do not make four in this place. Two and two make whatever the fuck the money buys. And whatever that is … well, it's empty. There aren't any good feelings here. I know you love celebrities and movie stars, and I'm not trying to minimize your love for all that or be some kind of a downer. I know you put these people on pedestals, but they are just people, Ben. And just as messy, ugly, and broken as the rest of us. I didn't tell you because I didn't want you to get overwhelmed beforehand or talk yourself out of coming or think that anybody here is better or more important than you, or that you don't belong. And this was half a surprise, too. All my feelings about Robert and flaunting wealth aside, I thought you would be happy to see the stars you always talk about. I think I saw that Olivia … Olivia something is coming tonight. She's your favorite, right?" Riley winked.

"You know her name! Don't tease me! Olivia Shaden! She is everything! She is everything! She is going to be here! Oh my god, she is going to be here! Help me, Riley. I can't, I can't believe it. Oh my god. My shirt! Riley, I have loved her forever! She is my favorite!"

"I'm well aware of that, Ben." Riley smiled. "You will have plenty of time to get ready before she arrives, but I need to go track down Robert at the Garden House. Wanna come?"

They slowly wandered down the path.

"What's a death party?" Ben gulped as they got closer and he saw what looked like a half dozen people at the Garden House.

"Oh, you'll get a kick out of this," Riley started as he studied an elaborate topiary display. "So, because Robert believes he is dying, he is throwing this pre-death party to celebrate and say goodbye. I know he privately hates everybody that will be here, but I think he is just gathering people up tonight to ensure there is an audience at his funeral. He will be on his best behavior, at least I hope. Wait, what's going on?" Riley looked down at the Garden House. "I'm sorry. I gotta run down there. There he is! I love you! One second!" Riley took off and began yelling, "Robert! What's happening?"

"Oh no!" Ben groaned and jogged after him.

As Ben got closer, he saw a handful of tired and sweaty men shuffling about, carrying garden tools, heavy-looking buckets, and bags of soil. One wiped sweat from his forehead, and others with long sleeves had them rolled all the way up. An older man, about Hugh's age, stood nearby with his hands on his hips, monitoring the workers. Ben looked to the Garden House and saw Riley arguing with an old man who was leaning against a wall.

"Oh my god. It's him. It's Robert." Ben stopped and waited. Riley looked up at Ben and waved him down. Ben took timid steps down the path. Riley's voice got louder, and Robert shook his head and turned away. Riley jogged up to Ben.

"Hey, are you okay? I'm so sorry about that," Riley huffed.

"I'm fine. But what happened?"

"I just … oh man, I can't believe him. So, for his pre-death party Robert agreed to incorporate planting, any type of planting—trees, flowers, herbs—whatever people wanted as a way to commemorate his life. I was going to lead the planting process with his guests, and each person would go home knowing they had planted something on Robert's estate, and they would have earth on their hands. That was the agreement, and I thought it would be lovely, but this asshole decided to have his landscape manager, Fred, that guy over there with the hat, pick up the cheapest labor he could find at whatever parking lot and have all the planting done before the guests even arrived. Plus, it's hot out, and I don't see any water!"

Robert slowly trudged over with Fred at his side. He planted his thin cane in the ground before each step. In his other hand, he held a mojito by the rim; a thin layer of muddled mint had settled at the bottom.

"It's him. It's Robert," Ben whispered without knowing it.

Riley and Fred looked at Ben.

"Oh hi. I'm sorry. I didn't introduce myself. I'm, I'm … Ben."

"Ugh! I'm sorry. Fred, this is my boyfriend, Ben. Ben, this is Fred, the landscape manager."

"Pleased to meet you, Ben." Fred held out his hand, but Robert interrupted.

"You are so ungrateful, Riley! I'm planting everything for every single guest tonight, and still, it's not enough!" Robert yelled without looking at Ben. He shook the glass in his hand.

Although weaker, Robert seemed just as powerful as he had seemed on television. But his shoulders were hunched, and it looked as though he was using his cane to hold back a full collapse. His silver hair still held small areas of its former dark potency, and a heavy white brow loomed over his penetrating eyes. The sleeves on his white shirt were rolled up, and he had on an open maroon vest.

"That wasn't the point, Robert. You and your guests were supposed to plant them with me. Instead, you have workers, and they are working in the heat. How long have they been out here? I bet you haven't even been paying them minimum wage. How much are you paying them? Did you see that they had been fed? No, of course not."

Robert looked at Fred and asked, "What's the minimum wage in California now, Fred?"

"Fred, don't tell him. He knows exactly what he has been paying them," Riley ordered.

Fred froze. Ben reached to touch Riley's back.

"Guess, Robert!"

"Guess! Guess! Guess! Well, I don't fucking know!" Robert shook his head.

"How much did you pay them last time?"

"He took care of that!" Robert pointed to Fred. "Besides, they need any money they can get!"

"You are the one who gives Fred the money! How are they getting back tonight, Robert?" Riley asked.

"Fred drove them all here in the pickup truck."

"In the back of his truck? All of those men?! That's not even legal!"

Some of the men had slowed down and were watching, while others had kept their eyes to the ground and were moving more quickly.

"How was the trip over here?" Riley called to the workers.

"The ride here was okay," one of the men yelled back. "We are used to driving in the back of a pickup."

"But it's not legal, and I'm sorry you weren't fed earlier. How much did either of these men promise you?" Riley asked as he pointed to Fred and Robert.

"They didn't say." The man paused. "But they said cash pay."

"Okay, I have heard enough! Everyone, your work is finished for today. Thank you so much! Go see the man with the hat, Fred, for full pay, and then everyone come and see me. Fred and I will be taking you back in a big black car, or possibly two big black cars."

The men nodded again but then looked at Fred and Robert.

"You heard him. Please put your supplies up against the house and come see me!" Fred hollered.

Robert stood still. Riley watched Fred pay them.

"Robert never goes anywhere, so he doesn't have a driver. I will have to drive them back. Ben, you okay if I run these guys back? It's just down in the Valley. I want to stop and get them food too, shouldn't be too long though. Or do you want to come too?" Riley asked Ben.

"Of course. I … I don't mind staying here."

"My gosh, I'm such an idiot. Robert, this is my boyfriend, Ben. Ben, this is Robert."

"It's great to meet you," Ben said. "I've been a lifelong fan. I've seen everything you have done and am so grateful for your work." Ben held out his hand.

Robert raised an eyebrow and looked away.

"I'm sorry for Robert, Ben. He will come to his senses later on," said Riley. "Follow us to the door? Fred, have them bring a car around."

The workers slowly followed Riley, Ben and Fred up the path, but they hadn't gone ten feet before Robert hollered,

"Don't let them in the house!"

Ben froze and watched Riley for a reaction. But Riley didn't turn around and he, with a dozen low-wage laborers, walked straight for the house, then through, the workers looking around for stories to tell later.

Riley reached for Ben's hand, and the group arrived on the driveway. A black limo had been brought up, the man driving stepped out, and Riley took the keys. "See you soon! Take care of yourself. You can go back in through the front and cool down if you want," Riley said as he squeezed Ben's hand again.

"Got it. I'll head up there now and wave you off!" Ben smiled.

Ben had made it to the front door and was waving as the workers jumped into the car. Just as Riley was getting in, a black SUV pulled up and a window rolled down.

"Hey, Riley. Are you leaving?" a woman's voice called out. Ben couldn't see who it was.

"Yeah, dropping some friends off. I'll be right back. Hey, Ben!" Riley hollered. "Would you please take Olivia to see Robert? She hasn't been here before."

Ben nodded but fell back into the door.

"Olivia, this is my boyfriend, Ben! He loves your work and might be your number one fan! See you both soon!" Riley yelled and smiled at Ben.

The SUV parked, and the driver, a serious man with a bald head, black suit, and black sunglasses, opened the back door.

"This is like the secret service," Ben whispered. As she stepped out, Ben went numb. "She's wearing gold! That gown, oh my god. Her hair, her heels, her jewelry!"

"Hi, Ben! I'm so happy to meet you. I would love for you to show me around!" She delicately walked to him. "It's so great to meet you, and I'm so grateful you like my work. I can tell I'm catching you off guard. I know the party isn't starting for a bit, but I like to be early—that's my secret." She held out her hand to a stunned Ben. "If I'm early, I get to connect in a more meaningful way with the host and scoot out when I want. I like to be home and have enough time to watch my shows for a bit. Ha!" Olivia laughed.

"Well, we have that in common!" Ben awkwardly laughed and felt himself sweating.

"I do not get the fashionably late crowd. I have seen people just waiting around, killing hours until it's the *cool* time to show up. They sit on their phones or bark instructions at the people who are raising their kids. God knows those of us who actually raise our kids need a break! I say, come early, leave early, get some sleep. We don't need to pace our arrival! Our egos could just squish in a little bit! There is enough room for everyone, right? Why is there so much emphasis on a grand entrance!" She waved her hand dramatically. "Look at me, complaining already! I'm sorry. Would you mind staying by my side this evening? Of course, I'll share you with Riley when I'm chatting with Robert, but outside of that, want to stick together?"

She took his arm, and Ben completely forgot about Riley as the door closed behind them.

"So tell me, have you ever been to a *pre-death* party?" Olivia asked. "What *is* it? Or is it just as it sounds? Is Robert truly dying? He seemed fine during filming, but that wrapped a year ago. Is he okay?"

"Oh, Olivia! I didn't even know this party was happening. I have never met Robert before tonight. I have no idea what's going on with him. You will have to ask Riley."

Ben escorted Olivia through the mansion and moved like it was just as normal to him as walking through his apartment. They walked up to Charlie, and Ben yelled, "Hi, Charlie! Do you know Olivia? Olivia, meet Charlie!"

All evening, Ben blissed out as he hosted and ushered

celebrities in and out, while Olivia kept close by when she wasn't down at the Garden House sitting with Robert. When Riley returned, he sneaked in through the back. He spotted Charlie, who was sitting down and having a drink.

"Ben can come over and take the reins anytime!" Charlie laughed as Riley sat down next to her. Riley watched his love weave in and out of conversations, connect with dazzling stars, make them laugh and feel at ease. At one point, Ben scanned the room, and Riley held up a drink to cheer him and nodded encouragement.

"Oh my god! I can't believe this!" Ben mouthed and touched his heart. He sipped down half a cocktail and winked at Riley as Olivia dragged him off to meet her co-stars. He glowed.

As the night wrapped, Ben showed everyone out. He gave his final hugs and passionate goodbyes and closed the door. He leaned against it and exhaled. Ben slowly shook his head.

"We did it, Ben!" Charlie called out from the couch.

"We did it, Charlie!" Ben smiled as he walked towards her. "Where is Riley?"

"Oh, once everyone cleared out by the Garden House, I think Riley went down there to talk with him. Aren't you exhausted, Ben?"

"The exact opposite! I'm buzzing! Thank you so much for this evening!"

"I'm the one who should be thanking you! Go on and find your sweetie. I'm going to rest for a minute."

Ben nodded and took off, nearly skipping through the mansion. He opened up the patio doors and looked out. He saw Riley and Robert sitting around a firepit that sat about forty feet from the Garden House. Ben pranced down the path but slowed as he approached.

"Ben! You are here!" Riley turned and stood to greet his love. He wrapped his arms around Ben and gave him a big kiss.

"I'm so proud of you! You handled everyone so beautifully, and you were supposed to be a guest. There were about fifty people here, my gosh! I want to hear everything. Were you able to share about yourself at all?"

"Oh, Riley! You wouldn't believe it!" Ben crouched down and let himself fall flat on the ground. "You wouldn't even believe it. Oh, my drinks are hitting me in waves. If you scrolled through my phone, you wouldn't recognize me right now. I can't feel my body! Did this day happen? I'm in a twilight zone of glamor and talent and power. I don't drink like this, Riley."

"It's okay. I'm here and only had one drink. Tell me more." Riley laid down next to Ben.

"You wouldn't believe it. I got to hear everything. I got to talk about the magic of it, Riley. Olivia is like my best friend now, after you, of course. I mean, I know not really, but tonight she was. I don't expect her to text me, but tonight I felt special."

"That's amazing, Ben! I'm so happy for you."

"And I got to tell people about my dream, my golf school. Riley, they actually listened to me, and even if they weren't interested, they acted like they were. A few even said to reach out to them if I ever need anything down the line. Oh wow, I feel dizzy." Ben closed his eyes and then remembered they weren't alone. "Oh, shit." he whispered. Robert was right there, eight feet away, facing the fire. He flushed with shame at how casual he had become in front of his childhood hero. "Shit," he exhaled and wiped his forehead.

"Hey, baby, it's okay. Don't let him scare you. You can be yourself," said Riley. "Having fun in front of him won't kill him, neither will being happy. Right, Robert? This isn't killing you, is it?"

Riley kissed Ben on the cheek. Ben then looked up at Robert who had turned and was staring at them.

"Back in the day, we didn't always have to show our

affection." Robert shook his head.

"Thank god, we aren't back in the day," Riley retorted.

Ben laughed and then covered his mouth.

"All the guests are gone, and it's getting late," Robert snapped. He lifted a thin arm and examined a heavy silver watch in the bright light of the flames.

"What time is it?" Riley asked as he sat up. He studied Robert and saw him wince.

"It's time for you two to go." Robert put his arm down and looked away.

Riley's phone beeped. It was a message from Charlie: *You two are staying here tonight! I'm not letting you drive this late. I'll deal with him.*

"Well, it looks like Charlie is not going to let us leave. And she is right, it's super late. Robert, I did not intend for this to happen, but can we crash here? I think there's room."

A moment passed before Robert responded, "Charlie will fix something up."

Ben looked at Riley, who nodded towards the house. The men stood, and Ben walked up to Robert. He put his hand out, but it was ignored. Fueled by alcohol, and an overwhelming desire to express gratitude, he patted the old man on the shoulder lovingly. Robert's eyes went wide.

"Thank you for everything, Robert! I'm going to go help Charlie. See you up there, Riley!" Ben walked lightly up the path to the mansion. "Thank you again for the time of my life!" he called back when he was thirty feet away.

"You're welcome," Robert mumbled, keeping his eyes on Riley.

Riley held out his hand next, but Robert didn't budge.

"You know, Ben's the reason this party went so well. Goodnight, Robert. Nice watch." Riley patted him on the shoulder. Robert didn't move.

Ben rolled over and saw Riley awake and on his back, looking at the ceiling.

"Riley." Ben reached out and touched his chest. "Where am I? Was last night real? Did all of that happen? I never drink. Did I get drunk and hallucinate the whole night? I had this dream that I was with Olivia Shaden. Nothing feels real. Just feel my hangover."

"I'm sorry for the hangover, love. Yes, last night happened. You can text Olivia if you don't believe me. Did you sleep alright at least?"

"Well, considering this room is bigger than my apartment, and this luxurious bed is bigger than my bedroom, I slept just fine. I could drown in these pillows and wouldn't care."

"You are so cute, Ben."

Ben furrowed his brow. "Oh no, some of it is coming back to me. Was I a total idiot? Did I offend your dad? Oh my god, I don't remember even talking with him."

"That's because you didn't, but you did thank him profusely and you touched his shoulder."

"What? I touched him? I touched Robert? Oh no ..." Ben pulled the cashmere blanket over his head.

"Hey, it's okay. If Robert has a little contact with humanity, it can only be a good thing."

"When can I apologize and when can we go home? I ruined his party."

"No," Riley said as he lifted the covers. He saw Ben's watering eyes. "Oh honey, you didn't ruin anything. You were the reason it was successful! You were the light and life of the party! It would have been a death-by-boredom party without your charisma. You were so graceful and kind."

"No. Robert didn't seem happy, and it was his party. I took

over and ruined it. I'm sorry."

"Robert is never happy. You made the party a celebration, which is what it was supposed to be. Robert ruined his own party by sitting down at the Garden House the whole night. People had to search for him and walk all the way down there to greet and worship him. What an ass!"

"I still feel bad and want to apologize."

"Well, you will have your chance. Charlie texted me before you woke up. She is arranging a brunch, starts in about an hour—just you, me, and Robert. We are going to eat on the patio, I guess."

"Shit! I gotta go shower! Do you have a sweatshirt or something I can wear?" Ben called out. He got up and ran to the bathroom.

∽

"Oh wow. What? It's already out there," Ben whispered. He opened the glass door to the patio.

"Good morning, sir, ummm … Mr. Lakes." Ben timidly walked up to the table. "My goodness! This is beautiful!"

"Hey, Robert!" Riley pulled out a chair and sat down. "Hugh really outdid himself this time."

Robert sat at the head of the table with a giant mojito. His plate sat empty despite the table being covered in fresh eggs, toast, pancakes, French toast, cereal, waffles, and fresh fruit.

"Hi, Hugh!" Riley waved as Hugh approached with a tray. He lowered it and put a giant green juice down in front of Riley. "My gosh! Hugh! This is just incredible! You worked way too hard! Please come out and eat with us, and have Charlie come too. And thank you for my favorite juice."

"I thought a proper brunch would suit you all well after the party last night," Hugh said.

"Thank you, Hugh! Yes, I didn't get to connect with you last night the way I wanted to. Please come out with Charlie and visit."

Hugh eyed Robert and then looked at Riley. "You are too kind, but I have work to do. Enjoy!"

"Alright, well, you are always welcome. You are part of this family, too. This meal is because of you. I appreciate you!" Riley smiled sincerely.

Hugh nodded and left.

"Well, what can I get you, love?" Riley turned to Ben.

"Everything!" Ben smiled and then gulped. "I mean, I'll start with some eggs. Thank you!"

Robert picked up his drink and looked out over his land. He rhythmically shook his glass.

"Oh, that's neat. Riley, your dad holds and shakes his drinks the exact same way as you."

"Huh, yeah. That's something. You are so observant, Ben." Riley smiled and reached for toast.

Robert put his cup down. He rolled up the sleeves on his white shirt and tsked.

"What did you think about your party, Robert? And what was that party truly about? Did you do it because you want a lot of people at your funeral, or are you finally trying to connect and be a person, a good person with meaningful relationships and friendships?"

"What do you think about what Riley does?" Robert put his head in his hands and peered at Ben.

"What do you mean, Robert?" Ben asked, trying to remain calm under his penetrating gaze.

"The carving, the logs, the knives, just trees." Robert waved his hand in the air.

"Well." Ben eyed Riley. "I know he is the most incredible and talented artist I have ever known or seen. I didn't appreciate how different trees were until I met him. Red oak and maple and poplar and cedar and birch, basswood, butternut pine, walnut, mahogany. Everything he makes is a unique masterpiece, like your films!"

"He's making something, but it's not money. The only reason he has ever had any money is because I had my actors call him to custom order. My network took care of him."

"Robert," Riley said firmly, waiting until he faced him. "Any money from your actors or your network went to charity. All got donated. Call it good deeds done in your honor."

Robert's face dropped. He picked up his glass and was about to shake it but instead took a drink.

"Do you know how long your son spent on your door? He started it when we began dating. It took him months. It needed to be perfect. That was an act of love, Robert. And I know for a fact he donated that money. You have a beautiful son, Robert. Riley loves me, supports me, shows me respect, encourages me, believes in me. He is safe and loyal and trustworthy. Riley is creative and passionate, tender and strong, and so hard-working. It's the best, most loving relationship I have ever been in. I feel so protected and safe and—"

"Protected? My son wouldn't swat at a fly," Robert interrupted. He picked up his glass.

"Yeah, I could hit you, Robert," Riley said without looking away.

Robert coughed and put his glass down before turning to Ben.

"Do you know how much money my last film made?"

"Robert, discussing the money you made is the most boring way of talking about your life," said Riley.

"Yes, actually. I do know how much money it made." Ben smiled and nodded eagerly.

"What do you do, Ben?" Robert asked.

"Right now, I'm an assistant manager at a golf course, but I'm working towards my certification to be an instructor. I want to open a golf school for youth that is accessible to everyone. You should see, Robert, when we play for fun. Riley carries my bag and in the other hand carries a block of wood that he studies until he sees what's there." Ben smiled adoringly at Riley.

"So, my rich friends are going to be funding this philanthropic venture now?" Robert asked.

"You think those people are your friends?" Riley smirked and shook his head.

"Why can't your type of gay take responsibility for their own problems? Instead of trying to intervene in the problems of others. You people are constantly trying to solve problems that aren't yours to solve. In my day, problems stayed personal and private!"

"My type of gay? You people? Do you mean I'm a plaid gay? I know I wear it a lot, but I also work with wood, so I have to maintain the look. Hence the beard, too." Riley winked at Ben.

Ben had remained silent but now found he could not contain himself: "Robert, I know we just met, and I'm trying to be respectful and kind, but I don't understand why you are treating him like this. We are actually living your movies, your love stories, and all I feel from you is hate and disgust. Riley and I both survived, just like you. The bullying. The discrimination. The disownment. The depression and self-loathing. Just like you. We struggled and have survived so much shit in this world. Just like you. And then we found each other and are in love. We are thriving. Just like in your movies. Why aren't you happy for him?" Ben demanded.

Riley looked stunned.

"You are so naive! I was selling something! Something people wanted to buy!" Robert furrowed his brow and put his head in his hands. He met Ben's eyes. Ben didn't look away.

"He was selling the one thing he didn't actually have in stock himself, the one thing he couldn't buy. The one thing he couldn't ever be vulnerable enough to try and find. That's why he is such an asshole."

"Oh I'm such an asshole?" Robert mocked.

"Yes," said Riley.

He was about to say more, but Robert cut him off.

"You young fools. Your understanding is vaporous, like the morning fog on a sunny day. Two plus two does not equal four. There is more to this living than what you have imagined. All of this show you're putting on for yourselves. Kissy, kissy. It's all a cinema trick. It's an illusion."

Ben dropped his chin to his chest, then looked back at Robert.

"Goodbye, Robert. It was great meeting you. Your work helped save my life when I was younger. I'll always carry that with me. I'm sorry if I ruined your party. I do wish you the best."

The men crossed the patio, but Riley paused before going inside.

"I know your vision has been going, Robert! You need to pay Charlie more since she is doing the typing for you now!"

⌒

Eight months later, a bundle of wood was delivered to Riley's door. The note on top of it read: *Come See Me.* Riley groaned and got in his car.

When he got to the property, he found Charlie crying. She pointed to the nearest bedroom, and he darted inside. Robert lay in bed with his eyes closed. He looked pale and thin and didn't move when Riley said his name.

"Oh my god," Riley whispered.

After a moment, Robert whispered, "Finally. Now you are taking this seriously."

"I didn't even know what was going on. You haven't told me or talked to me about anything. Charlie doesn't know anything either."

"I'm dying, Riley!"

"It's happening? Or do you just think you are dying? Look at me!"

"Riley!"

"What in the hell do you want? I moved here for you. I'm here for you! Every day I could have been here for you! I gave up my life in Oregon to move here and be here for you. But you don't want me around."

"I didn't ask you to move here! I never asked for you."

"That's not what I meant and not what I'm saying. You didn't ask me to move but you also didn't tell me what was going on with you. You kept me in the dark and you still keep me in the dark. Mom had to tell me. You never asked for me, and yet here I am. You don't see or accept my love. You don't love me. Why can't you look at me?"

Silence.

"Robert, I have two things to tell you. First, I'm going to propose to Ben this week. I'm not asking for your blessing, nor do I need it, but I wanted you to know. He is my true love, and I hope he says yes. I want to spend my life with him. He makes me so happy." Riley wiped his eyes. He then pulled a carving from his pocket and removed the blue cloth cover and put it down on the bedside table.

"And secondly, Robert, I'm going to reach for your hand. Please give it to me."

Riley gently lifted Robert's hand and rested it on top of the carving. He guided his palm and fingers over the smooth figure until he knew Robert had recognized the shape. Robert's closed eyes became wet, and his head softly rocked back and forth.

"I have seen every movie you have ever made, and I have never missed one of your award shows. Bravo, Dad. Bravo." Riley tenderly let go of Robert's hand, which clung to the wood carving. Riley took a step back and took a deep breath.

"And the award for best original screenplay goes to … Robert Lakes."

Riley clapped and continued clapping.

Tears streamed down Robert's face.

Riley bent down and kissed Robert's forehead.

"Riley," Robert called out as his son walked away.

"I know, Dad." Riley paused. "Goodbye."

WHY

" The two warriors drew in from the ocean.

They came by canoe with paddle in hand and, uh, moved back to the land.

They came by slow sea strides, and uhhh … cold waves crept up their loose sleeves.

They came bearing battle cry, slicing through white sea foam and cold, green water.

And they knew the way home, and they knew what to do.

But then there was, uhhh … a heave of darkness, and a storm broke over the mountain.

And they fought again. Two souls, lost on the field of angry water.

The hungry waves crashed again and again.

The waves kept coming.

The storm drowned them out.

No sound remained but the sound of their brotherhood."

Jonathan fell silent. He knew he wasn't getting the words exactly right, but he was getting the right feeling. Moved by his own recitation, he blinked back tears but kept rowing, his large biceps and broad chest flexing in rhythm with his motion.

"Oh my God, Jonathan, shut the hell up, just shut the hell up. What are you even talking about? You aren't some deep, lonely, warrior poet, you douchebag. Please, please shut up!" Chris shook his head. "You are not a man that knows battle; you are a man that knows greasy breakfasts and unemployment checks. You have never left home, never been anywhere. You read one single page from one of my fucking books and start reciting bullshit you don't even understand."

A growing morning light shone on Jonathan's face, illuminating his shame. But instead of turning away, he grimaced and paddled harder. Chris gripped the right side of the canoe and looked out across the water. Although they had just gone a short way out around the bay, Chris already ached to be home. He didn't want Jonathan's attempt at bonding.

"Okay, Chrissy," Jonathan muttered, groaning loudly in exertion.

"You are so ridiculous. There are no women here. Stop showing off, you asshole!" Chris rolled his eyes, leaned his head back, and groaned loudly in exhaustion. Jonathan stopped paddling and stared at Chris.

"Jesus, Chrissy. I'm trying to spend time with you, and this is how I'm treated? Anyone else in my shoes would have been done with you, would have hated you, would have never seen you again after what you did! Did you ever think about that— the fact I didn't say goodbye forever?"

Tears began forming in Chris's eyes, but he didn't want to cry, not while sitting there without possibility of escape.

"It wasn't my fault!" Chris declared. But within, his heart had been pumping guilt with blood for two years. He hated himself for what had happened, but he hadn't thought about how much Jonathan might hate him. "Why are you saying this now? Why are you doing this to me? Get me out of here!"

"Because you fucking did this to me. You did this to us! You are the reason we are alone!" Jonathan resumed paddling.

"What did I do? I didn't kill them! You think I wanted them to die? Our fucking parents, do you think I wanted anything bad to happen to them? I'm sorry!" Chris yelled, wiping at his eyes.

"You weren't there, and they died. You not being there killed them! Why didn't you go home?"

"I'm sorry! I don't know. But do you even understand how gas leaks work? We have no way of knowing if I would have even known about it. I could have just fallen asleep and died right there with them."

"I wish you would have!"

"Fuck you!"

"No, Chris, fuck you!"

Jonathan studied him in disgust—his stupid punky black jean jacket, the dumb patches with dumb words and dumb skulls, the trying-too-hard torn-up jeans, his dirty brown hair growing out under the puke orange dye job that oddly matched his life vest. His pathetic brother still didn't even know how to swim. The weakness disgusted him. He looked ten years older than his twenty-three years—all those fucking Marlboros and beers. Chris reached down instinctively for his cigarettes, but the life vest was in the way. Every gesture spoke weakness to Jonathan.

"Goddamnit, this is exhausting," said Chris. He closed his eyes and unsnapped the three plastic buckles and reached down into his pocket. He had preemptively turned the pack to protect it from the pressure of the life vest and he had been wearing the vest loose as well, but it had still flattened his cigarettes.

"Fuck!" Chris opened his pack to assess the damage.

"What's the matter? Cancer sticks got wet?"

"Fuck you, Jonathan," Chris said under his breath, just loud enough to be heard. He avoided his brother's eyes and tried to light a cigarette, but his hands were shaking, and it took him a few tries. He turned his head towards the water and waited for the relief of the first drag. Once it hit, he exhaled out the side of his mouth, so the smoke went in his brother's face. Chris ashed and peered at his brother through the corner of his eye, a burnt-out Abercrombie and Fitch asshole who peaked in high school. Five years had passed since his days of laying people out on the field and getting laid every Friday after the game, but Jonathan clung to those years like his shirt clung to his body. Chris knew Jonathan had intentionally ripped his expensive stoned-washed jeans to look like some kind of a rugged, outdoors guy. He saw his brother's full list of accomplishments as including the maintenance of perfect hair, the perfect body through perfect gym attendance, and, in general, being the perfect "bro." Chris inhaled and held the smoke. He looked at Jonathan and saw a big, dumb piece of muscle.

"Better buckle up, brother. You still don't know how to swim, right? Aren't you the only one in town who doesn't know how?" Jonathan smirked.

"Cheap fucking shot, *bro*." Chris closed his eyes, buckled his life vest, threw his cigarette, and reached for another. A memory flooded in.

Even though they lived in a port town, his mom fiercely believed in his freedom of choice and never forced him to do anything he didn't want to do, which included learning how to swim. On their eighth birthday, Jonathan had charged Chris, clumsily picking him up and throwing him off the dock. Chris had successfully avoided the water all of his life. The cold water shocked him. He screamed and struggled and thrashed and doggy paddled the best he could, but his slight and panicked body quickly became exhausted. He tried to float, but he felt an ocean of gravity pulling on him, and then a plant or seaweed or something touched his foot and he wailed even louder. Chris saw his father Greg and Jonathan standing there above him on the dock, watching him suffer. His brother began waving his arms wildly in all directions, mocking and laughing. His dad chuckled too. Chris resigned himself, let go and started to sink.

"Goddamnit! Go get him!" Greg had yelled at Jonathan. By that time, the weaker son was barely visible under the water. Jonathan dove into the water perfectly and within seconds pulled up a coughing and choking Chris, supporting his body as they moved to the dock. Once at the ladder, Jonathan guided his brother's hands around the metal poles and pushed him up, staying behind on the lowest rung so he wouldn't fall back in. Greg stood at the top of the ladder and extended a hand.

Even in his woozy terror, Chris didn't want his father to touch him. "Back up!" He coughed and gripped the ladder, without looking at his brother or up at his dad.

Jonathan let go of the ladder and fell back into the water, while Chris watched his dad's sandals take a few steps back. When he had enough room, Chris pulled his tired body up the ladder and onto the dock. He grabbed his blue towel and without looking up stomped past his dad. Greg yelled his name five times. Chris didn't look back. He stormed to the house and yanked open the screen door and yelled for his mother.

"Oh, honey, what happened?" Lisa asked as she hurried out of the kitchen. Upon seeing her son dripping wet and shaking, she opened her arms, and he ran right into her and buried himself in her safe embrace.

"Mom, why?" Chris sobbed into her thick coral sweater.

As a child, Chris asked "why?" to everything and everyone and would keep repeating "why?" over and over until he felt satisfied with the responses, or until he had answered the questions himself. Lisa had often walked in on him pointing to different objects in his room and repeating "why?" over and over and over. When her boys were older, Lisa had made the mistake of calling Chris her "little boy who cries why" at dinner one evening. She had meant it to be endearing, but Jonathan laughed hysterically. He latched on to the words and called his brother "the child who cries why" every chance he could. It took Chris only a couple minutes to come up with his own insult, and the next day he surprised Jonathan by saying, "You mindless meathead!"

Although wounded, Chris instantly forgave his mother. He had known throughout his childhood and teen years that Jonathan was jealous of their bond. Chris and Lisa were both intelligent, observant, naturally gifted with mathematics, music, and writing, and excelled at everything they tried. But they were also distracted and easily disengaged, quickly got bored, struggled with the mundane, and lived in their heads.

In response, Jonathan gravitated towards and forged an alliance with his dad, and through his early teen years, he walked with pride and didn't feel jealous or like an outsider. Jonathan saw himself and his father as big and strong men, not inclined to school, but good with their bodies and both carrying a commanding presence. But that bond fractured. Jonathan had shadowed his dad during the day one summer while he was working as a handyman, and he came to see that his dad also had smarts, like Chris and his mom. His dad completed rapid mental calculations, demonstrated incredible visual-spatial and assembly skills, and could easily multi-task and problem-solve any issue or dilemma that came his way. He came up short and was alone again.

‿

"Jonathan, humor me. Why weren't you there?" Chris pulled on his cigarette. He hated cheap shots, but right now, it was all he had. "Could it be?" he exhaled, turning to meet

Jonathan's strained eyes, "that our parents didn't invite you because they didn't really like you much? You are big, you are dumb, you don't do anything. You can't grow up, you can't keep a job, you can't even hold a conversation. You were never around, and then they never wanted you around. If it would have been so easy to save them, why weren't you there? Why weren't you over at dinner? If you are so perfect and strong and brave and helpful and necessary, why didn't they invite you to dinner? You would never have graduated from high school if I didn't leave my work around so you could use it for yourself. Did you think I didn't know? Hell, I did that for you, you mindless meathead. You are the twenty-three-year-old high school jock hero, so where the fuck were you? I want to hear you say it."

Jonathan looked puzzled and shook his head.

"No, fuck you, Jonathan. I want to hear you say it. Why weren't you invited, time after time after time?" Chris blew smoke directly at his brother's face, and even though he saw tears forming as it cleared, he didn't care.

Jonathan's chest rose and fell heavily, and he stopped paddling. "No, you know what, Chris, what are you doing with *your* life? You drink all day, mope around, smoke cigarettes, and dye your hair hideous colors! You are smart, but you don't do *anything* about being smart, so how is that better than dumb? You don't do anything. You call that living? You had scholarships, you could have gone somewhere, anywhere, you could have been something. You had the choice and chance for a life, and you didn't take it. Mom and Dad only spent time with you because they stupidly thought you would become something. You stay up all goddamn night all the time. Why didn't you go home and stay up all that night? Why didn't you do what you always do? Why didn't you? They wanted you home, but you selfish piece of shit chose booze and your friend instead. You could have sensed the gas leak, you could have saved them, you could have done something with your life. But you have done nothing, and you are nothing. You're just like me, but I didn't choose this, and you did! That makes you way dumber than me." Jonathan picked up the paddles.

Chris pulled out another cigarette and lit it as nausea spread across his body. He clenched his hands and crushed his cigarette and felt the heat from the burning ash as it slipped out of his fingers and into the water. Emotion came up in him and he couldn't hold back the tears.

"Fuck you!" Chris couldn't think of anything else to say. He didn't know how to cut his brother down any further while he was bleeding out.

"Fuck you!" Jonathan sneered.

Chris saw his brother's face, that horrible smirk, and something in him broke. He stood up and lunged at Jonathan. He didn't feel the canoe rocking violently beneath him. Jonathan saw it coming and positioned himself in the middle in a squatting position, trying to restore balance. He held his hands out wide, like the football player he once was, then took Chris and tossed him right into the water.

The cold water shocked Chris's body like a slap from all directions. He let the life vest buoy him up. He still didn't know how to swim and began doggy paddling while waves splashed against his face and neck. He knew if he kept his head up and kept his body moving, he would be alright, but every time a small wave hit his head, he held his breath and could hear his heart pounding against his temples. Jonathan had been yelling out his name and held out his paddle to pull him inward, but Chris didn't acknowledge him. He scanned the shore and guessed he was a couple hundred feet out.

"Grab the paddle!" Jonathan pleaded.

"Fuck you!"

"Chris, come on!"

"Fuck you!"

Chris doggy paddled, and tried to move, but his tight jean jacket limited his range, and he wore out quickly. He remembered this same exhaustion, remembered looking up at his brother, hearing his laughter, his mocking and his sneers. Chris remembered his dad. His dad. He should have stopped and hugged his dad. Tears stung his eyes, and he wanted to scream. He didn't want to doggy paddle to shore, but he couldn't let Jonathan get near him. Never again. Not like this.

"Chris, why won't you let me help you? You're upset and you're going to be completely fried swimming back that far."

"Leave me alone!" Chris yelled and paddled as hard and as fast as he could away from Jonathan. Land looked distant, and his body had been broken and become numb in the cold water, but he could only keep going. Soon, Jonathan fell out of his peripheral vision, but Chris felt the canoe behind him and knew his brother was holding back to give him space. Agonizing minutes passed, and he paused to catch his breath.

"Chris! What are you doing?" a familiar voice called out.

He scanned and saw his best friend Violet standing on the shore. She had a small inherited house that sat up on the hill overlooking the water and she was standing there in a black dress with newly purpled hair. At the sight of her, relief swept through Chris. Violet had her arms up in the what-the-hell-are-you-thinking position, and Chris could see the thin line of smoke from the cigarette in one of her hands. He just needed to get to Violet, get out of the water, and away from his brother. He waved at her and held up one finger, a sign to let her know not to say another word until they were together. Violet nodded, took some drags, and paced around.

"Chris!" Jonathan yelled.

Violet looked up, but Chris shook his head at her not to

engage his brother at all.

"You can probably put your feet down now!" Jonathan chuckled.

Chris closed his eyes when he heard that laugh, and his pruny hands balled up. He wanted to beat the shit out of his brother, if such a glorious thing were possible. He pounded his fists on the water, and his legs felt for the bottom. He could easily stand up and probably could have a few seconds before. "Goddamnit!" He stood and water poured off his body. Chris unsnapped his life vest, ripped it off, and threw it behind him. His legs ached with each excruciating step towards her, and his clothes hung as heavy as guilt. He didn't look back. The patches on his favorite jacket looked ruined, his cigarettes were trashed, and he didn't know if his industrial boots would ever recover. Chris pulled his hair off his neck and squeezed it.

"Dude, what happened?" Violet asked.

"That fucking asshole happened!"

Violet glanced past Chris and saw Jonathan paddling in the direction of the life vest.

"Give me a fucking cigarette, Violet! Please!" Chris held out his hand, water dripping from his arm.

"You'll ruin my cigarettes! Take your jacket off and dry your hands on my shirt."

"Let's just go. I'm coming over!" He started walking, but after a couple steps, they heard his shoes squish loudly.

Violet frowned and looked at his feet, but Chris kept walking. "Do you want to take your shoes off? Let me help you or carry something!"

"No!" he yelled, and she stopped walking. "I'm sorry, Violet. I'm fucking soaked and angry, and Jonathan is a piece of shit. I'm sorry."

"It's alright. I'm sorry too. Here, come here." Violet put her cigarette up against his lips, and he took a giant drag.

"Why didn't I think of that before? I'm fucking water-logged. Thank you!" Chris inhaled. "Oh, Violet, you're turning even more Violet!" He exhaled and smiled at her.

"Ha! Yeah, well, gotta maintain appearances. I just got fucking bored." She winked and pulled the cigarette back from his mouth and put it in hers. Violet pulled a chunk of her long hair forward to look at it and frowned. "This is really fucking purple though," she laughed.

"It looks great, but can we please keep walking? I can hear Jonathan pulling the canoe up."

"Yeah, sorry. Hey, you can stay over if you want. I still have some of your clothes … from before. I mean, oh fuck." Violet looked to the ground and wished she hadn't spoken at all.

"Oh yeah, thank you. Violet, I mean it, thank you."

She nodded, and he tried to smile, but memories of spending a month curled up in her bed after his parents died came flooding back. For weeks he couldn't move, couldn't sleep, couldn't eat, couldn't cry, couldn't talk, and couldn't be alone for too long. Violet had dropped everything and set him up in her room while she slept downstairs. She worked as a buffer to keep Chris safe when a drunk and raging Jonathan pounded on her door. Chris had protected Violet from bullies in high school, and they instantly connected. She had felt proud to be able to protect Chris. But now she worried—she saw how his anger and sadness fed upon each other. He had become his own bully, and she wondered what he would do to himself if alone for too long.

A couple hours later, Chris lay fully reclined on her couch in his old sweatpants and a T-shirt. He had showered, and Violet took his clothes and hung them up outside on her line, the sun beating down on his black jacket and pants. They were so heavy, she had to drape his pants over the line and used all of her clothespins for his jacket. She made a mental note to get him patches for his birthday.

"Thank you," Chris sighed as she came in the front door.

"Oh, don't worry about it." She waved her hand and walked into the living room.

"Can I make us some coffee and tea?"

"Sure!" Violet sat down in her brown recliner and watched him walk into the adjoining kitchen.

Chris puttered, turned on the stove, and got a kettle ready. Violet pulled some chunks of her hair forward to study them and started rocking.

"Do you want to tell me what happened?" she called out, pulling at a split end. Two minutes of silence passed, and Violet used her feet to swirl around and look up at Chris. He had paused in front of the fridge and was escaping into her metalhead stickers, crop circle collages, and incoherent magnet poetry. But now that she had her eyes on him, he opened the fridge and pulled out milk.

"Can we smoke in here?"

"Alright," she squinted at him, "but open a window. You'll only talk to me with a cigarette in your hand, huh?" Violet smiled.

Chris shrugged, and the teapot started hissing. He turned it off, poured her a cup, and grabbed a cigarette from the pack on the counter.

"Talk to me."

"Fine." He delivered a cup of tea to Violet and went back to the kitchen to make his coffee.

"Jonathan brought up our parents, and why I wasn't there, why I wasn't with them, why I couldn't save them. He trashed my life, and he's right. I'm nothing. Just a little void walking around." Chris spoke with his cigarette in his mouth and scooped the ground coffee into the filter.

"I could kill him, Chris! How dare he! After all you—"

"Violet, stop," he cut her off. "He's right. I'm not a living boy." Chris pressed the red ON button and ashed in the sink.

"I'm sorry." She fell back in her chair and sipped her tea.

"I'm at the end of my rope."

"What does that mean, Chris?" Violet sat up again. She thought he sounded different, like he didn't know he was saying things out loud. He put his forehead against the cupboard.

"I don't know. I need something to happen. I can't take it. It's too big now, it's become everything. Too many losses, and me too weak to do anything about them."

"What do you need to have happen? Haven't you been through enough?"

"That's not, umm … never mind. I'm sorry. I'm tired. Everything fucking hurts. I just need another cigarette and some coffee and some sleep. It's alright, Violet. Just forget I said anything."

Chris pulled the coffee pot out and poured himself a cup, even though it was still mid-brew. Drops of coffee hit the bottom of the burner, hissed, and evaporated.

Two weeks later, a storm rolled into their ocean town. Violet and Chris had a tradition of watching major weather events from her tiny, covered patio. But she couldn't find him anywhere; he wasn't at home, not at any of their hangouts, and he wasn't answering the phone. She decided to sit out back and wait for him and hoped he would show up. The sky grew dark, and the rain began pummeling the land and sea. The thunder was getting closer. Violet pulled out her phone to text Chris, and his voice ran through her head: *I can't take this much longer. I really, really can't.*

Her heart sank. *What has he done?* She got up and ran down the slick hillside through the torrential downpour. Then she saw it. A pitchfork of lightning across the sky, and then came a guttural thunder that shook everything around her. She wiped her eyes and tried to shield them as she scanned the shore. A movement by the water caught her eye. It was him. Chris looked like he was getting into the canoe, but she couldn't be sure. Lightning struck again, and she covered her ears against the thunder and began to run towards him, but a hole in the ground caught her foot and she fell. "Fuck!" she screamed as her legs went out and she tumbled down. The pain came instantly, and she knew her ankle was twisted. From the ground, she tried to look out and see him, but he had already left the shore. Crying, she hobbled up and dragged herself farther down. There was the canoe, getting into deep water, and the shadowy outline of Chris, fighting against the crashing waves.

"Chris! Chris! Chris! You'll die! Come back!"

Lightning zigzagged across the sky, and Violet couldn't tell if it hit the water. Chris didn't turn around. She screamed and cried, but he was fading into the darkness.

"Oh fuck, Jonathan!" Violet pulled out her phone and tried to cover it with her coat. Her trembling fingers pushed every button until his name came up. She squatted down and covered her head. It rang and rang and rang before finally he picked up.

"Jonathan! Chris took the canoe out in the storm! I'm so scared. Come get him now! I can't see him. He didn't look back at me. I screamed for him! Jonathan, help me! Please! He is going to die!" she shrieked.

"What?!"

"Get here! He's gone! You have to go get him! I can't see him. Please, oh my God, I can't believe this is happening. Get here. He left right by my place. You have to get him. I'm begging you."

Lightning struck again, and her phone went dead.

"Jonathan! Jonathan! Jonathan! Please, somebody help me!" Violet wailed and dragged herself closer to the water. Her ankle had swollen, and she gripped at the sand and tried to crawl closer to the surf. She cried "Chris!" again and again, until she lost her voice and she let her body slump to the sand where salt water was reaching her with its cold hand.

"Hey, I'm here! I'm here! Violet! I hear you!" Jonathan darted down the hill and found her. "I'm going to lift you, okay?" Jonathan bent down and picked her up and carried her about ten feet to a patch of grass. She didn't say a word but pointed to the water.

"Wait for me!" Jonathan commanded and ran towards the ocean.

"Chris! Chris! Chris!" He ripped his clothes off and dove into the water.

He swam into the dark. Lightning flashed and lit up the sky, then came again. The thunder was instantaneous.

"Chris! Where are you? Come home! Chris!"

He paused his swim, looking around for a sign of the canoe.

"Boy who cried why! I'm on your side!" he shouted.

"The angry waves kept coming. Uhh … the warriors, their canoe," Jonathan sputtered. Then he steeled himself and began swimming farther out, his muscles feeling like magic against the cold water. He was not yet exhausted. He thought the words as he swam.

The angry waves, the cold, green sea …
The storm drowned, why … a heave of dark …
No sound, no sound … the storm drowned, why …
No sound but the sound of their brotherhood.

HOT AIR BALLOONS

"Just have a daydream. Go sit at the French café in your mind. Tell me, what do you see?" she asked the man she had been sleeping next to for thirty-five years.

She shuffled her purse under the seat in front of her, double-checked the tray table even though it was securely latched, and closed her eyes to play along. She waited. He didn't respond. No surprise. The romance had fled as soon as they'd moved in together, all those years ago, but she still made small, desperate attempts to engage. *Even though we are empty nesters of love, we do have space to focus on other, important things*—she had reminded herself over the years. She believed it necessary to always try to be grateful and hopeful.

A moment passed. She opened her eyes. They had been kept closed for too long anyway. A glamour magazine told her a smoky eye helps with aging, but she didn't know if she had applied too much powder. Lines of insecurity and circles of sadness had formed on her face. She shook her head not to cry and looked down at her form-fitting, burgundy sweater. After decades of baggy cardigans, she had made a change. He didn't notice, but he hadn't been looking.

"Do you think many people get injured in hot air balloon accidents? I mean, in terms of death, what would you say?" he asked in response.

He had flipped through a hot air balloon article in *Arizona Magazine* and had become irritated and anxious to recline his chair. His feet were swollen.

She imagined Cupid stuck in the basket of a hot air balloon. This cupid couldn't fly because his wings had been cut, and arrows were being shot at him from all directions. He paced back and forth, his blue eyes full of panic and fear. Suddenly, an arrow hit him right in the heart, and he cried out before tumbling over the side of the basket. She could feel tears coming to her eyes, so she closed them again.

Then he remembered his wife had said something. She wanted to go to Italy, a restaurant, or something. So he pretended, "Uhhh … I can't see myself eating. I'm not hungry."

"Not right now you aren't, dear," she willed herself to smile, "but soon you will be."

He positioned himself to hold the magazine with his left hand and put his right one on her leg.

"Well, Idaho isn't France, but it is still nice to go somewhere. We have been to a lot of local places," she offered, trying to be optimistic. The boarding pass sat still in her lap.

Their plane hadn't moved. Somewhere up front, a baby started crying in pain. An arrow.

Tears came to her eyes, and she closed them again.

Thirty-five years, and they still hadn't taken off together.

FOREST

"Honey, Frances, you have to get up. You're going to be late."

"Hmmm … ?" Frances mumbled, half asleep.

"The alarm went off. I don't know how many times I hit snooze. It's almost six-thirty!"

"Why am I taking the early ferry again?" Frances rolled in bed to wrap their arms around Sara.

"You are taking an early ferry because she is expecting you late morning," Sara sighed. Frances groaned.

"I have to pee." Sara patted their shoulder. Frances lifted their arm, and Sara wiggled out. With half closed eyes, Frances watched Sara scamper to the bathroom.

"Oh my gosh," Sara exhaled in relief.

"You feel alright, love?" Frances propped themselves up on their elbow.

"Oh yeah, I'm fine. But I would feel a lot better if you would get up."

"Okay, I'm up. I'm up." Frances sat up and wiped their eyes. They reached for yesterday's jeans and put them on. "Get up.

Get up. This is just one day. Just one day. I can't do it, but it is just one day."

"You aren't going to shower?" Sara called from the toilet.

"No, I should just go." Frances pulled a light blue sweatshirt on and shook their head. They took a few steps to the bathroom door.

"You look beautiful, Sara."

"What? I'm sitting on the toilet. Don't, don't, don't. Ugh, I feel like shit!"

"Oh no. I'm so sorry. Please, I'll stay and take care of you."

"Are you kidding me? No, you are not getting out of this. You have put it off long enough. You said you would go this summer, and you didn't. You said you would go early fall, and you didn't. We are heading into winter. Cutting it kind of close, yeah? Even if she is a witch to you, at least you can say you tried." Sara reached for toilet paper and waved it at Frances to leave.

"Alright. I'm going."

Frances left the bedroom and headed for the kitchen. They pulled an egg carton and cheese from the fridge, washed off some grapes, pears, and apples, and as the eggs cooked, they cut up a fruit bowl. Right when they turned to put the eggs back in the fridge, Sara appeared.

"What are you doing?" asked Sara. She pulled a comb through her thin, red hair.

"I'm making my soon-to-be wife some breakfast. And you look so lovely."

"These pink pajama pants and this dingy white shirt?"

"You look great in my shirt." Frances nodded and winked.

"It's my shirt today. You have a set meeting time." Sara sat down at the kitchen table.

"She can wait."

"Yeah, but the ferry can't."

"This will only take a second. Please rest," Frances instructed.

"I just woke up. I don't need to rest. I can help. I'm not incapable of doing things."

"No," Frances paused and met Sara's eyes. "You are more capable and stronger than I ever could have imagined."

"Oh, Frances. I'm emotional enough right now. No need to make me cry." Sara blinked back tears.

Frances nodded and sliced into an apple.

"You are going to hurt yourself if you're not looking. Have you even had any coffee yet?"

"I'm fine," Frances replied.

"No, you do not want ferry coffee. And I'm going to make you something for the trip too."

"Sara, please."

"No. We are the boss. You are outnumbered." Sara walked to the kitchen. "Our baby might be from your egg, but they vote with Mommy now."

"Understood." Frances smiled. "Eggs are done."

"How much coffee will you drink for us?" Sara scooped into the filter.

"A thermos full is fine. Just do like four scoops."

"What are you going to eat?"

"Nothing. I'm going to be sick."

"You are going to take something, even if it's for later." Sara opened the fridge.

"Your eggs are getting cold," Frances declared.

"I'm overheating anyway."

"What can I do to help? I can stay. I'm worried about you."

"Nope. Go get your keys and coat, and I'll bring your thermos and snack."

"Alright. You're the boss."

Frances walked to the front door and briefly looked at themselves in the hallway mirror. They ran their fingers through their shaggy dark brown hair; it wasn't right, but it was going to do.

"Here you go, love." Sara handed Frances a black mug and a small, steamy Tupperware that held a toasted bagel with cream cheese.

"Thank you. Please eat your breakfast too. Can I get a hug?" Frances asked and turned to put their stuff down.

"No, no. You're all ready to go. I'll just hug you." Sara wrapped her arms around Frances.

"What are you putting in my pocket?"

"Nothing." Sara smiled.

Frances motioned to grab it.

"No, no. Just reach for it in moments of stress. It will be your good luck charm. I want it back though."

"You got it. Promise me you will be alright?"

"Yes, we will be fine." Sara lovingly touched her stomach and then kissed Frances on the cheek.

Frances took the elevator down to the basement of the apartment building and started their car. As they pulled out onto the street, Frances cranked the heat and peered forward. *Wow, winter is coming. Going to take the ferry in the fog—what a cliché!* Frances punched the radio to the '80s station and caught "I'm Gonna Be (500 miles)" by The Proclaimers. *Oh, fuck yeah, the best.* They sang along loudly and tried to forget who it was they were going to see. Frances eyed the clock. *Crap, gotta hurry.* They zoomed in their Subaru and rhythmically tapped on the wheel through the six songs it took to reach the tollbooth. *Oh good, not too many people here yet.* Frances eyed the cars ahead of them. As they approached the tollbooth, they felt in their left pocket for their wallet and remembered Sara had tucked something in the right one for good luck. *I bet I know what you are.*

"Good morning. Purchased online." Frances smiled at the attendant and handed their phone up.

"Hello, thank you." A young man with a Santa hat on reached for the phone to scan it.

"One adult, one vehicle." He eyed the car and the backseat and nodded.

"Not for long," Frances whispered.

"What's that, ma'am?" He handed back the phone.

"Ha! Haven't heard that in … oh, nothing. Thank you!" Frances grabbed the phone. "I like your hat! Happy holidays!"

"Thank you, ma'am. Be safe. Merry Christmas!"

"Okay," Frances blinked back laughter. "You too. You are very polite and good at your job."

Frances pulled forward and followed the hand instructions of the woman with a whistle and an orange vest. Frances turned off the car, undid their seat belt, and looked around. A whole fleet of cars were gathering. A van had pulled in right next to them. Parents got out and pulled the sliding doors open, and a handful of younger children wrestled free from their seats. Frances watched as two boys slapped each other; one girl ripped at another girl's necklace, which left them both scream-ing. "That's enough!" the parents yelled.

"That's a lot." Frances took a bite of bagel and tried not to stare. A fifth child, who looked to be about six but seemed just as annoyed by the others as the parents, popped out of the back.

"I choose you," Frances whispered with a quiet admiration, taking another bite.

"Kids, let's go!" The parents yelled in unison and slammed the van doors shut. The family trudged towards the stairwell that led to the galley and top deck. The fifth child walked be-hind the rest, looking around.

Frances touched the outside of their right pocket. *Every-thing's different now.* They took a sip of coffee and reclined the chair. *I'm going to be a parent. What the fuck. Wow. It's happening.*

Frances took another drink and held the thermos up in the air. "Goodbye, last coffee! I have to give you up in solidarity. The return with Sara will be glorious though!" Frances closed their eyes, and the comforting, residual taste of coffee faded. Frances licked their teeth and exhaled. They lifted a hand to their heart and whispered, "It's okay. Calm down, calm down." Something tasted off. *I gotta get some air. I'm gonna be sick.*

Frances got out, locked the car, and made it to the stairwell just as the ferry horn called out. *Here we go.* They gripped the handrail and began climbing. Once at the top, they scanned for the bathroom and kept their head low as they opened the door to the single-use family restroom and quickly peed. Frances came out of the restroom with their eyes on the floor, but then looked up and smiled. The galley was full of children. Frances walked across the dining area and watched as rambunctious kids ate donuts and stuck exploratory fingers up their noses. Others ran around while nearby parents laughed in exhaustion, or bickered, or ignored each other. Middle-aged couples sat together on the blue, plastic furniture, where some solitary folks read, or spaced out and quietly looked out the window to the sea.

My days like that are limited. Silence, I'll miss you. But I'm ready for this.

Frances pushed the door open and walked onto the deck. They put their hands on the railing. A biting wind wrapped around them, and they looked across the water to the looming mountain range, partially cloaked with fog.

"Keep coming, fog. Cover this up until it all goes away. I don't want to see those mountains." They closed their eyes and breathed slowly. *What is that taste?*

Frances walked back to their car and sat in silence until the ferry horned its arrival and docked. A few men with baseball hats talked loudly about a storm. *Oh god, no storm!* Frances was directed off the ferry and began the drive through the small port town.

"Even the weather doesn't want me here," Frances moaned, turning when they saw the sign that led up the dreaded forest road to the place they did not want to go. But even more worrying than their destination was the thought of being late, as the fog was growing thick and at times they struggled to see the road.

Forty-five minutes later, they took a final turn off the forest road, up a driveway to the house. Frances had made it, and right on time.

They stepped out of the car and into the imposing forest, and trudged to the front door. There they put their right hand on their right pocket for good luck and knocked with the left.

Silence.

"Please calm down," Frances whispered and put their hand on their heart.

Frances lifted the round, iron door knocker and tapped it twice.

Silence for a pregnant moment.

"Who is that? Who's at my door?" a deep, stern voice called out.

"Jesus, is she really doing this? Okay, I'll play, you witch. I know you can see me through the peephole," Frances whispered and then waved. "It's me! Frances!" They waved again and heard the barrel bolt slide, a deadbolt click, and then a second deadbolt click before the doorknob jiggled and the thumb turn unlocked. The dark wooden door pulled open.

"Oh, Franny, it's you. I wasn't expecting you this early." The older woman's dark eyes squinted at her tiny gold watch. A black shawl hung from her shoulders, and beneath it a black turtleneck cradled her face. Her graying, black, frizzy, shoulder-length hair was clipped halfway back.

"Please call me Frances, and this is the time we planned for. I'm on time. I know how you feel about people being late." Frances took another look at the advanced state of gray in the woman's hair, an unexpected sign of the time that had passed since they had last looked at each other. "Aren't you going to invite me in?"

"Fine, Franny, come in." The woman let go of the door and walked down the narrow, shadowy hallway.

"It's Frances! Why is it so dark in here?"

"And take your shoes off before you—"

"I'm taking them off right now. I won't spoil your rugs."

Frances quickly pulled off their sneakers and closed the door. They locked one deadbolt then hurried after the woman, but she had already made it down the long hallway. Frances paused where the hallway ended. Their mother was sitting in a leather chair in the living room, a few feet from the mesmerizing floor-to-ceiling windows that overlooked the lake. Frances glanced down the hallway to the left and eyed the open showrooms. Something was wrong. Frances took a few steps to get a closer look. Everything was dark. The display cases, the tables, and the shelves were neglected. The vases abandoned. The few remaining plants dead. Everything was covered in dust. *Why is everything forsaken?* Frances felt a shock of recognition—their mother was older and more tired.

This taste is making me nauseous.

"You alright, Mom?" Frances called out as they tiptoed back.

"Yes. I'm fine. Why do you ask, Franny?" The woman shifted her gaze out the window.

"It's just, I have never seen you without fresh flowers or lights on in your rooms. Your bowls and figures and sculptures and the whole grand show of it. I feel strange. It's like the house has forgotten who you are, and … or … maybe you have forgotten it. Everything is dark and dusty, Mom. Even your awards are covered in dust. This is not what I expected."

"Why are you here, Franny?"

"I was expecting the amazing artist and renowned educator, the innovator and visionary to still be keeping herself up. Are you really alright, Mom?"

"Why are you here, Franny?"

"I'm here to see you. It's been a few years."

"Why are you truly here?"

"Why can't you look at me when I'm talking to you?" they asked without looking at her.

Frances slowly walked into the living room which was adorned with luxurious leather sofas, elegant rugs, warm and regal coffee tables, elaborate candle displays, and a huge chandelier. But this room had also gone dim. The only light came in through the enormous windows, and through them Frances watched the peculiar fog drift across the water. An unending depth of forest circled the lake. Frances stood near their mom and glanced down at her through the corner of their eye.

"This place, your home. It's so still and beautiful. Doesn't it look like you could walk out there? The trees seem like people, standing together, solemn. It's strange for me to think that the forest is the only thing you see, and the forest is the only thing that always gets to see you, Mom."

"What are you going on about now, Franny?"

"Nothing. Please call me Frances. I was just saying it's amazing out here." Frances ran their fingers through their hair.

"Your hair is too short."

"That's one way of looking at it."

"Oh, Franny, you kill me!"

"Well, Mother, it looks more like you are killing yourself.

Are you eating right?"

The woman's eyes darted to Frances, but Frances was already looking at her. They straightened their posture. "What do you want to say to me, Mother? What do you need to get off your chest?" Frances raised their eyebrows.

"Franny, do you remember when you wanted to email Einstein? You were so smart for your age. I was in awe of you. But you failed to understand that you can't email dead people, and I didn't even know whose child you were."

"I was seven."

"You were old enough to show better understanding."

"Any other parent would have thought it endearing, but you were disappointed." Frances shook their head.

"I *was* disappointed! That's when I knew you weren't a genius!"

"Like you?" Frances asked, swallowing and aware of the bad taste persisting in their mouth.

"I didn't say that." Her hands gripped the armchairs, but her body didn't move.

"You didn't have to. You didn't want me around. You didn't try to understand me. You didn't spend time with me. You didn't like me because I wasn't like you," stammered Frances.

"I paid bills. I housed you. I dumped boxes. I poured cans. What more did you want from me?"

"I wasn't hungry for food, Mother."

"You didn't want for anything! I didn't want a coddled kid. Grow up. You can't blame me for all of your problems. That's all *got* to be water near a bridge though, right, Franny? *Finally?*"

"No, Mom, it's milk that has been souring under these rugs for thirty years."

"Why are you here, Franny?" she asked again and looked out to the forest.

Frances looked out the window, too, and took a deep

breath. "I'm here because I'm getting married, and I wanted you to know."

"What does he *do*?" she snapped and looked directly at Frances, leaning forward in her chair.

Frances shook their head and blinked back the burning that comes right before tears. *My God. She's amused.*

"No, Mom. You already know. I'm not doing that with you."

"Oh, I see. You are looking for my blessing." She maintained eye contact and slowly leaned back.

"No, Mom. I'm not."

She flinched.

"I'm not asking for anything. I'm telling you what's happening. I'm getting married to a woman, and we are starting a family."

"You and a woman, starting a family? What does that mean?"

"Really? That's the face you make. You are so committed to your confusion, it's impressive. Tell me, what do you think it means, Mom?"

Their mother shook her head.

"We are wanting to have children. That's what that means."

"Without a man? That's not possible. What kind of thing would that be?"

"Sperm donors, friend donors, adoption. Where do you live, Mom? Oh yeah, you hide in here." Frances raised their arms to the room.

"So, you are just going to take seed from a man, and he will have absolutely no say in what happens to *his* child, while two women raise it alone? *All alone?* What is this world coming to?" She shook her head.

"Wow! That was a lot. I don't even know where to start." Frances tried to swallow the sickly sweet, almost sour taste at the back of their throat. "Firstly, nobody is taking anything from a man. There are, in fact, good-hearted, generous people in the world who want to help others out. They don't want to be a parent, a father, or whatever. They don't want to have a say. They are wanting to help other families, though, as a gift. Do you get it? And how would we be alone? Can you explain that to me? Not having a 'man' means we are alone? The world is changing, Mom. This little world you built in here isn't changing, but out there, we are building greater love, acceptance, equality. We are fighting, Mom, every fucking day," Frances wiped at their eyes.

"None of what you are doing matters. Your work, you, all so insignificant."

"If I'm so insignificant, who in your life is significant? Can I please speak to the significant ones? Oh wait. You were alone, and you are still alone. That's you, not me. You raised me alone. But I'm not alone. I have Sara. Our work makes a difference, our love makes a difference. She is going to be the most amazing mother to our child, our children."

"Oh, *she's* the mom? And you are what? I repeat, what is the world coming to? Are you so woke that you aren't even a woman anymore?"

"You truly have no idea what you are talking about."

"Are you gonna correct me, Frances? Am I not using the right pronouns?"

"No, Mom. You just aren't a good person. I'm not gonna correct you, and I can't change you."

Their mother shook her head and kept her eyes locked on the hanging fog. Her wooden chair moved back and forth, and a soft, rhythmic squeaking sound filled the air.

Frances tightly shut their eyes and slid their right hand into their right pocket. "Mom? Mom? Why aren't you responding to me?"

A long silent moment passed.

"Mother." Frances opened their eyes and looked at her.

"You have always been a chair that rocks itself. I respect that. I have learned a lot from you, and for that I'm grateful. But now you are this big, pulsating person in my world, and I only ever feel you. It's so rare to actually see you. You are still fit to stand trial in this life, yet you hide away. A sentence hasn't been assigned to you. It won't be assigned to you. You have been forgiven. I have forgiven you. But you have been on this island for thirty-five years, collecting things that you used to take care of. But what I don't understand is, why couldn't you take care of me? Why didn't you want to? Because I can't go on a shelf? Because I can say no to you? Do you hate me now because I'm finally free of you?"

Silence.

"Look at me, Mother!" Frances begged. A sugary sickness crept up their throat.

"I can't!"

"Quit looking out your fucking windows. You need a mirror! What the fuck happened to you?"

"You know what, Franny? Your mouth moves too much when you talk, like a thousand thoughtless words are trying to get free. They spring from you all at once, and you make no sense. You have never made any sense! Just, please, for once, be quiet!"

"What? I stayed silent for decades to keep you happy. I'm not going to be quiet for you now."

"I have heard enough, and I have had enough, Franny! Please leave."

"Let me just ask you one question. Why did you make me swallow toothpaste?"

A moment passed.

"I was testing you."

"Testing me?" Frances shrieked.

"Don't yell in my house. And yes, Franny, I was testing you

to see what you would listen to: your mom or your gut."

"Who was I supposed to listen to? What was the right answer? You just made me sick."

"Well, you should have trusted your gut! When something feels wrong, it is wrong."

Frances stared at their mother. "What the fuck does that mean? All a kid wants to do is make their parents happy. You could have helped me, taught me, been proud of me. I know you saw how other moms did it."

"Yeah, I'm no smother-hovercraft. Those moms ruined those children. Made them soft." She tsked and faced the window.

"No, they didn't. They loved their kids."

Frances leapt and fell at their mother's feet and took her hands in their own. "Mom, please." Frances shook her hands and cried out, "Mom. Please, look at me. Please." Frances laid their head on their mother's knee.

"I have heard your news. I have heard what you are choosing for yourself. Please leave."

Frances looked up at her. "Mom, do you realize what you have done? Do you realize what you have missed? Please, please know I understand. It's in me too. The urge to isolate, to be alone, the pull to be away from people, from everything and everyone. I fight it every day. I learned it in everything I ever saw you do, and it has always been in me. The only part of my life that's a choice is that I choose not to be all alone. Please get help." Crying, Frances kissed their mother's hands, but she ripped them away and raised her right one in the air.

SLAP!

"What? You slapped me!" Frances touched their reddening cheek. It stung.

Their mother stared out the window.

"You fucking slapped me? I can't believe you." Frances

slumped back and fully sat down. They breathed slowly and closed their eyes and let a moment pass. *Calm. Calm. Be calm.*

Frances reached inside their pocket and squeezed on tight for good luck, for love. Frances sat up and opened their eyes. "I forgive you."

Their mother's head was bowed.

What, she's crying? Frances reached for their mother and studied the tears rolling down her cheeks.

"Mom. Mom. Please, look at me!" Frances shook her hands.

"What, Frances! What do you want from me?" She looked at her child.

"There you are! Mom, please, you don't need to be afraid. Just look at me. I love you."

She shook her head but didn't look away.

"I'm not a bad person. It's okay to care about me," Frances cried. And then they saw it. Something, a hint of something small, warmed or expanded in their mom's eyes. Frances's mouth dropped open in shock, and they were about to smile, but then it was gone. It fell. Frances shook her hands again, searched her face. Tried to bring her back.

"Frances, I keep myself away to keep you safe," their mother stated, clearing her throat.

"You keeping yourself away is destroying me. Having you in my life can't hurt as much as not having you does." Frances kissed the top of both of her hands.

Their mother pulled them back in disgust and fear.

"You know, that stings worse than your slap. But you know I'm not going to hurt you. It doesn't go that way. It tastes like toothpaste in here. I taste it all, the whole of my childhood, in my mouth, Mom. It wants to make me think that I will end up like you. I have to go."

Frances stood, wiped their eyes, and began walking away. After a handful of steps, they stopped and looked back at her.

She hadn't moved. "Mother, the only way to get anywhere with you is to leave you alone. That's the only thing I can do to make you happy. And yet you still seem pretty fucking miserable. Fighting for your love is like trying to heat the wilderness. It's trying to know the trees in the forest across the lake. It's trying to see through the fog."

Frances stomped through the hallway and put on their shoes. They grabbed the pregnancy test from their pocket and put it on the counter. "You need this luck more than I do. Goodbye, Mom."

The door slammed.

"Frances! Frances! Frances!" She jumped from her chair and ran through the house and down the hallway. She pulled the door open, just as her child's car revved and disappeared around the corner. She pressed the top of her hands to her face, hoping to feel the warmth from the kisses. She closed the door, and as she turned all of her locks, something caught her eye. On the table sat the white and blue pregnancy test. She picked it up and walked to her chair. She sat down and looked out to the forest.

"Congratulations, Frances," she whispered, barely able to get the words out before sobs broke out and ran through her body.

Frances cried and leaned forward in their car. They struggled to see through the fog. They thought about the good luck charm, that they should have saved it for this moment, that they should have it in their pocket. They wiped away tears and thought about their family at home. Though the forest, their mother's forest, seemed to press in all around, Frances smiled. They thought about the city, about their well-lit apartment. They thought about Sara's touch. The fog pressed in close. A decisive storm blew through the forest. They thought of finally escaping the dark wood, of being free, of being a parent, of being whole. They thought that sometimes the child escapes and sometimes the child does not. What if a tree fell in this forest, right into the road, thought Frances, and then one did.

GOUDA

"Oh, thank goodness you are here! Come in, come in! I have never hired someone from the internet to help me with anything, but I'm so pleased to meet you! My name is Carl!" The stout, older man outstretches his right hand, while the left pulls at his long, salt and pepper beard. His bright, beady eyes are smiling, but he seems anxious.

You step inside.

"Well, ummm … how do I say this?" Carl looks to the ceiling. "I need help grocery shopping."

"Okay." You nod but wonder if a different service would have been a better fit.

"I need to stock up on something, and I need someone to push a second cart. I can't bear to make two trips. How do you feel about following me in your car? The grocery store is three miles away, and I will reimburse you for mileage. I can even give you some money now to cover the gas. Does that sound alright?" Carl shoves his right hand in his pocket.

You nod.

"Here's fifteen dollars." Carl holds out the bills, and you

reach for them. He pulls on his beard again and nods his bald, round head. His mustache twitches. "Once we get back, I will pay you your hourly rate, plus a tip. Does that work?" Carl raises his brow in anticipation.

You nod.

"Great!" He smiles, and his shoulders relax. "Are you ready to go?"

You nod.

Carl adjusts his blue plaid shirt. "I just need to grab my jacket and keys. I'll meet you out there."

You turn to walk out the door and briefly glance back at Carl puttering around. Once you get to the street, you open your car door, sit down, and wait.

A minute later, Carl comes pouring out with what looks to be a dozen, folded, reusable bags under each arm. "I can't believe I almost forgot my bags!"

He waves as he is rushing down the sidewalk, and a handful of bags slip out. You motion to get out of the car, but he holds a hand up and smiles before shouting, "I got it!" You wave, start your car, and follow him to the grocery store.

Throughout the drive, Carl looks into his rearview mirror, and you nod at him. When you arrive, you pull up right next to him, and he gives a thumbs up.

"Perfect parking spots! I'm so happy you are here." Carl hands you all the bags from under one arm. "Grab a cart and follow me!"

You nod, and as you step into the entryway, you pull a cart from the rack.

"No, no," Carl shakes his head. "I'm sorry. I just think we will need a bigger one."

"That's fine." You push the cart back and pull a larger one. He pats you on the shoulder and pulls one for himself.

"Let's go to the dairy aisle! I need cheese!" Carl declares.

You nod and begin following him, but unlike Carl, you weave and pause to let other shoppers pass.

"What kind of cheese do you want?" you ask as he stops his cart in front of the cheese section.

"What kind? Ummm … well," Carl says as he wrings his hands, "I guess … let's see … ummm … all of it."

"Oh, like an assortment. Some from each kind?"

"No, well, not exactly. Just like, as much cheese as we are allowed to buy."

"So, like a lot of cheese?"

"Yep." Carl smiles, pulling on his beard. He takes a step forward and with two hands grabs eight bags of shredded sharp cheddar and drops them in his cart. Then he pulls a handful more of the same kind and places them next to the first ones. "Wow! These are perfect." Carl reaches for blocks of mozzarella and stacks five up before dropping them in the cart.

"You really don't care what kind of cheese?" you ask.

"Not in the slightest. I love them all! How many do you think we can get?" Carl reaches for some feta. "Oh yes. Just no cream cheese or cottage cheese."

You nod. You wonder what the fuck is going on. You reach for rounds of goat and gouda and look around at the other shoppers.

"Hey, Carl, can I chat with you for a second? I have an idea." You wave him over.

"I love ideas!" Carl exclaims as he releases six Parmesan wedges and seven packages of American cheese into his cart. He takes a few steps closer and glances at your tiny cheese pile. "What is it? What is your idea?"

"Well, I have a feeling the other folks here won't appreciate all the cheese being taken away. I noticed a few people in this aisle are already making strange faces."

Carl glances around and catches the eye of a woman a few

feet away standing in front of the milk section. She quickly looks away.

"Hmmm … I see your point. But what's your idea?"

"My idea is this: we get some cheese here and then we hit a few other grocery stores throughout town so we don't take too much cheese from one place. What do you think?"

"I like your thinking." Carl pulls at his beard and scans the rows of cheese before him.

"So, do you think we are done here? I don't know where other grocery stores are. Can you help me? Do you have time for all of this? I will pay you for the full day, plus gas and tip!"

"Yeah, I should be. Just let me take a look." You pull out your phone even though you know you are free and look for any notifications. Nothing. No dots, no emails. No dings. "Yep." You put your phone back in your pocket. "I'm all free until tonight."

"What wonderful news! I promise, I'm good for every penny." He pats your back, and you smile. "So, are you saying that you think we should leave at this point?" he asks.

"I think we are getting about there."

"Okay, well, grab more of those rounds and just let me grab some …"

Carl reaches for Brie and stuffs wedges under his arm, then grabs provolone and string cheese packages. He releases half the stack into his cart and half into your cart. Then he repeats the same motion and looks up at you. You reach for more rounds and drop them in your cart. Then you take a few steps and pull handfuls of pepper jack and American cheese packages for both of your carts.

"Will you also grab mozzarella, and then we can go?" Carl pleads.

"Sure." As you scan for mozzarella, you notice a man about five feet away staring at your cart. "Is this enough?" you ask, holding four orange-sized mozzarella balls up.

"Yes, drop those in my cart, and grab more for yours, and we are out of here! Oh, and please grab us some Swiss on your way out!"

You nod and scan the rows for Swiss, while Carl turns his cart around. You can feel his eyes on you, so you grab as many as you can and put some in both of your carts.

"Thank you so much!" Carl smiles, and you begin pushing your cart behind him. "Excuse me! Pardon me! Coming through!" Carl calls out.

You apologetically wave your hand at the people he is passing by. *This is so weird.*

"This line isn't too long. Let's go in here."

Carl turns his cart into checkstand three, and you follow. As he is unloading cheese onto the conveyor belt, you see the cashier's eyes widen.

"This is all together!" Carl points to your cart, and the cashier softens his gaze upon seeing you.

As he is handing Carl his receipt, the cashier chuckles and says, "Hope I get invited to your fondue party!"

"Ha!" Carl half waves his receipt in the air as he pushes the cart away. "Might be too cheesy for you!"

You nod at the cashier and say, "Thanks!"

You and Carl spend the next four hours purchasing cheese from five other grocery stores. Bags of cheese have filled up your backseat, and it's hard to see out the rear window.

When you get back to Carl's house, he asks you if you wouldn't mind helping unload. You take many trips carrying the bags of cheese inside and shove as many as you can into his fridge and freezer, leaving everything else on the counter. Carl is so pleased and so grateful. He pays you double your hourly rate, plus a $60 tip.

"Thank you so much! I couldn't have done this without

you!" Carl pats you on the back as you are heading to leave.

"No problem, Carl! While I couldn't have predicted what I would be helping you with today, I had a lot of fun. You are great to work with." You nod sincerely and feel a twinge of sadness.

Carl seems to read your mind, and as you open your mouth to ask about the cheese, he says, "Thank you again! I'll call you if I need anything!" and he shuts the front door.

You start your car. Your thoughts are full of Carl. You wonder about his life. You wonder about his past. You wonder what he is going to do with all that cheese. Now you can see clearly out the rear window. You can still smell the cheese.

Three weeks later, your phone rings. You pick it up and look at the number. It's Carl.

"Hi, Carl!"

"Hello! I'm so sorry for bothering you. I know it's Saturday. Are you free? Can you talk?"

"I'm not doing anything, Carl. Just reading. I can talk. Why are you whispering?"

"I'm at the hospital, and I don't want these people to hear me."

"What? You're at the hospital! Are you okay? What happened?"

"Shh ... I don't want these people to hear you!"

"Sorry, Carl."

"No, I'm sorry, I'm sorry. I need and want to get out of here."

"What happened?"

"It's too hard to explain over the phone."

"Then why did you call me?"

"I need help. They want me to stay here under observation, maybe for hours, or else they want someone to come drive me home. They don't trust me to drive myself, even though I drove myself here!" Carl shouts this last part for everyone to hear.

"I hear you, Carl. And I know this is frustrating, but they want you to be safe. I don't mind picking you up, and then maybe when you are cleared we can drive down and get your car, or I can bus down and get it."

"Look at how much time they are going to be taking away from you too! What a hassle, a hassle! And of course, I will pay you for all of this, but are hospital pickups in the scope of your job? I don't think so! They gave me no choice!"

"Carl, it's fine. Just tell me which hospital you are at, and I'll be there right away."

"Oh ummm … I'm downtown. You know the silly clown house on sixth avenue? The one with all the quacks?" Carl yells again.

"I know exactly where you are at. No need to yell."

"Humph!" Carl grunts.

"Alright, so where exactly in the clown house are you at?"

"I'm still in the emergency room."

"I'll be down in about twenty minutes, maybe longer depending on traffic."

"Thank you!"

"See you very soon, Carl."

"Wait, wait, wait!"

"Yes?"

"I told them you are my cousin, so act like my cousin when you get here."

"What? Cousin? And what does that mean: act like your cousin?"

"You know, family."

"Yeah … but do you want me to do anything in particular?" you ask.

"Just be my cousin."

"Got it. See you soon, Carl. Wait, Carl?"

"Yeah?"

"What's your last name?"

"Fredrick. Good catch."

"Thank you, Carl Fredrick."

"Thank you, cousin."

You arrive at the hospital, find parking at the end of the lot, and walk through the sliding doors of the emergency room. Dozens of solemn people hover around, some pace in distress, others sit in their chairs, staring off in sadness. You glance in each direction before you hear Carl yelling your name. He is standing close to the front desk and waves you over. His other arm is in a cast.

"Carl! What happened?"

"I'll tell you about it in the car. Hey, where is my nurse? My ride is here."

"Just a little patience please." The man at the front desk smiles and meets your eyes.

"You are here to … ?" He starts, turning to you.

"I'm here to pick up my cousin, Carl Fredrick, and take him home."

"Gotcha!" The man types away at the keyboard, picks up the phone, punches some numbers, and briefly speaks into it before hanging up.

"Your nurse will call you back in one second, Carl. You and your cousin can take a seat, and she will be right with you." Carl shrugs and pats your back, and you both turn to sit down.

"What happened?"

"I don't want to get into it."

"But, Carl, your arm. You look badly hurt, scratched, and bruised up. Of course, you wouldn't be able to drive home. I'm so worried about you."

"The only reason they won't let me drive myself is because of some silly outpatient surgery."

"You had surgery?"

"At some point today, yes. But it's been hours. I'm perfectly fine."

"Carl!" A nurse calls from the front desk.

"That's her! Let's go!" Carl stands and pats your back again.

"Hi, Carl! This won't take long. It looks like you have your family member here for that ride."

"Hi, ma'am! Yes, this is my cousin! Can we go now?"

"Not quite, Carl. Hi, I'm Lisa. And you are?" she asks you.

"Carl's cousin," you answer.

"Got it." She smiles and turns to Carl. "See, sometimes reaching out to friends and family can be a good thing. I'm glad your cousin was able to come." Lisa looks at you and smiles.

"Now, even though he is quite alert, the anesthesia is still in his system and could have an impact. Carl also has pain medication, so close monitoring will be crucial. He hasn't been awake for very long now. And you will be staying with him overnight, and for a full twenty-four hours, correct?"

"What?" you ask.

"Oh, you people!" Carl shouts. "I don't need pain meds, and my cousin is busy! I will be fine alone."

"Carl, we talked about this. It's a safety precaution after surgery."

"It's alright, Carl. It will give us a chance to get closer. I have been thinking about you anyway." You smile.

"Great. I will just need to go over a few things with you about aftercare," says Lisa.

"Of course," you reply.

Thirty minutes later, you and Carl exit through the emergency room doors.

"Freedom!" Carl yells.

Once you get to your car, you open the door for Carl, help him in, and put his seatbelt on.

"Getting personal, and I don't even know you," Carl chuckles.

"Well, we will have plenty of time to get to know each other this evening and tomorrow too."

"About that, I will not be needing your services, or any overnight observation. Just the ride home will do, and I will pay you, of course."

"Carl, I admit this is a strange situation, but I ethically can't leave you alone. And at this point, I have promised your RN and could be liable if I abandon you. So, unless you have a friend or family member that can stay over, I will be with you. But I do want you to be as comfortable as possible, so if you do prefer someone else, I totally get it, because you are right, we are strangers. Do you have anyone you want to call or want me to call for you when we get to your home? Family or friends?"

"Not that I know of," Carl mumbles. "Even though you are a stranger to me, and I'm a stranger to you, I see you as a friend now."

"And you didn't feel comfortable just saying I was a friend when we were there?"

"No, not at all. I said you are family so that they think I have a caring blood relative here and get off my back. They gave me such a hassle last time I was there. Is there anyone who can do *this* for you? Is there anyone who can help you out with *that*? Blah. Blah. Blah."

"What? Last time you were there? Carl, what? When was this? You won't even tell me what happened today."

"I'm not talking about it. The point is, they hassle you about the people. Who are your people? Where are your people? People! People! People!"

"That's okay. I get it. I don't have anyone here, either. But I hope me being here isn't too much of a stressor. I can sleep on the floor. I can sleep anywhere."

"Nonsense." Carl looks at you. "I have a couch. But we just have one little problem."

"What's that?"

"You'll see," Carl sighs.

"Well, whatever it is, I'm here to help. And you don't need to pay me for staying over."

"Of course, I'm paying you!"

"You really aren't in any pain right now, are you, Carl?"

"Can't feel a thing."

"Those must be strong meds then."

Carl shrugs. A few minutes pass in silence.

"Did I tell you about my hot tub?" He turns, beaming.

"Hot tub? Do you have a hot tub, or you just got a hot tub?"

"Just got a brand-new hot tub. I'm very pleased with it. You can take a dip if you like."

"Thanks for the offer, Carl, but I respectfully decline. My job is to be keeping an eye on you, not lounging in a hot tub. I don't think you should get in either with your medications and all."

"Whatever you say, boss. Guess in the future I will have to make up for lost hot tub days."

"I have no doubt you will have plenty of time to enjoy it! Oh, we are here."

You pull up in front of his house and notice the draft as soon as you step inside. "Carl?"

"Yeah, I know it feels like the outside in here. Well, the outside is in here because the sliding glass door in the back is shattered. The whole world has just been coming in and out."

"The entire door is shattered?"

"Yeah, I was running to my hot tub and didn't see the glass and ran right through the door. Old house, untempered glass."

He holds up his wounded arm.

"Oh my god, Carl!"

Carl pulls at his beard and shakes his head. He looks at his arm and utters, "Serves me right for getting too excited."

"No, it's not your fault. Just a terrible accident, and I'm so glad you got medical attention."

Carl nods and walks you through the house, to the pieces of glass scattered everywhere. Through the giant, frame-like opening that was his sliding glass door, you see the hot tub in the backyard.

"Oh god, Carl! Let me clean this up."

"No way! I am not letting you do that."

"Yes, you are in no position to clean it up. I want you to sit on the couch and just let me see what I can get done. Do you have gloves and goggles?"

"I'm sure I do, in the basement. I'll be right back."

"Nope, I'm coming with you."

You spend the next couple hours, dressed in a makeshift hazmat suit, sweeping up and removing glass. Carl pulls up a chair and sits nearby, watching and making small talk. He is drinking from a small cup, and though he says it is only two shots of whiskey, it looks more like four being poured for each of you. You take a few small sips but save the rest for after this is all over. Then you see large, jagged, bloody pieces of glass.

"Carl." You pause and look up at him. "Please tell me what happened last time you were at the hospital."

Carl gulps. "You're gonna think I'm nuts."

"No, I won't. I'm the nutty one! Think about it, I'm cleaning up bloody glass, pretending to be your cousin, getting ready to stay the night." You laugh.

"We can have some macaroni and cheese for dinner!" Carl lifts his cup in the air.

"Of course, we can!" You smile, and Carl seems to relax.

"Just don't drop that cup, Carl!"

"Ha!" Carl laughs and takes a huge gulp.

"I mean it, Carl. What happened?"

"I fell." He coughs and lowers the cup.

"You fell? Where, how? Just, like, you tripped, or what?"

"No. No. I'm not a klutz."

"Everybody trips sometimes, Carl."

"That's not what happened." He lifts his cup, but it's empty. He pours the last few drops in his mouth and looks at you. "Do you mind if I just go and … ?" He tilts the cup back and forth.

"Go ahead," you say. "I'll take a break and sit with you." You grab a chair and pull it close to him.

He stands and walks to the kitchen, grabs a bottle from the shelf, and pours for a good three seconds. "I'll bring you your cup. Do you want more?" he asks.

"Hmmm … I'm fine for now. Thanks."

"Well, you should have more before it gets too cold outside. I mean, before it gets too cold in here."

"I will."

Carl sits down with his cup and hands you yours. You raise your eyebrows and take a sip. He takes another drink and sighs.

"You are going to think I'm crazy. But I have this problem."

"I don't think you are crazy, and I think everybody has problems. I'm not going to judge you."

"You say that now, but I woke up one day, and everything was different." Carl shakes his head. "You know in the morning when you wake up and your legs and feet are cold, so you kick your blanket out so it covers you completely? Well, guess what happened to me?"

"What?" you ask.

"I wasn't cold, but I couldn't feel the blanket, so I thought I must be cold and pulled my blanket up over the middle of my body. I tried to kick it and spread it out, but after I did that, I still couldn't feel it. I couldn't feel my blanket anywhere and then I realized I couldn't even feel it in my hands, but I knew I was gripping it because I could see my fingers around it."

"*That* is so weird!"

"Tell me about it!" Carl takes another sip. "So, I got up, and throughout the day realized that I couldn't feel anything. I couldn't feel hot, cold, thirst. I couldn't feel pain, couldn't feel tired, couldn't feel anything. I spent a whole day trying to bring feeling back. I took a shower, smoked a pack of cigarettes, went for a run, stubbed my toe on every wall. I took eight shots of whiskey. Nothing. I pricked my fingers, watched sad movies, pulled hair out of my beard. I was losing my mind. I thought I was in a dream! I gave up on hurting myself and decided to eat something, but I couldn't taste my food. I kept eating and eating and eating and just shoveling it into my face, but there was no pleasure in that meal. But you know what happened at the end?"

"What?" You finish your drink while trying to keep your face as neutral as possible. "Do you mind if I just go and … ?" You tilt your cup.

"Go ahead," Carl smiles before taking a sip.

You mouth, *oh my god* while filling up your cup. You consider the length of the night ahead.

"What happened at the end, Carl?" you ask, walking back to him.

"At the end, at the end of it, I felt something!"

"What did you feel?"

"I felt full!"

"You felt … full?"

"Yes. After six plates of spaghetti, I finally felt something. Full! Full! I felt full! Satiation. It was a miracle!"

"Wow! What a bizarre day, Carl! So glad that's over." You shake your head and drink.

"No, you don't get it. It's not over!"

"What's not over?"

"I can't feel anything!"

"What?"

"Nothing!"

"Still?"

"Yes, that's what I'm telling you. I woke up, and it was gone. No sensation of anything, just full. I pulled out two teeth with pliers." Carl pulls his cheek out with a finger on his good hand to show you.

"Carl! Oh no!"

"Yes! I rolled down hills, hit my funny bone, watched sunsets, burned myself, watched horror movies, everything! I still have to make myself sleep; I never feel tired. For a long time, it was so disorienting to know I was holding things without even being able to feel them. I pull on my beard to seem normal, but I can't even feel it. It took forever to relearn how to drive! I tell you, I'm grateful, but I don't feel gratitude. I smile and laugh, but I don't feel happy."

"Jesus, Carl! You don't feel emotions or sensations? It seems like you are feeling emotions."

"I've been practicing. I know how to seem like a person. A real person with feelings."

"Jesus, Carl."

"I had fallen off a ladder. That's what led me to the hospital last time. I was going to jump off of my garage, but as I was climbing up the ladder, I lost my balance. Or, what seems like balance. There are quite a few feelings that go into balance. You can go on memory for a while, but eventually you trip up. Then you trip up again. My neighbors saw me, but I did not feel it and I did not yell for help. They called nine-one-one! Do you know what that ambulance ride cost me? Almost everything! And yet, I have to fake my aggravation!"

You shake your head.

"I only had four cracked ribs. They asked me what happened, but I guess I told the medic who showed up and the nurse at the ER two different things. I told the medic I was getting a football for a neighborhood kid, but that didn't make any sense because it would have just rolled off my roof. And my idiot neighbors were outside gardening, and I didn't see them. So, unbeknownst to me, they told the medic that I looked disturbing hiking up that ladder. I'm sure I looked disturbing, but I didn't feel disturbed. Anyway, they told him that they didn't know what I was doing and that there aren't any kids or toys in the neighborhood. Can you believe that? So, when I got to the hospital, I told the nurse I was getting a kid his frisbee, and that didn't compute. You know, I had to talk to a social worker for old people? My god!" He takes a drink.

"Oh, Carl, you didn't want to tell them what you were experiencing?"

"They would just call me crazy! There is no rational explanation for this!"

"I'm so sorry, Carl. And what happened today? Oh gosh … did you?"

"Yes. I ran right through that glass door on purpose. I thought there was a chance a serious injury could give me a serious feeling. I was bleeding but had no sensation of the blood pouring out of me. If I hadn't been looking at it, I wouldn't have even known I was hurt. It looked bad, but I felt nothing. I wrapped a couple shirts and a ton of rubber bands around it and drove myself to the hospital. They couldn't believe I had driven myself there, and they kept on looking at each other. One nurse kept looking at the other nurse, and he was frantically typing into his computer. I said, 'Please, please don't write bad things about me. Please just stitch me up and let me be on my way.' But I wasn't really having any reaction to anything, and that scared them, and they took more notes. I told them that my mother always told me to be strong and show no pain, so this is how I show up, and this is how I live! They were testing me! I had huge pieces of glass in my arm, and they had to put me under. As I was falling asleep, I told them I tripped and tried to catch myself, but I forgot I was right in front of my glass door, so I fell right through it. I told them it stopped me but left me bleeding. I woke up, and that's when they asked me to call you."

"You didn't trust one person who helped you?"

"I don't feel trust. I don't have that type of relationship with those people, or any people. You see, it's all about relationships. All of it. Everything. Relationships, relationships, relationships. Family and friends! But what about me? I'm all alone. To that, the social worker said an honest relationship with ourselves is the most important one. Bullshit, bullshit, bullshit. I don't need any 'look inside, feel better, and heal banter.' I can't feel it! I don't feel anything! I don't feel lonely! I don't feel pain! I don't feel honesty! I only feel it when my stomach is full. I know they were just doing their job, but no, I don't trust them. They will just take me from my home and put me in a *different* home. One for crazy people. One that has even less feeling than me."

As you try to get comfortable on the couch that night, you hear Carl talking in his sleep. You get up and walk to his room to check on him. He is repeating over and over, "Don't fuck with me, I can't feel a thing. Don't fuck with me, I can't feel a thing." You walk back to the couch and write your full name and address on a piece of paper. Below it, you write, "I'm your friend." The blue sheet you hang over the gap where the glass doors used to be; it moves in the wind. You think back to when you first met Carl. You had dropped two rolls of Gouda on his feet when you were loading his trunk. He didn't notice. A grocery cart was stuck in its row, and he pulled on it so hard that when it dislodged, it rammed right into his legs. Nothing.

A week later, your phone rings. It's Carl. You had been thinking a lot about Carl, and feeling sorry, amazed, confused, and many other things. But Carl had not felt anything about you.

"Hi, Carl!"

"Hi, are you free?"

"Yeah, just eating lunch."

"What are you eating?"

"A turkey sandwich."

"Sounds delicious!"

"It is." You feel a twinge and wish you hadn't said anything. "Do you need help, Carl?"

"Yes, if you are free today, but if not, tomorrow works great."

"Nope, I can be there in an hour or so."

"Wonderful! Thank you!"

When Carl opens the door, he smiles and pulls on his beard before giving you a big, one-armed hug.

"You alright? Is your arm feeling better?"

"I have no idea! But come on in!"

"What do you need help with, Carl? Oh wow, what's that smell? Is that … all the cheese?"

"Yes, it is! I am treating myself today. I am making a giant fondue in my hot tub! I'm going to eat and eat and eat and feel everything I can. I have plain water in there now, no chemicals. I'm going to melt all my cheese, and the tub is half open to keep everything nice and hot. I need help unwrapping, but if you get hungry, eat some slices! Drop the cheese in the buckets, and we can carry the buckets out and dump them in the hot tub. Since I'm one-handed, I might need help carrying them out, but don't touch my hot tub. I don't want anything to be contaminated. I'm keeping the cheese in there so I can reheat it and keep eating."

"Hmmm … okay, Carl. Whatever you say."

You walk into the kitchen and see the cheese on the counters, in bags on the chairs, and all over the dining table. Carl is saying things like, "Happy fondue to you!" and "Pour some cheddar on me!" He is letting out hollow little laughs. Hours later, plastic wrappers with cheese film residue have covered the floor, and the stench of melted cheese floods the air.

"Would you mind please going shopping to restock me for future fondues? Can you get everything you think I might need?" Carl asks. He hands you $300.

"Are you sure?"

"Yes, my friend, I'm sure." He holds out his hand, and you shake it. He smiles, and you feel weird.

"Don't worry about me," says Carl. "I must get in to get out. I used to feel disappointed when I got full, because I always did love to eat and didn't always want the experience of eating to end. But now the satiation is the end all be all. Do you feel me?"

You drive to the stores, load up on cheese, but something is spoiling in your gut.

When you get back to his house, you yell his name as you walk in the front door. You see the open doorway where the glass once stood, and there is the hot tub. All closed up. As you get closer, you see empty buckets and his black flip flops on the ground right next to the tub.

The cops tell you there was nothing you could have done. No way you could have known.

A couple months later, a lawyer calls you and says that Carl has left you his house. He also left a note saying he understands if you don't want to keep his hot tub.

GUT

I got stuff in my gut, stuff and gut and weight
accumulating, it grows on me
used to feel it in my bones, now I see it on my bones
stuff and time adding up
makes no sense to me, the stuff that sticks
flesh and gut and highway, this ain't
right, it does something to my humanity.
The road is open, but all the time in my life
it weighs on me, like a death sentence
my own damned design, I made it
gut and weight and flesh and open road
everything that feels like home and isn't
why my road go on and turn that way?
Stuff and gut and weight and time and history
all out there on the highway, like roadkill
but it ain't dead yet
no, I been left flailing and crying and wailing
a vulture that ended up prey
something went on and destroyed me

it ain't dignified, being out there on the pavement like that
ain't dignified for a person like me
time turned on me, and left me like that.

NOISE

What's that? Roy tilted his head.

Silence.

He resumed reading. But as he turned the page, he heard it again.

"What is that?"

He glanced at Abby, who remained undisturbed by the noise, and then looked around his living room. Silence. Roy burrowed himself against the couch cushion and pulled his legs fully under the fleece blanket.

"What is that?" Roy held still and waited. He was tired. He blinked and scanned the sentences.

"Oh, sweet Raskolnikov! Wait, what is that?" Roy threw the blanket back, stood up, and put the book down on the coffee table. He rolled his neck and looked at his watch. 11 a.m., late morning—three hours still his.

Roy walked down the hall to his bedroom and turned the light on. His eyes fell on his tidy bed with its evenly draped blue down comforter. He looked at the square bedside table, then at the matching dark wood dresser, and finally at his closed closet.

He turned the light off and took a few steps towards the door of his small office. He reached for the light and studied his antique wooden desk where an old black typewriter that had belonged to his father sat. Roy walked up to it and softly pressed down on the worn keys. He closed his eyes and exhaled. He opened them and looked down at his nearby laptop and his neatly stacked notebooks and journals. He heard the sound again, and he thought something must be falling down, that something must have come loose. He dashed over to a wall and checked each symmetrically hung frame, then examined the dozens of frames on the other walls. Nothing was out of place. He closed the door and meandered back to his living room. He raised his arms and stretched while Abby yawned.

"Exhausting, isn't it, love? I must be out of it, maybe I'm going mad." Roy smiled at the cat, and she closed her eyes.

He picked up his cup of coffee and shook it so the foamy white marshmallow swirl on top faded and melted completely. He went up to the windows and peered down at the street below. Cars honked, people shuffled along, speed walked, spaced out, or were busy texting. Roy took a big sip and sat on the couch. He put his cup down, lifted his thick blanket, and cuddled up underneath it. He grabbed his book and checked his watch. 11:18. He reread previous sentences and tried to focus on every word.

But the noise, again.

"Abby, do you hear that? Or are you immune from distraction during catnaps?"

She looked at him and rolled her head.

Roy put the book down. He waggled his fingers in both ears. He reached for his phone and went to the *BBC*, *The New York Times*, and then *The Wall Street Journal*.

As he scrolled, Roy heard the noise three times in a row. He tossed his phone down, folded his blanket, set it neatly on the couch, then finished his coffee in one gulp. He went to the kitchen and filled a tall glass of water and drank the whole thing before walking to the bathroom where he peeled off his tan drawstring pants and brown sweatshirt. He stepped into the warm shower. He rubbed his ears with his fingers, again, and then again with a washcloth while the hot water pounded his back. Silence. Roy smiled in relief. He put on a pair of jeans and a red sweater before combing his short black hair. He quickly shaved and put on his glasses and watch. The watch showed 12:20—he still had some time. He opened his office door and sat down at his desk. He looked at emails he had already read and re-reviewed assignments from his editor, Jenny. Roy picked up his pen and notepad and read his notes. As he began writing, he heard the noise. He groaned and rubbed at his ears, hoping to dislodge any shower water that might still be there. He decided he would leave early. He tucked his notebooks under his arm, closed the door, and walked back to the living room.

"Abby, I see you got my spot. Please keep it warm for me. I'm leaving early but will be back in late afternoon. Text me if you need anything, and if you hear that noise, please pretend it's a mouse and catch it for me. If you decide to read, don't read ahead too much."

Abby blinked at him before licking her fluffy white paw. Roy put on his coat and shoes and picked up his leather bag. He slid his notebooks inside and felt the outside pocket. His wrap of tin foil was there. He locked the front door and walked to the stairwell exit. As he pulled the heavy door open, the noise came again, loud this time.

"Goddamnit!"

"You alright, Roy?" an old woman's voice called out from down the hall. It was Mrs. Frank. She wore a pink polka dot nightgown and her white hair sat up in a bun. One arm held a pink-and-gold checkered cane, and under her other arm she held her plump tan Chihuahua, Mrs. Sprinkles, who had on a matching pink polka dot onesie.

"Hey, Mrs. Frank. Hi, Mrs. Sprinkles. Yeah, I'm fine," he said hurriedly, not wanting an elongated encounter with Mrs. Frank. "I just pinched my finger opening the door."

"Watch out for those doors." She pointed her cane at him and shifted her weight. "Wish we could keep the doors open, keep air flowing, keep it welcoming. Let it in and let it out. It has gotten ridiculous—the security, the locks, the monitoring. If somebody needs something and I have it, my door is open to them, and it will stay open. People break things when they are out in the cold and doors keep closing on them." She shook her cane in the air.

"I hear you, Mrs. Frank, and I agree. You are one wise woman." Wanting to leave, Roy bit his lip, still holding the door open.

"What can I say? I have been around eighty years, more or less. Let's go with less!" She chuckled.

"Ha! Good to see you again, Mrs. Franks." Roy smiled, but Mrs. Franks didn't move. He stared at the unmoving Mrs. Sprinkles. "How's your baby?"

"Oh, Mrs. Sprinkles is doing alright. She peed on the carpet over there, but don't say a word." Mrs. Franks looked down at Mrs. Sprinkles, who looked up at her before looking at Roy and blinking. "Come over for crosswords and coffee sometime soon if you aren't too busy. How are your stories going? Are you still saying what needs to be said? Are you telling the people the truth? This world has totally lost it. Tell them it doesn't need to be this way. Tell them, Roy. Tell them I said so," she pleaded while stabbing the air with her cane.

"I'll do my best, Mrs. Franks." Roy twitched. The noise again.

"Thank you for always calling me Mrs. Franks and not 'Widow Franks.' Just because my Georgie insisted on dying doesn't mean I have lost my title, or my first name. I'm a widow, yes, but I'm still married."

"Of course."

"How many years have we known each other? Mrs. Sprinkles, how long have we known Roy?"

"At least seven years, Mrs. Franks," Roy said.

"Exactly! So, you should be calling me Robin by now. Good heavens, dear. You have been standing there holding that hefty door open, listening to me blabbering off. You are trying to go about your business! Your arm must be tired! I'll see you later, Roy. Do come over sometime. I'm going to check the mail."

"No worries, Mrs. Franks, I mean, Robin. I didn't even realize I was holding it. I always enjoy seeing you and Mrs. Sparkles. I'll come by soon." Roy smiled and waved and tried to ignore the noise as Mrs. Franks nodded and trotted down the hall.

As the stairwell door closed behind him, he rubbed his ears while hustling down the last steps. The noise. Soon he was in the alley, where a row of half-mauled bags of wet trash greeted him.

Roy turned the corner and joined the bustling sidewalk of people: families trying to stay in a group, single folks scrolling and texting, bewildered and offended tourists, the downtrodden and lost begging for change and mercy, and busy, self-important professionals so addicted to their routine they find themselves walking their work commute on the weekend. Roy checked his phone: 12:50.

He walked the three blocks to his favorite place, a quaint, out-of-date café. A giant Starbucks had opened directly across the street and had lured many folks away, so he almost always had a guaranteed seat. Roy pulled the front door open, listening for the familiar chime of the tiny bell that hung from the top. He raised his eyebrows in acknowledgment of his favorite waitress, Judy, and she smiled. It was busier than usual, but he saw three people at a booth in the corner motioning to leave, so he strolled over to claim it. The noise came, and he vigorously shook his head, like a wet dog. He saw a woman, mid-bite, flash him a look of disgust. Roy tried to quickly play it off by raising and shuddering his shoulders, as though he simply had a chill. Before he knew it, Judy stood right next to him and was reaching for the previous customer's plates. Roy's body spasmed slightly at the sound of the noise but began helping her by collecting the silverware.

"Oh, Roy, come on. I got it."

"I'm sorry, Judy. I wasn't rushing you."

"No, I want you to take this spot before a family of five squeezes in and then complains about the room. I assume you are waiting for Lane?" Her short, gray-blonde ponytail bobbed.

"Yeah, waiting for Lane. I love your blue eye makeup. And it matches your blue?" Roy pointed to the top of his head.

"These are scrunchies. Everyone says they are out of date. But I love them. And I just got my eyelashes done, thank you for noticing. If I'm going to be here another twenty years, I might as well do it in style. Besides, it gives me a boost. Roy, are you alright?"

"Yeah, yeah. I'm sorry if I made a face. I have a terrible migraine that I can't kick."

"Oh, sweetie, I'm so sorry. Those are the worst. Take a seat and relax. I'll be right back to wipe this down and bring you some coffee. Alright?"

"Thanks, Judy."

She glanced back and saw his face wince again. Roy closed his eyes and attempted to focus on the sounds of the café, but the noise came again, and then again. It took an effort to sit still;

his body wanted to resist the noise by moving in strange and distracting ways. Roy slowed his breathing and put his hand on his heart. He didn't hear Judy as she came up to the table, put a mug down, and filled it with coffee.

"Heeelllooo, anybody home?" Fingers rattled on the table.

"Oh, hey," Roy flinched and opened his eyes.

Lane slid into the booth and put his bag down. "You jumped even though you knew it was me. You alright?" Lane raised his eyebrows.

"Yeah, I'm sorry. Just tired. I have a bad headache." Roy shook his head.

"Did you and Abby party too hard last night? Why didn't you call me?" Lane winked.

"Ha. Yeah, I'm fine." Roy sat up and tried to smile. Lane nodded and glanced around as Roy studied him. Everything from his well-worn leather jacket to his tousled sandy hair, from his soft blue eyes to his faded blue jeans, everything permeated ease. Even though he was highly attentive and engaged, he always remained calm.

"Well, if you want me to run and get you an Advil, Tylenol, something?" Lane met Roy's eyes.

"Thanks, but I'll be okay."

"Or if you need to go home—"

"No, I wanted to see you. I mean, I wanted to stick to our meeting time," Roy stammered.

"I don't see a single marshmallow in your coffee yet. You must be hurting." Lane winked again.

"What? Oh, what?" Roy winced and looked down. The noise grew. "What? When was Judy here?" He looked around, and tried to play it cool right as she approached the table.

"Hi, Judy! Good morning! You look great!" Lane beamed and leaned back to face her fully.

"Hey, Lane. How are you?" Judy smiled and began pouring

him a cup of coffee. "You know, I'm doing okay. Did I tell you both that I have three grandchildren with me now? Did I tell you that?" She put her hands on her hips and shook her head. "Don't get me wrong. They are a blessing, and I would do anything for them. But my god, it's a lot! Earl is home with them right now. Who knew his retirement would be raising children? I'm just happy to be working day shift. Night duty with the kids works great for me. Anyway, my goodness, I could talk at you all day." She wiped her forehead, and then started laughing.

Roy watched Lane listen, nod, and shake his head compassionately at her circumstance. Roy flinched and cleared his throat, hoping the cough covered his awkward movement.

"You two are just the sweetest, and I will let you get back to it. You probably have lots of projects to go over. I'll be back by, or I can get your regular order started on your third cup?"

"Nothing for me today. Thank you, Judy." Roy tried to smile.

"Oh, honey. You are hurting. If you need a doctor to feel your forehead, I'm here. I have never been wrong about the presence of anything in the mind or body of man. How long have you two been coming here?"

"I'm unsure. But thanks, Judy. I'll let you know." Roy nodded and looked down at his cup.

"Regular is great. Thank you, Judy. We have been coming here for five years," Lane said.

"Five years? I'm getting old! Point is, you can trust me. Well, you know what I mean." Judy grinned at Lane, but Roy still hadn't looked up as she left.

"You are always paying attention to people." Roy crossed his arms, hoping he could hold himself still when the noise came again.

"Yeah, but so are you. We just do it differently. You are looking for their story, their history, their pain, and the present moment. I'm looking for their angle, their essence, their past and their future." Lane lifted his cup and waited for Roy to meet his eyes before taking a sip.

"How many pictures did you just see?" Roy asked, determined not to flinch at the noise.

"No less than seven. Maybe five good ones, three usable. I'm still listening when I'm looking."

"I know you are, Lane."

"Well, outside of your massive migraine, how are you?"

"Don't be fooled. I'm fine. And I always come bearing marshmallows." Roy reached inside the outside pocket of his bag and pulled out the small roll of crinkled aluminum foil. He unfolded it and picked out two fluffy, partly squished marshmallows before placing them on top of his coffee. "To love me is to love my marshmallow," he smiled.

"There you are!" Lane clapped. He opened his mouth to add something more, but Roy interrupted.

"These are always, always, available to you." Roy held his tin foil roll-up.

"Well," Lane touched his heart, "I appreciate that greatly. But as Judy said, we have been coming here almost every week for five years, and I will continue to decline your marshmallows for all foreseeable Saturdays. More for you! Just don't let anyone steal your bag. They would be weirded out."

"Fine. No one will steal my bag. And Judy didn't say anything about five years. You said that." Roy flinched while rolling his tube back up and then picked up a spoon and slowly pushed down on one of the marshmallows. The noise, he didn't flinch at it. "How are you, Lane?"

"I'm fine. Things are good." Lane smiled and picked up his cup.

"How are you always fine and good?" Roy took a swig of coffee.

"I'm not always fine, but today I am. I'm happy to see you, but I'm sorry for your pain."

"Thanks. Want to get to it for a bit?"

"Sure." Lane half-smiled as his friend winced again.

"What do we have coming up?" Roy asked, even though he knew.

"Good question." Lane nodded, playing along. He reached into his own bag and pulled out his iPad. Then he grabbed three folders full of pictures, two small notebooks, and a pen. "Okay, so I heard through a contact about a demonstration at that elite art gallery that just opened. It sounds like this gallery was built on about half a block of land that was supposed to stay public property. And we have a march for city union workers in a week and a half, but this Tuesday is the tenants' rights march. I'm sure we will have no problem finding people to interview. I wanted you to have the opportunity to talk with a management company or a landlord, so I called buildings near the march, but no response. I doubt we'll get an appointment or quote, but we'll see. Hello, Roy, anybody home? Your marshmallows are melting." Lane snapped his fingers.

"What? Oh, sorry," Roy blinked and shook his head. "Yeah, whatever you want sounds great."

"What? No, Roy. While we are a team, I just take the pictures. You are the one interviewing and writing. This is not a 'whatever I want' situation. I don't have word limits to contend with."

Roy nodded and then slowly looked around the café. The noise had come several more times.

"Roy, you're trembling. Please let me get you something." Lane reached out but immediately pulled his hand back. Roy hadn't noticed.

"I've taken all there is to take. I'm okay. I mean, I'll be okay. Just more coffee might help."

"I'm sorry. Let's not talk about work. It might actually be nice to just sit here and not obsess over articles, stories. Everything gets done anyway, and all we do is work. All we talk about is work," Lane said. He started putting his stuff away. "Well, now here I am rambling on. Ha! You usually do the talking. I'm not comfortable with this role." Lane smiled and winked, but Roy didn't respond. "Roy?"

"I'm sorry, Lane. I'm here. You said there were protests?" Roy shuddered.

"Didn't you hear? Wake up! News flash! We aren't talking about work today. Your migraine could be the catalyst for a whole new way of experiencing the weekend, a whole new way to live! It could break the pattern of our chronic work addiction, get us talking about ourselves. We can learn about each other. The possibilities are endless," Lane practically sang.

"I appreciate what you are doing, Lane. I'm sorry I'm so out of it." Roy lowered his eyes.

"No, I like migraine Roy. Migraine Roy makes regular Roy slow down and take a break."

Roy frowned. Judy came up and filled their cups. No one spoke, but Lane nodded a thanks.

"Hey, I'm done. I'm sorry. Please let me help, let me do something. You are my dear friend. I care about you." Lane looked away as soon as he had finished speaking.

Roy studied Lane's face. The noise seemed to come from his face, then from behind his head. Lane stared back quizzically.

Judy came up to their table with a giant serving platter and said, "One veggie omelet, one side of French toast and syrup, and a cup of orange juice." She put the plates down in front of Lane.

"Heaven! Thank you as always, Judy!" Lane smiled and looked down at his steaming plates.

"Are you feeling any better, Roy?" she asked.

"Yeah, a bit, thank you," Roy lied and lifted his cup and began drinking to cut conversation.

"There is nothing better than dipping French toast in this whipped butter," Lane sighed.

"Only marshmallows." Roy put the cup down.

"Oh boy. He's coming back!" Lane laughed, but Judy just stared as she topped their cups off.

Roy winced twice, his face furrowed, and he closed his eyes. He wanted to cry out.

"Do you think it's one of those cluster headaches?" Judy mouthed to Lane.

"No idea. Can I please have a box and the check?" he whispered back.

Judy nodded and left.

"Sorry," Roy mumbled, opening his eyes. He searched for something to say. "You know, it's so impressive how you always finish both plates, and how you mix cuisines so seamlessly."

"These cuisines aren't mixed. It's all breakfast food. It's all the same thing. Besides, as you well know, this is my one weekly indulgence. This is how I live large! We don't drink, we don't smoke, we don't eat out besides this. I look forward to it every week." Lane took a bite of omelet and saw Roy's eyebrows raise, so he continued. "Yeah, I mean it. Sometimes I'll be at the grocery store, and eggs will be looking at me, and even though it pains me, I have to say, 'Sorry, can't do it. It's not Saturday. I trust you will find a warm plate to sit on soon.'"

"I like this talking Lane. He's funnier than I remember." Roy attempted to smile.

"Well, I'll be here every Saturday." Lane winked.

"Here you go." Judy came up to the table and handed Lane a box and Roy the check.

"Wait, we are leaving?" Roy asked, then flinched again.

"Yes! I'm not going to sit here while you are suffering.

You need Tylenol, one of those hot neck pillow things, sleep. Thanks, Judy." Lane nodded at her.

"But you were just saying that this is how you live large?" Roy reached for his wallet, pulled out his card, and handed it to Judy. "Thank you so much." He smiled and turned back to Lane.

"Roy, I can live large at home. Besides, I want to find out if Felix likes eggs. I just need to finish my orange juice." Lane scooped his food into the box.

Judy returned with the card and said, "Please look out for him, Lane. Good to see you two! Until next time!"

Lane and Roy stood, and each pulled a twenty from their wallets. Lane handed his to Roy, who stacked it on top of his own and folded them both under the coffee cup. As they grabbed their bags and headed out, Roy heard the slight jingle of the door chime and felt it far away, so light and full of life compared to his noise.

Once on the sidewalk, Roy turned and asked, "Lane, have you ever heard an unknown noise, over and over for hours?"

"Hmm, like your ears are ringing? Tinnitus?"

"No, not like that. It's not constant, but it repeats. And it's not ringing. It's something else."

"Sometimes I hear, like, a high-pitch sound, but that's when my ears ring. Like that?" Lane asked.

"No, not really." Roy shook his head and looked to the ground.

"What does it sound like?"

"I can't describe it. It's not going away. It's just this, this noise. I hear it every fifteen seconds. Other times it's minutes apart, and then longer, and then it will come several times in quick succession. I don't know where it's coming from."

"Is it happening right now?"

Roy met Lane's eyes and nodded.

"You have no idea what it sounds like and can't figure out the source? I bet it's the migraine."

"My head only hurts because this noise won't stop. Wait, wait, did you hear that?" Roy looked around frantically.

Lane froze and leaned forward and listened intently. "I … I think I can hear it."

Roy's eyes widened as his heart beat faster. "What? You can hear it?"

"Wait, wait, nope. That's just New York City. Damnit." Lane laughed and patted Roy's shoulder.

"I don't need this, Lane." Roy gulped.

"Hey, hey, I'm sorry. I was just trying to make you laugh. Is there construction by your place?"

"No. I don't know. It's not loud and it's not like construction."

"So, it's a soft noise?"

"I don't know, Lane," Roy snapped. "It's zippy and metallic, but also soft, and also not any of those things. I'm sorry, I'm exhausted. I'm sure you are right that it has to do with my migraine. Alright, see you later. Sorry for ruining our breakfast. Pet Felix for me."

"Okay, see you Monday, Roy. Please get some rest. Call me if I can do anything."

Roy darted away from Lane without acknowledging his words. Baffled, Lane watched his friend move slowly down the block and saw him freeze, look around anxiously, rub his ears, and finally, when he was about to be out of sight, Lane saw him lift his arms to plug his ears.

⌒

The next Monday, the staff huddled in a conference room for their weekly meeting. Roy and Lane's colleagues scrolled or griped or bragged about their weekend while they waited for

8:30. Lane looked at the clock and then the door. 8:27. No Roy. He had never missed a meeting.

"Alright, we ready to start?" asked Jenny. She walked in and took a seat at the head of the table.

People nodded, quieted down, and put their phones away while Lane kept his eyes on the door. No sign of Roy.

"Hi, team. I hope everyone had a good weekend. So, who's going first? Beth?"

"Sure." Beth flicked her pen back and forth in her hand. "I have undercover PETA, destruction of homeless encampments, discriminatory hiring practices, and the Taxi Union, who made the switch to Lyft and Uber, who didn't, why, and so on. Everything's on schedule, and remaining photographs will be processed and submitted this Thursday."

"Great. Please let me know if you need anything, or any help from anyone else. Those all sound intense and powerful. I look forward to the drafts." Jenny scribbled something and looked up. "Roy? What do you have?" Her eyes scanned the room. "Roy?" she asked again.

"Oh," Lane started quickly, "he's not here yet, but he just texted that he got stuck in traffic."

"Wow, he is always the first one here. I always thought he was immune to traffic," Jenny laughed and made a note. "So, Lane, maybe you can speak to your projects then?"

"Yes! Demonstration at the gallery, tenants' rights march tomorrow, city workers next week."

"I'm sorry. I'm so sorry!" Roy burst in. "Traffic, I got stuck in traffic!"

"Hey, Roy, glad you made it. No worries. Lane was just filling us in." Jenny smiled.

Roy pulled out a chair and pretended to fumble with his bag to avoid any form of contact, so Lane continued. "We are hoping for some interviews. I'll submit the photos ASAP."

"Wonderful. As always, I'm here. Just make sure we get everything by the fifteenth." Jenny jotted something down and turned to Roy. "Roy, are you alright?"

"Yeah, I'm sorry. I just don't feel good." Roy slumped in his chair and struggled to look up.

Some of their co-workers leaned subtly back in their chairs.

"Hmmm … yeah, you don't look great. I know you just got out of traffic, but if you need to take the day, or want to work from home, go ahead. Do what you need to do to take care of yourself."

Roy closed his eyes. "It's just a migraine. Can I go sit at my desk if that's alright?"

"Of course." Jenny nodded emphatically.

Roy kept his head down as he grabbed his bag and left.

"Mind if I join him?" Lane said.

"Go ahead. Please keep an eye on him. I know the tenant march is tomorrow, so keep me posted."

Roy had just sat down in his cubicle and had put his head in his hands and plugged his ears. As Lane slowly walked up to Roy, he heard him whispering, "Stop. God. Damnit."

"Hey, Roy. Stop what?"

No response.

Lane stood two feet behind Roy and saw his friend plugging his ears and shaking. Lane reached out and touched his back.

"What!" Roy yelled and jumped.

"Jesus, sorry." Lane leapt back.

"You scared me!" Roy twitched. The noise.

"Roy, what happened? Did you sleep at all this weekend? Your eyes are bloodshot, you look exhausted. I have never seen you unshaved. While you finally look like you fit in in this city, this isn't you. You look lost."

"What?" Roy whined. He began frantically looking around.

"I asked you if you slept this weekend," Lane said softly. He pulled a chair from the adjoining cubicle and sat next to Roy.

Roy blinked a couple times and looked down at his desk.

"Does your head hurt? Do you have a fever? Want me to touch your forehead? I might not be as capable as Judy, but I can feel warmth."

Roy turned and met his eyes.

"Hey, why are you looking at me like you don't know me? It's me, Lane. What's happening?"

"I'm sorry. I'm sorry. I'm out of it." Roy shook his head and looked back at his desk. "I haven't slept for two nights, and unlike the hipsters, I feel it." He faked a grin.

Lane chuckled but saw his friend's face go dim. "Is the noise still happening?"

Roy's eyes widened, and he quickly looked around before leaning forward. "You hear it … too?"

Lane leaned forward. "Why are you whispering?"

"You are making fun of me." Roy sat back. He stood and reached for his bag. Lane grabbed his hand but immediately let go. Roy looked down at his hand and shook his head.

"I'm sorry. I just, what are you talking about? I wasn't mocking you. I would never, ever do that. I think you need a doctor. If you're leaving, I'm coming with you." Lane stood.

"Don't!"

"Yeah, I'm coming to keep an eye on you. We'll get something to help you sleep, and then we can work. I'll go tell Jenny. Don't leave without me. Promise?" Lane begged.

Roy shrugged.

"Thank you! Be right back." Lane darted to Jenny's office, and Roy started walking. As Lane explained the situation to Jenny, he saw Roy through the glass door, heading to the elevator.

"Jenny, I'm sorry. He's leaving, and I have got to grab him."

"Keep me in the loop, and thank you for looking after him. Protect yourself, too," she called out.

"Will do! Thank you! Roy, wait for me!" Lane ran out of her office to grab his stuff as Roy pushed the button for the elevator. It was closing just as Lane ran to it. The men looked at each other for two seconds as the metal doors shut. "What the hell, Roy?" Lane yelled.

Roy stared at him blankly and then flinched.

Lane punched the button and tapped his foot. "Fuck! Should have just taken the stairs."

The door dinged its return, and Lane hopped inside. When he hit the street, he scanned each corner and intersection searching for his friend.

A message from Roy popped on his phone: *I can't impact you like this. Stay here. I feel terrible.*

Lane shook his head and put his phone back in his pocket. He scanned in all directions and said, "There he is!"

Roy had made it to the end of the block and had crossed the street. He stood waiting for the light with his head down.

"Fuck! What should I do?" Lane looked up and down the street. "Yes! Please stop!"

He stepped out into the street and waved his hand. "Come on, come on, come on!"

The yellow taxicab driver nodded at Lane and pulled over. Lane hurried in and quickly said, "Thank you so much! We are picking up my friend. He just took a left up there and is proba-bly only about two blocks away right now."

"He is walking away? Does your friend know you are pick-ing him up?"

"I'm surprising him. It's his birthday. Please take a left if you can, and we can grab him."

"Got it. It's okay. I'll have to stop where I can. I need a des-tination once he gets in."

"Thank you. I'm so sorry about the inconvenience. I promise to leave a big tip."

The driver turned, and as they moved up the block he said, "I'll have to stop up here for a minute."

"Understood. We are just about to pass him. I will yell for him before we stop. Thank you!" Lane rolled down his window and yelled at a distraught Roy, "Roy! Get in! He's pulling over."

"What!" Roy's body twitched. The people around him stared as Lane waved at them, smiling.

"Happy Birthday, Roy! Surprise! Now get in the car!"

Roy glared at Lane.

"I know you've been out all night partying! Now get in! Roy! We will take you home!"

"Okay, we gotta go!" the car driver yelled.

Roy huffed and trudged toward the car. He opened the door, slumped inside, and shook his head.

"What's your address again? I promise I knew it, but it's escaping me," Lane asked.

"Ugh." Roy looked out the window for a moment before leaning forward to give his intersection.

As they climbed the stairs of Roy's apartment building, he paused. "Tell me you don't hear that."

"Roy, I don't hear anything except for our feet. I think you have tinnitus."

"No. I don't hear it in my head. I hear it outside of my head. It's not a ringing, not a buzzing, not a sustained anything. It's not tinnitus. It comes from different directions. It comes and goes."

"Do you think you could try to describe it? What does it sound like right now?"

"No idea. It's fuzzy, crunchy, maybe like a scratching noise. No, wait, that isn't right. It doesn't make any sense."

They arrived at Roy's floor, and Lane pulled the hallway

door open for him.

"How do you know it's not coming from inside your head?" Lane questioned as they walked.

"I know what's in my head and what's not in my fucking head!"

"Hi, Mrs. Franks!" Lane patted Roy's back as he yelled and nodded ahead.

"Oh fuck," Roy whispered. "Hi, Mrs. Franks!"

Mrs. Franks had a blue polka dot dress on. She held her cane firmly in one hand, and Mrs. Sparkles hung underneath her other arm. She covered the little dog's ears.

"Roy! What language! Mrs. Sparkles doesn't like swear words." She leaned against her door.

"Sorry, Mrs. Franks … er, Robin. I'm getting sick. I'm not myself right now." Roy wiped his forehead.

Mrs. Franks took a big step back into her apartment and stroked Mrs. Sparkle's head.

"Well, I'm sorry, but I'll have to keep my distance, dear. If you need anything, any meals, I can leave them outside your door. I make a mean casserole. Everyone goes on and on about soup, but a casserole is not only warming, it fills you up. People need energy to fight illness! Energy!"

"Thank you, Mrs. Franks." Roy tried to smile, but the noise came again, and he hunched over.

Mrs. Franks stepped back a few more inches.

"Don't worry, Mrs. Franks," Lane eyed Roy nervously, "I'm going to take good care of him."

"You're a good pal, Lane. It's great to see you. Are you taking good pictures? Are you showing the people what they need to see? Are you, Lane?" She peered forward. Mrs. Sparkles blinked.

"I'm doing the best I can. Thanks for the reminder." Lane smiled.

"Don't be afraid to show them. People need to see!"

"What do they need to see, Mrs. Franks?"

"The truth." She squeezed her dog a bit tighter.

"I'd love to hear more. What does the truth look like?" Lane asked, meeting her eyes intently.

"Well, I don't know. But people know it when they see it, especially in pictures, especially with words. They know it in their heart." She tapped her chest with the hand holding the cane.

"You know what, I think you are right, Mrs. Franks. Thank you." Lane nodded sincerely. He caught Roy in his peripheral vision, wincing and staring at Mrs. Sparkles. Roy was wondering about Mrs. Sparkles' own auditory events.

"I would love to chat more with you about the truth, but Roy is really sick. I'm so sorry. We have to get him home." Lane patted Roy's back.

"Oh, good heavens, that's right. Here I'm going on and on. Get some good rest, Roy. Do let me know if you boys want anything, or if you are feeling better and want to come over for *Wheel of Fortune*. See you later, boys! Say, bye, Mrs. Sparkles!"

"Bye, Mrs. Franks, and bye, Mrs. Sparkles! Come on, Roy, let's go." Lane waved.

Mrs. Franks shook the dog. Mrs. Sparkles blinked. Mrs. Franks closed her door.

"Hey, zombie, give me your keys!" Lane commanded.

Roy blinked and reached into his pocket. "Did you hear that?" he asked, while holding the keys out to Lane. He eyed the hallway.

"Nope, just the sound of my soon-to-be sleeping friend hallucinating from exhaustion!"

Lane grabbed the keys from Roy's still outstretched hand.

"We are almost there! Keep walking!"

He pushed Roy forward and looked for the front door key.

When they arrived, Lane grabbed Roy's shoulders and leaned him against the wall, then he opened the door and pushed Roy in.

"What are you doing?" Roy asked.

"I'm downloading Instacart to get you NyQuil."

"I don't need that. I'm not sick. I have no flu or cold symptoms. I'm fine."

"Ha! Says the man who has been hearing strange noises and hasn't slept for days. Please just do as I say today. Deal? Let's get you better before the march tomorrow. People who are fine don't hear things other people don't hear. Right?"

Roy nodded in defeat before standing and haphazardly walking to the bathroom.

"You look lost in your own home. After your nap, we are calling the doctor. Or right now?"

"Later," Roy hollered.

Lane pushed deliver on the Instacart app and then downloaded the DoorDash app and scrolled through pho places. "My god! This is amazing! Add to cart! Add to cart!" Lane pushed deliver and smiled at himself.

"What are you doing?" Roy stood freshly showered in the hallway. He had combed his hair.

"Get into bed!" Lane put the phone down in his lap.

Roy walked over and sat down on the couch. "I'm not going to just leave you out here. You are company. I have company," Roy huffed.

"If Felix was here, yeah, you would have company. But this is just me."

"Lane, you are missing work to sit here with me."

"Not true. I'm going to be sitting here with Abby, working while you sleep. Jenny said I could have a 'work from home' day. And I'm simply working from *your* home." Lane winked.

Roy didn't say anything but stood and began walking to his bedroom.

"Text if you need anything!" Lane hollered.

Roy waved, and Lane saw him plug his ears.

"Okay, Abby. Let's feed you." Lane headed to the kitchen and emptied a bowl of wet food. As he put it down for her, he pet her back. "I'm going to go check on your daddy. I'll be right back."

Lane tapped on Roy's almost fully closed door. "I'm coming in."

Roy was sitting up in bed, reading. In his hands was *Crime and Punishment*. He paused and looked up at Lane.

"I'm losing it. This is my punishment, but what is my crime?" Roy moaned.

"You can't just … ignore it?" Lane wanted to sit next to Roy on the bed but stopped himself.

"What in the hell do you think I've been doing?" Roy slammed the book shut. "I'm sorry. Wait, do you hear that? Do you hear it?" His eyes widened, and he leaned forward and looked at Lane.

"Yes, I heard that. It's Instacart, though. I'll be right back," Lane nodded and watched Roy fall back into the pillows and then look away. Lane softly patted his leg and said, "I'm sorry."

Five minutes later, Lane stepped back into the bedroom. "What a spunky kid! Here you go."

Lane handed Roy two NyQuil capsules and his cup of water. "I really hate that you are going through this, Roy. It's so strange. I'm so sorry. I hope it passes soon, whatever it is."

"Thank you, Lane. Tell me the plan for tomorrow." Roy took the NyQuil and put his cup down.

Lane began reciting the next day's plans but looked and saw that Roy was fast asleep. He got a bit closer and picked the book up. Underneath it were pieces of twisted-up tissue that

Roy had shoved in his ears. He put the book on the table and saw a small row of smashed ear plugs. Lane shook his head and pulled Roy's blanket up. He looked at Roy one more time and closed the door.

"Hmmm … I have never seen his office. I don't think he would mind. I want to be close," he whispered. Lane pushed the door open and turned the light on. He put his bag down by the desk and studied each wall. "I'll be damned. Every single one, framed."

His eyes fell on his photographs, the black and white, the color, the portraits, and the articles from their stories together, their years together. Lane wiped a tear and walked to the desk. He sat down, opened his laptop, plugged headphones in, and got to work. Hours passed.

"Lane?" The door pushed open, and Lane jumped.

"Roy lives!" He took his headphones off, leaned back in the chair, and smiled at a groggy Roy.

"What time is it?" Roy rubbed his bedhead. He didn't notice Lane closing a doc on his screen.

"Ummm …" Lane looked at his computer, "Seven p.m. You seem a bit better. Nice flannel pajamas."

Roy nodded, then winced and closed his eyes as he heard the noise again.

Lane sighed and decided not to ask about it. "Hope it's okay I'm in here. I wanted to work and be close," Lane said.

Roy swallowed, opened his eyes, and looked around the room. "No, I don't care. Now you can see I truly have no life. All I do is commemorate work highlights, powerful days, moments. I promise, I do love, like, other things besides work."

"Yeah, I know, Roy." Lane tapped his fingers on the desk.

"I'm starving. I think I have some chicken I can thaw," Roy said without looking at Lane.

"Really? You think you are going to thaw some meat and

cook tonight? No way. I can see you twitching right now. The noise is back. Don't worry about cooking. I got us delivery anyway."

"What?"

"I splurged. Go get on the couch, and I'll shut this down and join you. We didn't call your doctor, either. Do you want to do that tonight and leave a message, or—"

"No, I can't even think about that right now. I'm sorry. I need to go sit down." Roy tapped the door to indicate he was leaving.

"I'll be right there, Roy."

Roy took a few steps but paused and walked back to the office. "Thank you, Lane."

Lane sat in the office for a moment, surrounded by his own photographs, reminded of their collaborations. He stood, closed his computer, and shut the door behind him.

"You got soup?" Roy asked as Lane approached him in the kitchen.

"Not just any soup—pho. The soup of the gods." Lane grinned and reheated it.

They ate in silence in the living room. Although Roy inhaled his meal, Lane saw him shudder and close his eyes.

"Do you think Abby and Felix would ever get along?" Lane asked, watching Abby stroll nearby.

"Ha!" Roy laughed and shook his head. "Abby is the queen of the castle. Maybe if she needed a personal assistant, but I don't think she's in the market, so probably not. Why do you ask?"

"I don't know. Just making conversation." Lane smiled. "Well, what I do know is, Felix and Abby would love to eat this chicken together." Silence. "Are you feeling any better, Roy?"

"Yeah." He stirred his pho. "I feel better that I slept and I'm eating, but it's still there."

"Really? You hear it this second?"

"Yeah, I hear it. It's not in my mind. It's not a ringing in my ears. I hear it beside me. I look, and it moves. I hear it above me and look up to the ceiling. Nothing. It changes locations and stops. Sometimes the noise goes in and out, and I hear different parts of the noise at different volumes."

"My god! How crazy and annoying! I want to try something. Tell me when you hear it again."

"Well, it just stopped, but it will be back again."

"Where did you hear it?"

"Behind me." Roy tilted his head back.

Lane put his bowl down and walked behind the couch where Roy sat. He stood a few feet back from him, and Roy didn't look back. They waited.

"There. Did you hear that?" Roy asked without moving.

"Where is it? Where was it?"

"I can still hear it behind me. It must be right next to you, but I can't tell what side."

Lane scanned the room, looked to his left and right, and leaped back and forth while clapping.

"Go away! Your noise isn't needed here! Be gone!" He clapped and jumped around for a minute. "Be gone! Noise, go away! Leave, now!" Lane yelled.

"You're a good friend, Lane." Roy cleared his throat and avoided Lane's eyes.

"Yeah, a good friend who is really out of shape." Lane winked, but Roy wasn't looking. Lane stood and grabbed their bowls and headed to the kitchen. "It's almost nine. You should crash."

"Yeah, it's getting late. You wasted all day here. I feel terrible. I bet Felix misses you."

"Felix is fine," Lane hollered from the sink. "I'm staying

over. I'll crash on the couch, and if anything gets worse, we are going to the doctor."

"In the middle of the night? Here? I'm not going to the hospital to complain about a noise while people are actively bleeding, have broken bones, have been shot or are overdosing or dying."

"Your health is just as important as anybody else's," Lane said, walking back to the living room.

"Yeah, I know that, Lane. But I'm not going to the hospital tonight. Not over this."

"I'm still staying over."

"That's fine. Take my bed? I'll sleep out here. It makes sense. I don't know if I can sleep more."

"Nope. Gonna dose you up with NyQuil again. There are more capsules on the table by your bed."

"I feel awful that I don't have a guest room. Uhhh. Let me grab you blankets from the cupboard."

"I'll grab them, thank you. Maybe I'll get lucky, and Abby will cuddle me."

"Lucky cat. I mean …" Roy shook his head. "I mean lucky guy. Abby gives the best cuddles."

"Yep. Goodnight, Roy. I have everything I need out here. We'll head out around nine a.m."

"Sounds good. Night. Thank you, Lane. I'm sorry."

Lane waited thirty minutes for Roy to finish before he hopped in the bathroom. As he stepped out, he tiptoed up to Roy's room and listened. Silence. Lane smiled to himself and cuddled up on the couch with Abby. Not an hour later, and then throughout the night, Lane heard Roy pacing around, going in and out of the bathroom, and groaning in frustration and rage.

Abby turned and looked and wanted to jump down, but Lane held tight to her.

The next morning, Lane sat at the counter with a bowl of

cereal when a haggard Roy stumbled into the kitchen. Lane tried not to react to his appearance.

"Hey! Good morning. I was just going to wake you. Did you sleep at all? I just made some coffee. Let me pour you some." Lane grabbed a cup and quickly glanced at a jittery Roy. His alert, bloodshot eyes had bags forming underneath them. He looked desperate and lost, almost scared.

"You don't have to do that, Lane."

"Did the loud traffic last night keep you up? I'm sure it didn't help." Lane handed him a cup.

"Yeah, the city is loud, but those are known sounds and don't bother me. *The* noise bothers me. I'd love to be in this loud city forever. If only it was loud enough to muffle *the* noise."

Lane called a Lyft, and soon they were at their destination. The driver took them within a handful of blocks of where the march was due to start. Roy and Lane got out and meandered closer to the growing crowd. Hundreds of people in the street held signs, bystanders on the sidewalks cheered, families with young children sat on steps, and some elderly folks in wheel-chairs watched with their hands raised. Dozens of the marchers had microphones, and they rallied the crowd as everyone marched and chanted in unison.

"Affordable housing now! Stop extreme rent hikes! End predatory practices! Stop slumlords!"

"Okay, Roy. Want to meet at this intersection? Maybe in an hour or so?"

"Sure," Roy said, but his eyes started wandering. The noise was getting louder.

"Hey, hey, are you sure you're okay? We don't have to do this." Lane searched his eyes.

"Yeah. Lane, I'm fine. Let's do this."

People pushed between them. They nodded at each other. Lane turned away to melt discreetly with the crowd while Roy stayed on the sidewalk. After a while, Roy walked and took in the people and their energy. The force of the crowd kept distracting him from the noise. He approached an elderly man with a cane, sitting contently on a middle stair.

"Hi, my name is Roy, and I'm with *Know This, New York*. I'm covering rent hikes, inflation, cost of living, and what people are dealing with right now. I'm curious if you are open to sharing your thoughts and experiences, with the possibility of being quoted in my article? I will be recording and have questions ready. All you have to do is share what you feel and what's been happening."

"Pleased to meet you, son. My name is Bill. And sure, I have a lot to say." He adjusted his cane and stood. His short white hair stuck out in all directions, and he wore a faded black jacket. His discolored white button-up shirt was unbuttoned at the bottom for his belly, and he had dark blue corduroys on. White stubble covered his slightly bloated face, and his tired eyes looked watery.

"I really appreciate it. Thank you for taking the time," Roy said as he pulled out his phone and hit the recorder app. He opened his mouth to ask a question, but Bill started talking.

"Well, I have lived on this block since the beginning of time. My parents lived on this block. We were 'grandfathered in' with rent control, as they say, and now I'm a grandpa. But the rates go up, the rates go up, the rates go up." He pointed his finger in the air higher and higher and higher. "I'm in a tiny one bedroom. I have social security and did tuck some pennies away over the years and thought it would be enough. I raised my daughter alone and gave her everything I could because I thought I would be protected here. I thought I would be safe. If it all comes down to it, I might need to go push a cart. I don't know what other job I could even get. I sure don't mind working. I worked for fifty years, but I don't move like I used to. I don't even know if I could move quicker than the patrons shopping. That would be humiliating!" He stammered and stomped his cane down. "I don't have any skills with technology. I have been retired for eight years. Of course, I'll do whatever it takes, but I'm in my late seventies. I don't want to be ashamed. I don't want to be made fun of. I don't want sympathy. How can I have pride while I'm breaking my body? Nothing is worth not being able to pick my granddaughter up, and I struggle with that as it is. Son, are you okay? Are you okay, son? What's going on with you?"

"Yeah, yeah, I'm fine. I'm sorry. Having pride in our work is so deeply important, and I hear the struggle, the conflict you are facing. It is so hard. You thought you were safe, and you retired after being in the workforce for decades. You are living modestly, and you want to be there and be well enough, strong enough, to enjoy these years with your granddaughter. I'm so sorry. What, if any, contact have you had from your landlord or management company?"

"I haven't spoken to a human in years. Where did they all go? And this started before everything happened, before everybody got sick with corona. I only get notices, shit in the mail. Oh, pardon my French. You can take that off the record." He hung his head in embarrassment and tapped his cane. After a moment, Bill cleared his throat and looked back up at Roy.

"No one is telling the truth. Everyone is money hungry. I do get some of that because if my home was filled with coins, I would try not to let any escape, but this is too much. Some raises make sense. Everything in the world is going up. I know landlords have huge bills too, but increases need to be steady, steady, and reasonable." He lifted his arm and raised it one even inch at a time. "What do they expect me to do? I know you don't have the answers. But tell me, what am I supposed to do? I can't leave, I have nowhere to go. I'm on so many waitlists for assistance. My daughter can't take me in. She has my granddaughter, and there isn't any room."

"How do you get by every month?"

"Well, I have food banks, which I'm grateful for. But it's always a hassle to find someone to help me carry. I cut my meds in half, or sometimes keep my phone turned off. My daughter doesn't really call me anyway, so it's no problem," he chuckled uncomfortably. "Son, are you sure you are, okay? Does your head or something hurt? You're shaking."

"Yeah, I'm so sorry. Just a bad headache. I am fully present, and I'm hearing every word. Please don't think I'm not listening. I appreciate you being vulnerable and honest with a stranger."

"Those headaches are awful. I get them right here." He pointed to his temple. "I think it's stress. Stress from all of this. Are you stressed? Could it be stress for you too?" Bill leaned in.

"Yeah, I see. So, you understand." Roy nodded. "And yeah, I'm sure you are right. It's stress. This has all been so hard, and so stressful."

Bill nodded in satisfaction as though he had diagnosed a disease that had baffled medical experts.

"How do you deal with the stress?" Roy asked.

"I used to not deal with it. There was no time! I was more in a state of responding to everything that was happening to me. Stress was dealing with me, not the other way around. Now I hope it's mostly getting bored of me, although there are flare ups sometimes, so I get headaches. Now, I try to take things head-on. I remember my family, and I keep fighting. That's why I'm here."

As the men wrapped up their conversation, the noise grew louder.

"Thanks again, Bill." Roy winced. "Here is my card. Please never hesitate to contact me."

"Pleasure. Good luck with the article! I'm here if you ever need to talk again." Bill smiled.

Roy continued on and spotted a woman who stood on a bottom step waving a bright red sign that read: *Housing is a Human Right! Affordable Rent Now!* The middle-aged woman had long brown hair and kind, tired brown eyes and clothes at least ten years out of date. Roy asked, and she agreed to answer a few questions. He thanked her and pulled his phone out.

"My name is Sheila. So, I have been living here for about fourteen years and had my daughter a year after I moved in. I have two jobs and I can't afford daycare. My mom watches my toddler during the day, but he is so much, and she is an old lady! My young teen watches him at night so I can work. The elite like to say, 'Why did you have so many kids that you can't afford?' Well, you know what? I did everything in my power to stay protected from this happening … wait, if this is too much information, please stop me right now." She waved her hand and paused.

Roy shook his head, so she continued. "But my blessing pushed through those birth control barriers and came through anyway. He wanted to be born, and I wouldn't change him for anything. When I had my daughter, I could afford her. And you would think that with two full-time jobs I could afford two kids. I'm using a few hours of sick time to be out here fighting, protesting, making noise. I have to do something. My son is upstairs, and my daughter is at school. She takes the bus by herself. She is mature and understands, but I don't want that. She doesn't deserve that. Some mornings I can commute with her, but not if I get called in early. I want more training and education, and I went to college, but it's not enough. I can't afford school, and there's no time. I have nothing more to give, and it's never enough. I want to give my kids the best life possible, and it feels impossible. Sir, sir, Roy, are you okay? Is something happening? Are you dizzy? What are you looking for?" Sheila reached to steady him.

"Yeah, I … I …" Roy's whole body was shaking. His eyes darted frantically.

Lane ran through the handful of people between him and Roy. He grabbed Roy's shoulders and jumped in front of him. "Hey, hey, Roy, Roy, Roy, it's me. It's Lane. I'm here. I'm here." Lane nodded at Roy. "Can you see me? Nod if you can see me, Roy."

"Who are you?" Sheila asked.

"I'm sorry." Lane met Sheila's eyes without removing his hands from Roy. "We work together. We are here together." Lane looked at Roy, and he lifted one hand from his shoulder to reach for the credential info around his neck.

Sheila nodded. "I think Roy is getting sick. I pray to God he will be okay. I can't afford to get sick. That's the truth," she said.

"No, I promise. He's not contagious, he's been having terrible headaches. Damnit." Lane's eyes flashed at Roy to make sure he heard.

"We were just having a conversation, and then he started looking like he was getting sick. He looks scared and confused, too." Sheila shook her head.

"Thank you so much for paying such close attention," Lane replied, his hands still on Roy.

"Roy, Roy, look at me. Focus your eyes on me. You are breathing hard. Try to slow down. It's getting loud here, but focus on me."

After a moment, Roy found Lane's eyes. "I'm okay. I'm hearing *the* noise."

"Can you sit down?" Lane asked. Roy didn't budge. Lane raised his eyebrows and gave a look that said, 'I could be calling an ambulance. You don't want that, so don't challenge me.'

"Here, take my spot. It is really loud out here," Sheila said and reached for his arm to help him sit down.

Roy scowled and sat down. Lane hunched over to look at him, and Roy grabbed his jacket. Roy had never touched him before. Lane glanced at Roy's hand and then up at him.

"Finish my interview," Roy whispered.

"No way! What?" Lane leaned back to stand up more fully, but Roy held onto his jacket.

"Please, Lane. Finish my interview," he whispered, half-begging and half-commanding.

"No, you are resting for a minute, and we are getting out of here."

"Lane," Roy said sternly, "Sheila has been kind enough to take a few minutes from the very limited amount of time she has to talk with me. I want to honor that. Finish the interview."

Roy pulled his phone from his pocket and held it out.

"Where are you at in it?" Lane asked.

"Going to ask about communication from management, next steps, the future. But anything she says or wants to share matters—her thoughts, her truth, everything."

Lane nodded and took the phone and clicked on the recorder. He turned to Sheila, who was giving them space by watching the crowd, although she still had been discreetly tracking their movements and words.

"Sheila, my name is Lane. What an introduction!" He grinned and shook his head at the whirlwind. "Do you happen to have just a couple more minutes for me to finish up Roy's interview? Are you comfortable with that? If not, or if you have to go, I completely understand."

"I'm so glad you were here to help him. That means everything. I have a few minutes." She smiled.

"By the way, I'm coming back over," Lane said as the men sat down in their Lyft.

Roy was looking out the window, but his eyes occasionally darted about.

"What about Felix?" Roy asked.

"Felix is fine. I prepared him for this, so he is probably eating himself stupid, but he will be fine. Can we please go to the hospital now?"

"Don't ask me again."

The driver eyed them in the mirror and said, "If we are going somewhere else, tell me now."

"Our destination is the same." Roy smiled. "I'm sorry about any confusion."

"Well, I'm coming over!" Lane insisted.

"Why can't he drop me off and then drop you off?" Roy grunted before squeezing his eyes shut.

"You refuse medical help. You barely let me help you. Why won't you let me take care of you?"

"You have been!"

"Yeah, only what you will tolerate. If I had lost my shit and was hearing sounds, you would insist I get help. But somehow, you don't need any! How is that fair!" Lane demanded.

The driver glanced up at them again. His eyes had gone wide.

Lane smiled uncomfortably.

"It's not a sound. It's a noise. I wish I could hear a sound. This is all noise," Roy whispered.

"Okay, gentlemen, where are we going?" the driver asked, studying them intently.

"We are going home," Roy said firmly and looked out the window.

Lane's eyes shot at Roy, who was still looking away. Lane watched Roy for a moment and then turned and looked out his own window. Lane mouthed the words 'we are going home,' smiled, and closed his eyes. Once they arrived, Lane opened the apartment door and guided Roy inside.

"Give me your phone and insurance card. Tell me or write down your social security number and then go take NyQuil. I'm making you a doctor's appointment. Is your birthday still the same?" Lane winked.

"Yeah." Roy scribbled his info down. He walked to his bedroom and closed the door.

Lane cuddled Abby for a few minutes before setting up his computer in Roy's office. He wrote an email to Jenny: *We went to the march. I'm requesting to help Roy with this story. He is still sick.*

Three hours later, he got a message back from her: *Sounds good. Glad you two made it. I'm looking forward to the draft. Keep me posted.*

"Thank you, Jenny!" Lane plugged headphones into Roy's phone and listened to the interviews. He took notes, listened to the interviews again and again, took more notes, reviewed everything, and started typing. Hours, and then the day, passed. Lane took breaks to make coffee, eat, and stretch. It was dark and late out when a drowsy Roy knocked on the office door.

"Lane, what are you doing?" Roy rubbed his eyes and scratched his head.

"I'm so relieved you slept. You look better. If you are hungry, please let me make something for you. I just need a couple minutes to finish this up."

"Finish what up?" Roy's eyes grew more alert.

"The story for today. Jenny gave permission. I just sent her the draft. You don't have to worry."

"What? Why? Why did you do that? You shouldn't have done that! That's not okay! It is my job. That was mine to write! Why are you in my house, in my office, writing my articles?"

"Roy, I'm not going to raise my voice in response. Why are you yelling? I'm worried about you, and I don't know what's going on. I'm trying to help you. You would do the same for me."

"No, I wouldn't. I really wouldn't, Lane." Roy cleared his throat and clenched his teeth.

"Well, that makes me really sad, Roy. I guess we aren't as close as I thought." Lane looked down.

"No, we aren't. You worry about and take care of you, and I'll worry about and take care of me."

"You know what, Roy? No wonder there is nobody in your life. You have been alone since I met you. I can't get past this noise, but you have never let anyone in. And you don't come out. And here I am just another noise to you, trying to get your attention." Lane closed his computer, picked it up, and slid it into his bag.

Roy swallowed but didn't move or speak.

Lane took a few steps past him and paused. "Somebody really did a number on you, Roy. Whoever, or whatever, made you feel like a burden really fucked you up. Maybe after all the noise is gone, you can get some therapy and look at that."

Roy clenched his teeth, the noise came hard at him from above, and he let out a wail.

Lane touched his shoulder, but Roy shook his hand off and looked away. Lane sighed and kept walking. He paused and said, "Your doctor's appointment is on the twenty-second at ten a.m. Jenny approved that morning off. Good luck."

Roy waited, and a minute later he heard his front door slam. He stood motionless in the office for a long time as the noise infiltrated the room.

Roy wasn't at the office the next day, or the next. Lane watched the door all day for him.

Finally, Lane knocked on Jenny's door. "Can I come in?"

"Sure, Lane! How are you? How do you feel about my edits

and feedback?"

"Got them. Very helpful. I'll make those changes. Thank you again for letting me contribute! Have you had much contact with Roy? Did he reply?"

"Yeah, he's working from home for the time being to fully get over his illness. But, of course, you already knew that." She smiled and nodded. "You two have the City Workers Union story coming up, and I know he wanted to be fully recovered before that."

"Oh no, absolutely. Yeah, I have been in contact with him. I was just tracking his communication with you. He was a bit looped when I saw him last." He smiled, but Jenny frowned, so he quickly added, "He seems much better now. It was like he had one of those twenty-four-hour flu things that got him pretty bad, and it's been hard to recover. But we texted this morning, and he got your email."

Lane walked back to his desk and began a text to Roy: *Hey, Jenny said you are working from home. Please let me know what I can do. I'm still banking on breakfast on Saturday unless I hear from you otherwise. I can also bring it to you, but we don't even have to go if you aren't up for it. Just let me know. If not, I can just see you next week at the City Workers March?*

A message from Roy beeped back an hour later: *No to this Saturday. See you at the March.*

"Ouch," Lane sighed, before texting back: *Thank you for letting me know. Take care of yourself, Roy.*

Roy read the message and then put his phone down and continued pacing. He lifted his earmuffs to adjust the earplugs underneath them. He fantasized about a life without the noise. He would go to the café with his friend and be fully present and alive. He would walk casually around his neighborhood. How he would enjoy himself. *The* noise came. Roy went to his living room and pulled his curtains shut. He turned off all of his lights and ripped the cords out of every outlet. He dove into bed and buried his head in pillows. He cried.

"What's happening to me? Why are you doing this to me? Please stop!" Roy turned and turned and turned under the covers. He threw them back and ran to the shower. He pushed and pushed and pushed on his ears under the hot water. "Where are you coming from? Stop it! Stop it! Stop!" Sobbing, Roy dropped down and wrapped his arms around his legs. When he eventually got out of the shower, he looked out his bedroom window and saw it was getting dark.

"I'm going to find it! Yes, that's it! I'll find it!" He dressed quickly and hustled to the door. "Bye, Abby! I'll see you later." Hope rang out in his voice, and he skipped down the hallway.

Roy searched all night. He went down alleys, ran down streets, looked behind dumpsters.

He circled street lamps, hovered near parked cars, leaned against trees, and tried to hear it.

Roy followed people until they looked back. He stood in front of buzzing neon storefronts.

He tumbled into bars, weaved around dancing bodies, lifted up the lid on dirty toilets, and peered in. He studied graffiti and watched a building get tagged. He wondered if spray cans made the noise. Roy listened to buses, stray animals peeing, and young people laughing, screaming, and fighting. Roy went down every aisle in every convenience store. He crinkled bags of chips to see if that could be the noise. He then paid for the bags of chips. Roy assessed the demands and cries and confusion of people pushing their stuffed carts down the sidewalk.

Could they be making the noise?

After sunrise, Roy stumbled behind executives, important walking suits screaming into their phones.

Could it be them?

His whole body ached, and his feet burned in pain. He

licked his cracking lips and wiped his eyes. Roy crawled seven blocks to his café and pulled the door open. The bell chimed above him, and he jumped and burst into tears. Everyone looked.

"Oh, my days! Roy, come here, hun. What happened to you?" Judy motioned for another waitress to take over the table she had just seated, and she shuffled over to Roy and reached for his arm. "Come on, dear. Let's get you comfortable. Just relax. I'll get you some coffee right away, and you look hungry. Can I—?"

"Yes, please. Thank you, Judy. I'm sorry." Roy sat down at a table and put his head in his hands.

Forty minutes later, Roy had consumed five cups of coffee and was cutting into his third Belgian waffle. The door chimed, and Roy looked up. There was Lane, standing in the doorway.

"Really?" Lane said loudly enough for Roy to hear.

People turned. Judy hustled up to Lane and pulled on his arm.

"Lane, I need to tell you. Roy came in here looking totally delusional and lost. He was crying. I don't know what's the matter with him. Can you please go talk to him? He seems much better now that he ate, but Lane, he looks so … so broken."

Lane briefly looked at Judy and nodded before meeting Roy's eyes. "I've tried to talk with him, Judy, but he doesn't want to talk to me," he replied without looking away from Roy.

Lane then looked at Judy and pulled out a twenty and handed it to her. "Here. In case he forgets. I'm sorry if he scared you. He's just having a bad week that started with a bad migraine. It will be okay. I'll see you next Saturday. Thank you for looking out for him."

The door chimed as Lane left. Roy put money on the table. He hurried past Judy and yelled, "Thank you!" before she could ask any questions. He ran in the opposite direction from home.

Five days later, Lane texted Roy: *I haven't heard from you or seen you since Saturday. You weren't at the City Worker's March. I got permission and am writing our article, but I refuse to do that again. You are going to have to figure it out with Jenny.*

A day passed, and Lane's phone beeped with a message from Roy: *I went to the doctor. They can't help me. I've been searching for the noise. I'm turning my phone off.*

"I'm taking off early today. I'll make up for it tomorrow!" Lane yelled as he grabbed his jacket and bag. A few of his colleagues glanced up and nodded before lowering their heads again.

Lane took a taxicab to a grocery store and filled up two bags. He hailed another one down and gave the driver the intersection. Lane hopped out and ran across the street from Roy's window.

"Hey! Roy!" Lane cupped his mouth and screamed. "Roy! Roy! Hey! I'm here! Roy! Look out your window!"

A middle-aged man on a different floor yanked his window up. "Stop yelling!"

"This is New York! Why aren't you yelling?!" Lane yelled back.

"I'm going to report a disturbance if you don't shut the fuck up right now!"

"Fine!" Lane lifted his hands to show he was done, but a motion in the corner of his eye distracted him. A dark curtain on Roy's window had been pulled back, and it swayed a bit before settling back in its position. "Roy?" Lane scanned the other windows for any signs of movement. Nothing. Lane grabbed a bag of marshmallows from his grocery bag and ripped it open. He pulled a handful of marshmallows and began throwing them up in the air to try and catch them with his mouth.

They mostly landed on the ground, but some hit his face as he jumped and danced around.

"Woohoo!"

"Darn it!"

"Almost!"

"Ahhhh!"

People walking by stared and laughed and pointed. Lane kept his eyes on the windows as much as possible but addressed their gawking by yelling, "I'm not a street performer. I'm in love!"

He paused when he thought he saw a rustling of the curtain. He waited for a sign of Roy. When there was nothing, he threw more marshmallows back in the air and leaped around for them. Two teenagers stopped and pulled out their phones.

"Don't make me a TikTok!" Lane called out.

Lane soon got sick of marshmallows and stood watching the windows. He watched for hours. He thought of trying to call Roy one more time, but instead he slumped against a tree.

❧

A few weeks later, Lane buzzed Mrs. Franks' number on the intercom, and she curiously asked, "Who is it?"

"Hi, Mrs. Franks. It's Lane. I was in the neighborhood and I figured I'd see if you were up for a visit. Perhaps we can watch *Jeopardy!*? If you want coffee, I can pick some up right now?"

"You have made my day! I will make a casserole. Come on up!" She buzzed the entry button.

Lane exhaled and pulled the door open. When he got to her and Roy's floor, she was standing in the doorway with Mrs. Sparkles under her arm. They wore matching yellow polka dot dresses, and she hurriedly beckoned him in before he could put his ear or a knock to Roy's door.

"Hi, Lane! I'm so happy you are here. This means so much to me." She nodded and smiled.

"I'm so happy I'm here too. You know, I just love the matching outfits that you two have!"

He stepped inside, and she sat him down at her table while she made coffee. Mrs. Franks put Mrs. Sparkles down on the chair next to him. She barked at him twice and blinked.

"Mrs. Sparkles! That is our friend, Lane. Show some manners. I'm sorry, Lane. She is acting strange. You know, I haven't seen Roy for weeks. I don't want her to forget who he is too."

"Oh really?" Lane cleared his throat. "You haven't seen him?"

"No! Can you believe it? If I didn't know better, I would think he was avoiding me and Mrs. Sparkles. I left a huge serving of casserole for him at his door, and I knocked and knocked. No answer. Do you know how many days that casserole sat out there? Three days! Three days! At night I brought it back inside and put it in the fridge, so it didn't go bad, but every morning I put it out there again for him. He didn't touch it. I don't even know if he saw it. I finally gave up and brought it back inside, and Mrs. Sparkles ate it."

"Really?" Lane's eyes grew wide, and he looked at Mrs. Sparkles, who was looking at him. "I'm impressed, pup! Lucky lady got some good casserole." Lane smiled at Mrs. Franks.

"Lane, how do you feel about tuna fish casserole?"

"You know, I love it!" His stomach flipped. He turned to Mrs. Sparkles. "This is our lucky day."

Four hours later, Lane stumbled out of Mrs. Franks' apartment. His belly hurt, and he felt exhausted by watching so much *Jeopardy!* He trudged to Roy's door and knocked. Silence. He knocked again. Silence. Lane slumped down against the wall by the front door and sat for a few more hours.

〜

Three weeks later, Lane stood in the same spot across the street from Roy's. He had earmuffs on and a to-go box full of Belgian waffles.

"Roy!" He cupped his hands and yelled again.

"Roy!"

"I brought you breakfast!"

"Please let me come up! Let me at least drop this off or visit Abby!"

"Please let me help you! Please stop hiding away!"

"Please! I wish I could hear it, so you didn't have to!"

"I'm sorry."

〜

One evening two months later, Lane stood across the street holding a stack of giant cardboard signs. He rotated them for hours so that if Roy did look out, he didn't miss it. When his arms gave out, he used one to hold the sign while the other one rested. He never stopped. The sun came up.

Lane felt his body wanting to quit, so he yelled, "Roy!"

"Roy!"

A neighbor yelled out through his window, "Give it up, pretty boy!"

"Please, Roy!"

The curtain was drawn back. There he was. Lane saw Roy. His beard and hair were wild, like a bum, or a wizard. He looked pale and sickly. He looked like Lane's true love.

"Come on, arms. Come on, arms. One more time." Lane began crying and rotating the cards. He smiled and nodded with each one.

I LOVE YOU.

I HAVE LOVED YOU FOREVER.

CAN I PLEASE HOLD YOUR HAND WHILE YOU GO THROUGH THIS?

I WANT TO HEAR EVERYTHING WITH YOU.

I WANT TO HEAR YOU.

PLEASE LET ME TAKE CARE OF YOU.

YOU ARE THE ONLY PHOTOGRAPH IN MY HEART.

OURS IS THE ONLY STORY I CARE ABOUT.

I LOVE YOU.

Roy wiped tears from his eyes.

His room was completely silent. He looked down at Lane. He had always known Lane.

The noise was gone.

AERATE

"Eeeeemmmmeeeeetttt!" Barbara shrieked. She threw thick slabs of ham on the skillet as the hot oil squealed and hissed. She grabbed two eggs with one plump hand, cracked them against the pan, and poured them in. Barbara eyed the meat and scooted it over with tongs to give room for the white run of the eggs, then she wiped her hands on her flour-flecked apron. She cut wide slices of homemade bread, put fresh strawberry and blackberry jam on the table, and pulled the hash browns from the oven. Tall glasses of orange juice were filled, and coffee cups were poured alongside a pitcher of milk so fresh it seemed to still be warm from the cow. A small white bowl of sugar cubes was placed next to the rooster-shaped salt and pepper shakers.

"Eeeeeemmmmeeeeetttt!" she shrieked.

Upstairs, Emmett sat on the bed. He ran his tired, withered hands over his balding head. His shoulders ached with the lifting motion, so he lowered them back down again. *At least I got my overalls on without too much hassle today. How will I get through the next ten hours?* He stood and took a few steps to look at himself in the full-length mirror. Raising a dirt-stained finger to the bag under his right eye, he pushed at the shriveled skin. *What happened to me?* Emmett tried to straighten his back, but the pain was unbearable, and within seconds he bent into a curve again.

"Eeeeeemmmmeeeeetttt!"

Why does she always need to yell? He had never missed breakfast, not in over fifty years, though he had never woken hungry in all that time.

"Be right down, Barbara!" he bellowed as loud as he could down the stairs. His voice would soon give out. He worried about his body, not his words. He couldn't chop without pain, couldn't haul without pain, couldn't lift, couldn't shear, couldn't milk the cows, couldn't dig, couldn't plant, couldn't bend, couldn't turn the compost, couldn't harvest without pain. His joints were stiff and swollen, and days passed where all he felt was exhaustion and numbness. The doctor told him he had symptoms of rheumatoid arthritis and to come back for more tests. When he'd shared the news with Barbara, she told him he was simply becoming soft and weak. When he told her he was hurting, she shook her head.

Emmett gazed up at himself in the mirror again. He reached for his black comb on the nearby dresser and pulled it gently across his head.

"I have one comb tooth for each strand, might not need this anymore," he chuckled and put the comb down. He walked out of the bedroom and stood at the top of the staircase. Bright, warm light poured up the stairs through windows below. Emmett paused and smiled.

What a glorious day. How I would love to be lying in a field of tall grass, motionless, while the sun and the clouds passed over me. Emmett reached for the hand-carved railing he'd made fifteen years ago and admired his craftsmanship. Even back then,

Barbara demanded support of some kind while she went up the stairs. She said she simply didn't want to fall, but he knew she could no longer make it up by herself. Many times, he would offer to hold her hand, but she always patted it away and insisted he go first. He knew Barbara had been gaining weight and felt self-conscious about it. She didn't want him to look up at her rump as he walked behind her.

"I would never disrespect you, Barbara," he mumbled once, sensing her discomfort.

"Shoo!" she replied.

Emmett had eagerly gotten to work, designing and carving a perfect railing. The handsome, healthy, and smooth wood felt as sturdy and vital as he did in those days. There was no pain. He was proud. He could do anything. But when he'd presented his gift to her, she'd folded her arms and looked at it as though expecting more. The thin line of her mouth didn't move.

"The Richards have an iron railing, Emmett. Everyone does," she'd sighed.

"Well, Barbara, this is wood. I brought part of God's nature indoors, for you. It was free, well, mostly free, and it really goes nicely with all of the lovely wooden furniture you picked out for our home." He'd shifted the toothpick in his mouth and smiled, but her arms remained crossed. Her reddish-brown bun of hair moved as she shook her head.

"I want iron, Emmett."

"I understand, Barbara. I just don't know how we would pay ..."

She'd looked sternly at him, and her round cheeks flushed.

"I understand, Barbara."

Emmett took thoughtful steps down the stairs, caressing the railing. Turning the corner, the familiar sight of the morning feast greeted him. His stomach flipped. He was not hungry.

He walked past the abundant breakfast table and stood in the doorway of the kitchen.

"Morning, dear," he smiled at her, but she looked at him blankly.

"Emmett, take this!" She handed him a warm, covered bowl of sunny-side-up eggs, and he continued on to the table. He sat down and quickly added one egg, one piece of toast, and one piece of bacon to his plate.

"Emmett, don't forget your ham steak! You'll need the energy for your work!" Barbara shuffled up next to him and pulled the lid off the center plate. The strong smell of warm, heavily seasoned ham filled the room. Emmett stared as she forked the biggest piece and slapped it on his plate. A huge helping of hash browns followed, and he sighed as she slid two more watery eggs onto his plate.

"This looks especially beautiful today, Barbara. Just like a painting. In fact, I wish it was a painting so we could admire it every day, and you wouldn't have to do all this work."

"You can't eat paintings, Emmett. What are you talking about? You don't like your breakfast?" She impaled a huge chunk of ham and shoved it in her mouth.

"Good heavens, Barbara. Not at all. I just meant, this is all so beautiful, it could be a painting. Like a work of art, you know, and could be in a museum for all the world to see and admire." He smiled and nodded to see if she understood, but she didn't respond and kept eating. Minutes passed. Emmett took a bite of toast.

"What are you going to work on today, Emmett?" Her cheeks jiggled as she chewed.

"I had some ideas, but why don't you tell me? You always have the best ideas, Barbara." Emmett pushed his plate forward, propped his elbows on the table, and rested his head on his palms to listen.

Barbara looked at him and stabbed at the last big bite of ham, sliding it around her plate to absorb the remaining blobs of jam. "Emmett, how would you get on without me? What would you do if I wasn't here to set you straight?"

"I don't know, Barbara. It's too painful to think about."

"That's right, Emmett." Barbara's fork went in her mouth, and she nodded in satisfaction.

"Here, let me clean up. Wonderful as always, Barbara." Emmett stood and quickly picked up the two plates and headed to the kitchen. He hurriedly scraped his runny yolks into the trash and pocketed the toast for the animals. She started hollering as he opened the back door.

"Eeeeeemmmeeeeetttt! Feed the chickens and go fetch me eggs!"

"Eeeeeemmmeeeeetttt! Plow the fields!"

"Eeeeeemmmeeeeetttt! Shear the sheep!"

"Eeeeeemmmeeeeetttt! Check on the fields!"

"Eeeeeemmmeeeeetttt! Turn the compost!"

"Eeeeeemmmeeeeetttt! Plant those seeds!"

"Eeeeeemmmeeeeetttt! Isn't it time to rotate some crops? Rotate, rotate, rotate!"

"Eeeeeemmmeeeeetttt! Milk the cows!"

"Eeeeeemmmeeeeetttt! Harvest!"

"Eeeeeemmmeeeeetttt! Fill up these baskets!"

"Eeeeeemmmeeeeetttt! Aerate!"

"Eeeeeemmmeeeeetttt! Stack the hay up straight!"

"Eeeeeemmmeeeeetttt! Cut more firewood!"

"Eeeeeemmmeeeeetttt! Winter is coming. Why are you slowing down?"

Emmett always put his ax, pitchfork, shovel, rake, sack, wheelbarrow, rope, sickle, seed, haystack, vegetable, or cow teat down when she called and would wave his hands at her or take steps in her direction until he heard his orders.

Two years passed.

Emmett gripped the hand railing, but his old hand against the healthy wood startled him, and he pulled it back. Instead of becoming wrinkly, the skin on Emmett's hands had become tighter over the years, as if it was being pulled and stretched thin. The joints in his hands hurt. He could barely take it. The pain had a numbing effect. He panicked when he could no longer feel his grip, couldn't feel the pitchfork, the shovel, the seeds in his hands.

"Barbara," he started, as she shoveled bacon onto his plate, "I think I need to rest today."

"Oh shoo, Emmett, you just haven't gotten any eggs in you yet. You need some protein; it'll do you right. We can't get behind, and there is so much to be done out there." Barbara tsk-tsked and slid three sunny-side-up eggs on his plate. She sat down and scooted her chair forward and took a large bite of hash browns.

"Barbara, might I say something?"

"Speak your mind, Emmett."

"Barbara, would you ever be open to making … scrambled eggs?"

"What do you mean, Emmett?"

"Scrambled, like whisked up and cooked. That fluffy type of eggs."

"Emmett, you love sunny-side-up." She stared at him, bewildered.

"Barbara, you know I love your cooking. It's just, I think I could use a change."

"Humph! Scrambled eggs! Nonsense!" Barbara shook her head and started cutting her bacon. The knife went through it so quickly that it scratched across the plate. Emmett winced.

She only cut her bacon on these plates, the plates his mother had given them as a wedding gift. Barbara didn't like it when he brought up his mother, so he never said a word about her.

"Emmett, I don't know what has gotten into you, but I don't like it one bit." She cut into a strip of bacon the long way. Emmett looked at her, bewildered, and then at her plate. Barbara picked up the spaghetti-thin slices of bacon and took tiny bites. She glanced at Emmett. He pushed his plate forward. His hands hurt.

"Barbara, you know what they call you at the store?"

"What, Emmett?" She pursed her lips and poked the yolks on her plate. The golden liquid ran.

"They call you Bossy Barbara." His eyes widened at his own words. He covered his mouth.

Barbara dropped her fork.

"Oh, Barbara, I didn't mean that." Emmett shook his head.

"What in God's good name is going on with you, Emmett? If I didn't know better, I'd think you were unhappy and ungrateful to be here, with this 'Bossy Barbara' and scrambled egg nonsense. My daddy gave you this land fifty years ago because he had faith in you. You had nothing, Emmett. We took pity on you. I took pity on you. My daddy told me to have faith, that you could shape up. That you could be a *real* farmer. You had no other potential, Emmett, and now I'm having my doubts. If you didn't want to do this work, you should have said so."

"Barbara, please forgive me. I don't know what's gotten into me. I don't feel right."

"You aren't acting right, Emmett. That's for sure."

"I'm going to go lay down, Barbara." He gathered some plates and stood to leave.

She scooted her chair back, and it scratched against the floor.

"Emmett, what about all the work to be done?"

"I understand, Barbara. I'm going to put on a fresh shirt. I think that will help me."

"Burning daylight, Emmett, and you didn't even eat your eggs. What's gotten into you today?"

"I'm sorry."

"Shoo, Emmett."

Twenty minutes later, Emmett came back downstairs and walked past her in the kitchen.

"Emmett, I thought you were going to change your shirt."

"Oh yeah," Emmett mumbled, looking at his shirt.

"Do you think these kinds of problems go on at the Richards' farm?" She crossed her arms.

"I don't know, Barbara. I'm going to get to work. I'm burning daylight." Emmett nodded a goodbye at her, opened up the back door, and started walking outside. Barbara called out at him.

"Eeeeeemmmeeeeetttt! Harvest the corn before morning ends!"

"Eeeeeemmmeeeeetttt! Cut more firewood!"

"Eeeeeemmmeeeeetttt! Stack more hay!"

"Eeeeeemmmeeeeetttt! Feed the chickens and gather eggs!"

"Eeeeeemmmeeeeetttt! Time to fertilize!"

"Eeeeeemmmeeeeetttt! Harvest apples! I need apples!"

"Eeeeeemmmeeeeetttt!"

"Eeeeeemmmeeeeetttt!"

"Eeeeeemmmeeeeetttt, where are you?"

Barbara stood at her back door and covered her eyes to protect them from the hazy light of the setting sun. No Emmett. She huffed to the stairs and gripped the handrail that had never hurt her hands, not once. When she made it to her bedroom, she stomped to the window to get a better view of her farm and scanned for Emmett. She couldn't see him anywhere. She opened the window and yelled, "Eeeeeemmmeeeeetttt!"

She saw all the work had been done, but there was no Emmett. Barbara turned to head back downstairs and saw a piece of paper on her dresser.

Barbara,
I have always done everything you ask, but now I need to aerate. I need to aerate.
I'm sorry.
Love, your Emmett.

FACTS OF THE AIRPORT

Passenger 28A peered out the small window to his left and into the dark. He spotted a woman driving a small cart and saw a man with a bright orange baton waving and walking and studying the plane. The passenger then looked down at his notebook, picked it up, and began softly murmuring to himself as he reread his own writing. Although the exact words were inaudible, the man in the middle seat, passenger 28B, had heard. Passenger 28B paused and discreetly looked over before clearing his throat, sitting up a bit, and resuming his reading. 28A set the notebook down, grabbed his pen, and scribbled a few more lines at the bottom of the sheet. When he reached the end, he flipped the page over and continued writing on the back for half a minute. 28A picked up the notebook and murmured to himself again as he read what he had just written. His head shook in awe, and he reached up to cover his smile before turning back towards the window.

28A closed his notebook and lifted his tray table. He bent over to slide his notebook into his dark duffel bag that sat half-tucked under the seat in front of him. While 28A leaned over,

28B scooted his legs in a bit to give extra space. As 28B did so, he glanced over and his eyes fell on passenger 28A's spine, which protruded through his sweater. Sensing something, passenger 28A rapidly clipped his bag closed, shoved it under the seat, and turned to meet passenger 28B's eyes. But passenger 28B had fully returned his attention to his journal. He nodded at the man glancing at him and offered a small grin in return. Passenger 28A appeared pained but smiled back before turning and looking out the window. He studied the clouds huddled together. *It's getting lighter. Pretty clouds. Would clouds be coffee or tea drinkers? Hmmmm … why have I never seen the sky before?* He exhaled slowly and closed his eyes to hold the tears in place. *I need to rest.*

Passenger 28B pulled his bookmark out. It was made from thin strips of blue construction paper glued to cardboard, and lopsided pink clouds had been cut and glued on top of the blue paper. He rotated it and read the misshaped words, 'Love you daddy!' that were written at the bottom by his six-year-old child, Sally. Beneath it, his wife's handwriting read, 'Miss you, travel safe! XOXO!' His finger ran across the bookmark, and he rested his head back against the seat. *Sally must be waking up soon for her special blueberry pancake Saturday. Jessica is probably prepping right now.* He looked at his watch. *My sweetie didn't get any sleep at all.* He sighed and tucked the bookmark in his economic and financial analysis journal and then slid it into the mesh magazine pocket in front of him. He closed his eyes.

A voice came over the intercom.

"Good morning, everyone. This is Captain Williams speaking … Our flight time today will be nine hours and forty-five … The estimated arrival time at Heathrow Airport is … The weather is cool and cloudy in London with …"

Minutes later, flight attendants dispersed throughout the plane, and a woman's voice came over the intercom. "… now we request your full attention as the flight attendants demonstrate the safety features of this aircraft. As we prepare for takeoff, please … fasten seat-belt sign … carry-on luggage … seat backs and tray tables are in their full upright position … Although we never anticipate a change in cabin pressure … an oxygen mask will … Place it firmly over your nose and mouth … If you are traveling with a child or someone who requires assistance, secure your mask first and then assist the other person … Do not remove the oxygen mask until a crew member states you are no longer necessary."

"Wait? What?" Passenger 28A's eyes popped open. "Are you kidding me? Another one! This is too much!" He chuckled. 28B smiled but kept his eyes straight ahead, and 28A laughed even louder. He shook his head and bit his lips, but laughter squeezed through anyway. He leaned forward and glanced at the opposite seats, while 28B eyed his movements. 28A then craned and looked behind him, and through the space between his and 28B's seat. He scanned everyone he could, searching for reactions, before finally giving up and meeting 28B's gaze.

"You heard that, right?" 28A pleaded while laughing.

"Yeah, I did." 28B nodded and smiled.

"Thank God! That was hysterical! And all these glazed do-nuts missed it!" The words came out jumbled between laughs as he motioned at their fellow passengers. The man covered his mouth and spoke between his fingers. "That's too much! Too much! Don't remove the oxygen mask until someone tells you that you are no longer necessary." His laughter bellowed and broke through his fingers. His eyes watered, and his face reddened.

Two passengers in the row ahead looked back at him, and the woman tsked.

28A mouthed "I'm sorry" as tears streamed down his thin face, and he shrugged to show he was just as baffled by his laughter as they were. He clamped down hard on his mouth, but it didn't help, and he began making noises like he was hyperventilating.

28B had tried not to stare, but now he couldn't look away as 28A's body heaved and shook in the seat. Finally, 28B patted 28A on the shoulder and gently asked, "Are you okay? Seriously, are you? I can get you some water?"

28A gave a thumbs up and panted, "I'm truly fine, just having a laugh attack."

28B nodded but wondered why it was taking him so long to regain his composure. Passengers across the way had leaned forward and whispered loudly, "Is he alright?" Even the grumpy young man in his aisle seat looked up from a device that should have been stowed by now. 28B fielded all the irritated glances and murmurs and waved his hands, mouthed "he's gonna be fine, just laughing" and redirected their attention by pointing to the flight attendant who was still providing instructions.

The voice on the intercom said, "Flight attendants, prepare for take-off."

The flight attendant closest to the passengers in row 28 walked up to them. "Sir, sir, are you okay? Do you need anything? Can I get you a drink? Are you able to breathe?" he asked.

28A gave a thumbs up and wiped his eyes. "I'm so sorry," he choked out. "I just, I just … it was something funny, and it got to me. I'm so sorry. I didn't mean to be disrespectful."

"It's okay. Laughter is much better than being upset." He smiled but still looked concerned.

"I promise you, he's fine," 28B interjected. "Just having a laugh attack."

"Gotcha! Well, once we get into the air, press the button if you need anything. And young man, please put your phone away." The attendant turned to the aisle seat passenger, who groaned before complying.

28A gave a thumbs up and looked out the window in hopes it would help him calm down, and the attendant continued down the aisle. *Think of anything else. Think of anything else. Think of anything else. Think of something serious. What's serious? What's serious that I can think of? Oh … ummm … death. Death is serious. Right? Think about death.* He closed his eyes, put his hands on his chest, and exhaled out the last small hiccups of laughter.

"I think you laughed for all of us there," 28B whispered.

"Sure did. Thanks for helping me with the masses." He wiped his eyes and pointed around.

"I didn't do anything."

"Sure, you did. You helped me during my epic ab workout."

"As long as you can breathe, work out all you want." 28B smiled, but something had changed.

"Huh, yeah," 28A sighed and patted his chest. A few moments passed, and the plane turned on the runway and then lifted off.

"I need to rest, sorry," 28A sighed and closed his eyes.

"Nothing to apologize for. It's really early. It's wise to sleep some of this trip away." 28B looked over, but the man seemed to be half-asleep already. 28B pulled his journal out and read a few pages before tucking it back in the mesh basket. He was drifting off to sleep as the voice on the intercom announced, "It is now safe to move about the cabin."

When 28B woke, he saw 28A was awake and had a manila folder opened up on his tray table. On it lay pamphlets, papers, packets, and a book. 28A noticed the man next to him had woken, so he slowly but intentionally closed the folder back up, scooted it to the left side of his tray table, and casually laid his arms across it. 28B kept his eyes straight ahead; he knew that 28A wanted to keep his folder private.

28A was about to put his folder in his bag, but the same flight attendant pulled his heavy cart up and asked, "Anything to drink? Any snacks?"

The young man in the aisle seat shook his shaggy hair, and the flight attendant nodded and turned to 28B.

"I would love some coffee. Cream and sugar please."

"You got it." The attendant began pouring. "And for you, sir? Glad to see you have recovered."

"Thank you." 28A smiled. "I'll actually have the same. Could I please have some water too?"

"Of course! We have these small water bottles." He reached in his cart. "Here you go."

"Thank you," 28A said, reaching for the water bottle, and then after a moment, his coffee.

After the attendant had gone, the two men sipped their coffee.

"You know what's funny?" 28A asked, turning to 28B. "I noticed most people can't wait until they get free coffee on the plane, especially on early flights. They need to get it ASAP at an airport café. I get it, I'm in that boat. People want to be awake, all that, so the lines are always so long. And there is this knowledge that people want 'good' coffee. But sitting here, drinking this, after spending an arm, leg, and a hand for coffee before we boarded, I can't taste a difference. Can you?"

"No." 28B chuckled. "But because we are only comparing drip coffee, no."

28A smiled and made eye contact with 28B. 28B smiled back, but the intensity of the man's gaze caught him off guard, and he tried his best to casually look away. *His eyes. What is happening? Is he okay?*

"I'm terrible at conversation. I need to rest some more. I'm sorry," 28A sighed.

"No problem. We still have more than eight hours to go.

Sleep off as much as you can," 28B replied.

28A picked up his coffee, finished it, and put the cup down in the shallow holder. He closed his eyes and turned to face the window.

"Shit, I hate this. I hate turbulence," 28B murmured to himself as he gripped the armchair. A movement caught his eye. He looked down as paperwork and a pamphlet slid out of the folder and across 28A's tray table. His eyes went wide at the bolded titles before him: **Die on Your Terms, How to Prepare for Death, We Are Here to Help When It's Time to Let Go, How to Be at Peace with the End.** *Oh my god, what? What?*

He studied the man's body. 28A seemed like any other 30-something with thin brown hair. *His spine was sticking out, but really? His eyes seemed tired, but what? Is he … doing this?*

He tapped 28A's shoulder. "Excuse me, your papers are slipping," he stammered, keeping his eyes away from the words. "Sir, sir." He tapped again, but 28A's body was fully turned and facing away. "Sir. I'm worried about your papers. Is it alright if I hold onto them?"

No movement.

A voice came over the intercom and instructed everyone to stay in their seats with the seat belts securely fastened.

Crap. Crap. Crap.

28B hesitated but reached over and grabbed the paperwork the moment before it slid off completely. He tucked everything back in the folder, lifted it up, dropped it in his lap, and delicately closed the tray table. He put the stranger's coffee cup on his own and slid them into the mesh pocket.

The plane shuddered and dropped.

28B gripped both of his seat's arms as his body jostled back and forth, and he looked over to see 28A completely undisturbed. Twenty-five minutes passed with the folder on his lap. He couldn't put it in the man's bag, and he didn't want to put it in his own. His mesh pocket held his own magazines, wrappers, and coffee cups. The folder held importance, and he didn't want it to get bent or dirty or splashed on by anything. He looked over again. No movement.

Fifteen minutes passed. He looked down at the folder and then back at the man. No change. With his left hand, he slightly opened the folder and scanned as much as he could.

Medically assisted suicide? Lethal dose? Completely painless? Sleep and die peacefully? We will help you on this journey? Physician supported?

"You know, you can just ask me. You don't need to waste your time with reading. I've already read it all," 28A sighed and gave a sly look.

"Oh my god!" 28B dropped the folder and flushed. "I'm so, so sorry. We had terrible turbulence, and your papers were sliding out. I didn't want them to fly everywhere so I took the folder and put your table up. I was just putting everything back together. I'm sorry. Here you go."

"Thanks," 28A chuckled, reaching for the folder. He bent over and slid it in his bag.

28B kept his eyes straight ahead. His mind raced. 28A coughed. 28B exhaled and bit his lips.

Half an hour passed.

28B faced 28A directly and said, "I'm sorry, I can't take it anymore. What? Just what? What is that?"

"What is what? What are you asking?" 28A replied flatly as he looked and met the man's eyes.

"That!" 28B pointed down to the bag. "That thing! That folder! It's not my business, but what? Are you doing that? Or is it just research, or what?"

"I thought you just said it's not your business," 28A grinned.

"Uhhh ... you're right. I'm sorry. I got up too early, and these flights are too long. It just caught me off guard. Turbulence jumbles me up, but you slept like a baby." 28B's face reddened again.

"Yep. I've never had trouble sleeping on a plane," 28A said.

28B bit his cheek and nodded. *Think about anything else. Think about anything else. Think about anything else. Think about something funny. What's funny? Think about Sally being bossy. That's funny.*

"Are you?" 28B asked. As the words left his mouth, he didn't feel conscious or aware of them.

"Okay, fine. Yes. I'm doing this."

"When? Like right now? Or way down the line … at the end of your life?"

"I'm at the end of my life."

"What?" 28B's mouth dropped.

"Yes. I'm at the end."

"What happened? What's wrong? Are you sick? Why are you doing this?"

"Yes," 28A stated calmly yet firmly. "I'm sick. It's deep and it has spread, and nothing can be done. Six to twelve months. Maybe longer, maybe less. But it's going to turn, and I'm going to go down rapidly. I'm not going to let that happen. I'm going to lay down on my own," he swallowed and met 28B's eyes.

"What about your family? You have to have some family! Parents, spouse, kids, friends, relatives. What about them? Where are they? Do they know you are doing this? Are they here on the plane?" 28B looked around frantically.

"No. No one is here."

"What? Why not? Do they know?"

28A rolled his neck and sighed. "No, they don't. I only have parents. Not married yet and never will be, which might make it easier. I … I don't know. No kids. Never will have any."

"Oh god. Oh my god … I'm so, so sorry." 28B hung his head.

"It's okay. Please look at me. It's okay. Well, I mean, it's not, but it has to be."

28B shook his head, searching. "Are your parents still alive?"

"Yeah."

"Well?" 28B demanded.

"Well, what?" 28A asked softly, although he knew what was coming.

"Do they know?"

"No."

"What?" 28B half-yelled.

28A's hollow eyes flashed wide, and he shook his head.

"I'm sorry." 28B dropped to a whisper. "What about your parents? They didn't even get to say goodbye to you? What kind of son does that? They aren't with you. They aren't stopping this!"

"You don't understand. They wouldn't let me go. They would fight me and fight me. It would destroy our relationship, and it would destroy them. I have written long goodbye letters. It seems you want me to live just because we are talking, just because we are sitting next to each other right now. What if we had never spoken? You don't know anything about me," 28A sighed.

"No parent should have to bury their child."

"I agree. But no parent should have to watch their child die an excruciating and debilitatingly painful death. And no person should have to stay alive and suffer just for another if they don't want to. Often, it ends up hurting the others more, seeing their loved one in agony," 28A said.

"But why aren't you fighting? Why aren't you fighting it? You could win. You could survive."

"No, you don't understand. I don't need to fight it. I don't want to fight it. I won't survive, and staying alive in anguish and unbearable pain is not winning. I have had a good life, and although I haven't done everything I wanted to do, I have done enough. I don't think many of us are able to do everything we want to do. Or we think we are doing everything we want to do, but when it gets to the end, it turns out we weren't doing the right things, or enough of them. It's been hard, I'm not lying. But I'm at peace. If there has to be a winner, it's me. Going out on my terms is winning."

"I just can't believe you are doing this," 28B shook his head. *So fucking sad. Don't get upset.*

"Okay, let me ask you this. Are you a parent?" 28A asked.

28B nodded.

"Imagine your kid, or actually your partner if you have one, or anyone else you truly, truly loved. Imagine if they were suffering, imagine if they were in agony, imagine if nothing could be done besides waiting. Waiting through minutes and days and weeks and months or possibly years of excruciating pain and helplessness. Imagine them losing themselves completely to a disease, a cancer, anything. They can't do anything, can't connect, can't do what they love, can't pursue their passions, or fulfill their life's purpose. Imagine the only thing they could do was to wait in hell, in pure torture, until it ended. Would you want that? Would you want your kid to suffer, especially if they were begging and crying and wanting it to stop? That it was destroying them? What kind of life is that? How is that worth staying alive for? What would you say to your child if the only thing they experienced was torment and loss of self? Would you want them to stay alive for you? Do they owe you their life? Or do they owe themselves the choice to let go when they want to? Let go with a shred of themselves intact, able to comprehend and make their own choices. I'm assuming your child or children aren't even close to adulthood, but imagine they were, imagine them my age. Fully informed and able to decide for themselves. What would you tell them?"

"I don't know. It's not right. I don't feel good about it. None of it," 28B snapped.

"Yeah, you aren't alone."

"Jesus Christ, I'm sorry. I didn't mean to … oh fuck."

"It's okay. I get it. It makes me angry too. It's not right, and it doesn't feel fair."

"It's not fair! You're a young man who should have his whole life ahead of him!" 28B exclaimed.

"I agree with you," 28A lifted his hand and slowly lowered it. "I'm really sorry. I'm really tired. I need to close my eyes now. I will see you in a little bit."

28B nodded but didn't say anything. He spent the next hour flipping through his journals. He tried to read a book, he even tried to sleep, but he couldn't distract himself. He closed his eyes and ran over the conversation in his head.

"Excuse me." 28A tapped 28B's shoulder. "I need to use the bathroom."

28B nodded, stood, and tucked himself as far back as possible. As 28A stepped past, the aisle seat passenger frowned, ripped his headset off, and shook his shaggy hair.

"I'm so sorry," 28A murmured to the aisle seat passenger as he passed. No response.

28B watched the young man. *I'm going to strangle that kid if he doesn't show some respect.*

As if reading his mind, 28A flashed 28B a look and slightly shook his head.

Fifteen minutes later, 28A returned and mouthed "I'm sorry" to the aisle seat passenger who huffed, stood momentarily, and then plunked back down and shoved his headphones back in. 28B stood and smiled and tried to make as much room as possible.

"I can't believe how kids are these days," said 28B. "The attitude, it's incredible." *Fuck. Why did I say that?*

28A smiled, sensing the man's embarrassment. "I was a kid once. And you know, it's not just kids. It's all of us," 28A said as he sat down. "Plugged in and pushing each other away."

"Okay. Fair enough," 28B sighed.

"I wanted to tell you, but I forgot earlier. I'm not going to be buried."

"What?" 28B turned and searched the man's eyes.

"I'm going to be cremated and have my ashes spread under my favorite tree in my favorite park in London. It's the place where I have felt the most peace in this world."

"So, are you just going to send your parents a picture of a tree in the mail?" 28B scoffed.

"You know, I hope so. That's a good idea. Show them where I'm at. Or maybe they can come visit me. Anyway, tell me about your life. You read journals and magazines about business. You obviously hate turbulence. What else? What else bugs you?"

"What? You are asking about me? You are going to die."

"Sooner rather than later, thank god." 28A winked.

"Yeah." 28B shook his head. "Well, I can't complain to you, a person who is on a trip to die. I haven't known anyone who was going to commit suicide. I feel weird about it."

"We are all on a trip to die! This just happens to be the end of my trip. You could see it as an expedition, not suicide. And why not talk to me? If anyone has the ability to listen, it's me. I'm not busy, and it's not like I'm going anywhere." He smiled and looked around. "Here, just imagine I'm dead and start talking. I'm a good audience. Tell me. Tell me everything you want me to know about your life."

"Well, I'm in finance. Married to Jessica. One daughter, Sally. Lived in Seattle my whole life," 28B answered shortly.

"Fascinating! Tell me more about finance!"

"It's not fascinating, and it's not worth talking about right now. I do it for the money."

"Ohhhhhh …" 28A sighed. "I see. Yeah, we do what we have to do. This a business trip?"

"Yeah, I fly on the weekends to give myself time to adjust to the jet lag. Have meetings Monday through Thursday, fly home Friday. I travel somewhere a couple times a month. I still haven't gotten used to it. But I'm not complaining. I'm very lucky, I mean …" He shook his head.

"You sound really dedicated to your job. You are probably pretty important."

"I am dedicated. And I don't know if I'm important, but yes, I worked my way to the top."

"Why is your company flying you in economy seats then?"

28B shrugged to hide embarrassment. "Well, I could ask you the same thing. This is your last flight. Why are you flying economy?"

"I was a teacher!" 28A grinned.

"Oh … really?" 28B asked. "What grade did you teach?"

"I taught third grade for five years. This was my last school year."

28B swallowed. "My god, I'm so sorry," his voice trembled.

"Me too."

"Are you, ummm …"

"Yeah, early thirties. I don't look it anymore though. Got my master's in education, landed a job at an amazing school. I wanted to be established and have myself figured out. That was important before dating, before marriage. And then it was too late. Probably for the best, but still." 28A shrugged.

28B blinked back tears and coughed to hide his watering eyes.

"Enough of that." 28A wiped his eyes and smiled. "What kind of TV does your kid watch?"

"Ummm … I don't know," 28B shook his head, "Jessica knows that stuff. It changes all the time."

"Mmmhhhmmm …" 28A nodded softly without judgment. "Sure does."

"I'm a good father. I take care of my family. They are my priority."

"I know you are. You work so hard for them, and you love them so much. I can tell."

"Now I'm the one who needs to go to the bathroom. I'll be right back."

Once in the stall, 28B splashed water on his face and wiped his neck with a scratchy paper towel. He sat back down as casually as he could, but 28A saw his face was red.

"If you could wake up tomorrow doing something else, what would it be?" 28A asked.

"Hmmm … I would be a philosophy professor. That's what I always dreamed of, but I struggled in college. My parents told me I was missing a certain depth and wouldn't be successful, so I changed majors. But in a heartbeat I would do it."

"That's so hard. I'm sorry. I loved being a teacher. I'm sorry you didn't get to experience it."

"Yeah," 28B exhaled. "It's okay. I'm doing okay. I made a choice; the choice wasn't made for me. I'm not complaining."

"I didn't say you were, only asking what else you would want to be doing."

"The one thing, though, is I fear that all my daughter knows about me is that she misses me. That I'm not there. I worked for almost a decade to get to where I'm at. I can't change jobs. I can't let them down. My family needs me, and I need to take care of them. I do whatever I can, but I'm traveling all the time. The world has changed so much, it's expected of me to be everyone, all the time. It didn't used to be this way, not when I started. My wife does everything: the kid, the house, the errands, the cooking, the cleaning. We have another kid on the way. My wife is proud of me, but I hate being gone. I'm proud and grateful for her. But I miss her, and I miss my child."

"Ohhhhhh …" 28A sighed. "I'm so sorry. My god, that is so hard. You have so much."

28B wiped his eyes and sniffled. "I hate these long flights. Turbulence throws me off."

"I understand," 28A said gently.

For the remaining hours of the flight, the two passengers embarked on an animated discussion of their childhoods, their parents, their fears, their relationships, life in Seattle, teaching, finance, politics, religion, globalization, music, the universe, UFOs, the future, the election, art, the rise of fascism, the supply chain, inflation, the pandemic, climate change, violence, mental health, poverty, current and impending wars, the medical system, young people, technology, and AI.

Then they each shared their favorite birthdays ever.

"If you could die a different way, what way would it be?" 28B asked. "Oh my god, I shouldn't have asked that. I am so amped from talking that I wasn't thinking."

"It's okay." 28A smiled and softly rolled his head side to side while he thought. "I'd probably want to be eaten by a lion. It might sound strange, but I wonder what it would be like to be part of a strong body. I thought I was just weak and built differently, and I was teased and tormented for looking like the runt of a litter growing up. So as an adult these last few years, I thought this weakness was simply how I was. But it turns out I was just sick for a long time. I thought that what I was experiencing was just my job, the germs, the burnout, the learning curve, the late-night planning, getting the hang of it, you know? I thought that what was happening was normal, or just really bad covid. The hospitals were overwhelmed, I never went in. Anyway, I have never been strong, you know, in my body."

28B nodded and cleared his throat. Heartbreak radiated through him. He wanted to comfort the man, he wanted to reach out, he wanted to do something. He wanted to make it stop.

Voices called out from behind them.

"Well, quit showing your tits to the plumber, Amy!"

"Well, quit being yourself, Steve!"

The two men looked at each other and burst out laughing. 28B was still chuckling as 28A turned on his screen to look at the flight tracker. The tiny plane on the big map had moved an inch.

"This life journey, all this work, all this progress. Even though I know how far I have gone, everything I have seen and done, I have barely moved an inch. And now I have to be done. I have nothing to show for it. Nothing except for myself. I'm being taken out. I was just getting started in life. And it's all over." 28A touched the tiny plane on the screen.

28B listened but didn't say anything.

"Now I feel that all I have accomplished is planning this grand trip," 28A said with a lighter tone. "So, I have been noticing strangers and picking up parts of them, parts of them that will comfort and amuse me and stay with me forever until the end. Can I show you something?"

"Of course."

28A reached down into his bag and pulled out his notebook.

"I finally got the nerve to try stand-up, which was a dream I had, and now life is standing me up. The irony! Wish it was funnier! Can you read this for me? Tell me what you think?"

"Of course." 28B smiled and reached for the notebook.

He began reading:

Before my big flight across the ocean, I was sitting at the airport, and I started seeing things. Seeing facts. Facts like death and life and too much time and not enough time. I feel I'm ready to share these truths with you. These non-negotiables, these facts.

These are the facts of the airport:

The happiest person who has ever lived and will ever live is the kid who just kicked a watermelon-printed beach balloon across the dirty carpet at my face. His parents missed it, unfortunately.

I passed an old woman telling her phone to turn on. She yelled three times and looked like she was going to throw it. If possible, every elder at every airport would take us back a hundred years.

I saw a woman coming out of the bathroom, frantically wiping the germs off of her phone. She walked right into a post. Wiping your phone will not widen your view. It will not fix your tunnel vision.

Everyone has touched, is going to touch, and is touching everything in the airport: every railing, every counter, every kiosk, every seat, and every drinking fountain. This cannot be avoided. Don't try to.

There is truly no stranger danger at the airport. Everyone here suffers the same. We suffer together and we are stuck together. But here's the thing: we ask the stranger sitting next to us to watch our stuff because the stranger five seats away is unsafe. The way to build trust is to move four seats, but nobody wants to get up for that.

85% of the people in wheelchairs can walk; they just want a ride. I can't blame them. Everyone wants a free ride when they can get it.

No price can be put on small comforts at the airport, so the price of a bagel is $17.95. But at least the napkin is free. For now.

Everyone is trying to be sexy at the least sexy place on the planet.

Airports are the only way we can meet other people from around the world without having to go anywhere. It couldn't be *easier. Why aren't we meeting each other?*

The benefit of bonus miles is negotiable. Are bonus trips the cause of all of our ailments?

The names announced over the intercom for 'left behind items' are entirely made up. It's a trap to see who is wanting to commit theft.

The air at the airport is deprived of 23% of its oxygen. This makes everyone drowsy, so they can inflate coffee prices. A 12-ounce drip is $15. Free stir stick.

Once on board, the flight attendant instructs us that following an emergency, we can remove our oxygen masks if we are no longer necessary. Turns out no one is necessary.

Why do they use the word terminal? Doesn't it have a morbid ring to it? Of all the words out there, they had to pick one that means impending death. I think about explaining our words to non-English speakers. Terminal means death, the end … or, where our important methods of transportation arrive and depart. You get to figure out what we are talking about.

Life would be better if we saw our bodies as airplanes, moving around until we find the terminal with our name on it.

My name is Airplane. Nice to meet you. Oh, you got to go? I understand. I'm leaving too.

"That's pretty good. Thank you for sharing that with me," 28B laughed and handed it back.

"Wouldn't that be a good, final act?" 28A reached for it and smiled. "No joke I told was a lie."

"You are absolutely right. Well, now I need some shut eye. I'm sorry," 28B shrugged.

"I understand. I'm feeling tired myself. Thanks for the talk. I needed that," 28A replied.

28B nodded and closed his eyes. Within moments, tears streamed down his face, but he kept his eyes shut and cleared his throat and adjusted himself in the seat to try and regain some composure. A moment passed. 28A reached out and rested his hand on 28B's arm.

"It's alright, and I'm alright. I'm at peace," 28A whispered.

28B sobbed. He couldn't open his eyes. He cried and wiped his eyes and cried some more. He reached across with his right hand and gripped 28A's hand in his own.

Other passengers on the plane leaned forward and looked down the aisle. They peered at the crying man and shook their heads and murmured, "What's wrong with him?" Others sat up and looked behind at him and waited for him to open his eyes.

"He's okay. It's okay," 28A mouthed to the gawkers. He fielded all their stares and confusion. He gave a thumbs up to reassure them that he was there, tending to the situation.

28B didn't let go of his hand, and soon 28A watched as his new friend fell asleep.

When they departed the plane, 28A held his hand out.

28B grabbed his hand and pulled him in for the gentlest yet most powerful hug he could give. He held the man as long as he could and stumbled over words of gratitude, of sadness, of adoration. He gave his goodbye.

28A smiled as tears filled his eyes.

Hours later, 28B put his briefcase down in his hotel room. He took a shower, cried, ate, cried, drank two beers, and tried to sleep. He couldn't get the stranger and his story out of his mind.

Just get up. Check emails. Make some coffee. Do something.

He sat up and walked to the desk and pulled out his laptop. Out with it came a folded piece of paper.

What is this? His heart raced. *Oh my gosh. It's from him.*

The top of the paper read:

If you happen to want a picture of my new life, email my friend at this address. He is the only one who knows about this and is helping me with the process. Tell him Brian Tree. He will make sure you get a picture. Or better yet, you could come visit me. This is the address of the park. And here, would you mind please doing this for me? I'm afraid I'm not up for it. Good luck with your life, good luck with your family. In the coming days, our time together will bring me laughter.

I love you. Thank you.

The man, 28B, meandered past the line of people outside the club smoking, drinking, laughing, yelling, and hugging each other as though they had been separated by destiny, not that it had only been a few days.

He stepped up to the window and asked, "Is it too late to sign up for the open mic?"

"Nope." The woman blew a pink bubble that matched her eyeshadow. "Just go talk to—wait, he's right there. Hey, Oliver!" she yelled through the window at a nearby man who was about to head inside. He was built like a football player and was dressed completely in black with spiky black hair. "Oliver. This bloke wants to sign up. He's gonna follow you in."

Oliver nodded.

"Cheers, mate!" she yelled at the man.

Oliver waved 28B over.

"Thank you so much!" 28B smiled and waved and turned to follow Oliver. He put his name on the list and navigated through the darkness, the red lights, and the tables. He trudged over to the bar.

"Three shots of whiskey, please."

The bartender raised his eyebrows.

"I'm just, I'm nervous. I'm about to go up, and it's my first time," 28B yelled way too loudly as he leaned over the counter.

People at the end of the bar looked over, and he timidly waved.

"Got it. You'll do great. Cheers, mate!" The bartender slid him a tall glass.

A woman with bleached hair complained about the dilemma she was in with the man she was dating and her dog, who won't let him get near her. An older man described a situation where he thought his grandchildren were talking about Tic Tacs and finally learned what TikTok was.

28B's name was called. He felt his armpits and heartbeat and walked to the stage. People clapped, but he couldn't see anything. He held the microphone up and swallowed before reaching in his back pocket and pulling out the sheet. "I have got some truths, some non-negotiables to tell you. Something that most of us experience, but few talk about. These are the facts, the facts of the airport."

Six months later, 28B was on a plane.
He sat in first class.
A picture sat in his lap.

See you soon, Brian.

JANINE

The person whose age is the exact median of the total population in the fourth-largest suburb of Seattle is a woman named Janine. Janine sat on an old, wooden barstool by the counter in her tiny, yellow kitchen and waited. *What does he know? What if he doesn't know? What should I tell him?* She picked at a painful hangnail on her pointer finger until it bled and then applied pressure to stop it with her thumb. *Fuck, fuck, fuck. I guess I did something wrong, but what was it? I did everything exactly how I was told. Why did Scott just tell me to go home? Should I go back and talk to him?* She looked at her watch. *I can't go now. Jack will be here any second. Crap! Maybe Scott has already told Jack what happened? I don't want him to be mad at me. Fuck. He'll know what to do, though. He always knows what to do. Why don't I ever know what to do? Why can't I do anything right?*

Ten hour-long minutes passed.

BUZZ!

BUZZ!

"Oh my gosh!" Janine jumped at the sound of the buzzer.

Jesus Christ, Janine. Calm down. She walked to the door and pressed the blue intercom button and hummed "Hello" into the box.

"Yep," Jack answered.

Janine pressed the tan button to allow entry and exhaled. *He sounds mad. Fuck, I bet he knows.* She groaned and opened the front door an inch before trotting back to her barstool.

A few minutes later, Jack pushed the door open. Janine put her head down on the table.

"Hi, Janine. I can see you," Jack uttered slowly.

Oh god, he knows. "I'm so sorry, Jack." Janine looked up and shook her head. Jack held a gray carrier tray stuffed with two large coffees and one closed, round, white paper bag. A beautiful, dark leather messenger bag hung across his shoulder.

Did he bring cupcakes? Janine eyed the white bag.

He placed the tray on the counter and sighed.

"I don't know what happened. I tried my best. I'm so sorry, Jack," Janine said, her eyes welling.

"Please don't worry about it. I do want to hear everything, but first, let me give you a hug." Jack smiled and put his bag down. He took a few steps towards her and opened his arms.

Janine remained on her chair but wrapped her arms around him. "I mean it, Jack. I don't know what happened. I tried my best."

"Janine, it's okay. Scott isn't mad, and *I'm* not mad. You have nothing to be ashamed of or worried about. It's important we try different things and find the best fit for us. It can take a while, and if something doesn't work out, it doesn't mean there is something wrong with you."

Janine pulled back from the hug and looked up at her brother and nodded. Jack kissed her forehead and gave her a squeeze before walking back to the other side of the counter. He picked up a coffee and leaned against the cupboard.

"What do you want to say? What's going on in there?" he asked, taking a sip.

"You didn't have to try different things! You always just knew what you wanted to do, and it all just worked out. It didn't take you a long time! I want that. How do you do that?"

"Well, Janine. Everybody's different. And comparisons aren't helpful. Just because I didn't struggle as much with work doesn't mean I didn't, or haven't, struggled with other things."

"What have you struggled with?"

"Really? Are you serious?"

"No, I'm sorry. I'm just jealous and a fucking loser." She put her head down on the counter.

"No, you aren't. Here, have some coffee. Just don't knock it over." Jack pulled her coffee out and put it by her head.

"I'm such a loser," she mumbled as she wrapped her hand loosely around the cup.

"Stop it. Sit up and eat a cupcake."

"What?" Janine shot up, and her eyes widened.

"See! You'll be okay." Jack shook his head and took a sip. "Of course, I got you cupcakes."

Janine grabbed and felt the bag, and met Jack's eyes.

"Yes, dear sister, they are both for you. Lattes are my only sweet indulgence."

"I hear you." Janine nodded quickly and pulled the cupcakes out of the bag. "Yes! Vanilla and chocolate frosting! Oh, thank you! Oh my god, yes!" Janine briefly closed her eyes in bliss and smiled. "Can you please hand me a knife?"

"Oh, Janine!"

"What? I'm in my home! I can do whatever I want."

"Fine. I'm sorry. Here." Jack turned around and pulled a drawer open. He grabbed a butter knife and handed it to her.

"Thank you!" Janine reached for it and began scraping the frosting off her cupcakes. Jack watched her wipe it onto a napkin in big, messy chunks. She then quartered her cupcakes, picked a piece up, and dipped it in the frosting. "So good!" Janine popped it in her mouth. "And, by the way, I can tell you have been working out. You look great! So hip and handsome with your stylish hair. I love your shoes, that black shirt, and those tight, tight jeans!" Janine raised her eyebrows and picked up another piece of cupcake and plunged it into the frosting.

"Hey!" Jack sassed.

"I'm just kidding, kind of. And you have been tanning too, huh?"

"Yes! Thank you for noticing! You could come with me! It could be our thing."

"Nope! Not for me!" she said with her mouth full. "I have told you that those spaces are too small. Once they make tanning beds the size of huge rooms, I will be there."

"Well, I'm glad to hear that's your primary concern about tanning," he winked.

"Yes! I'm so pale, I'm see-through, but I can't imagine lying in one of those things. Or even standing in a little corner with somebody right on you spraying you with that stuff. Strange! You stay sun-kissed, and I'll stay inside and eat cupcakes." She popped another chunk of cupcake in her mouth.

"You are still really into your cupcakes, huh?"

"I can't help it." Janine shrugged.

"Tanning, cupcakes. We do what we gotta do, right?" Jack smiled.

Janine nodded and looked down at her crumbs and chocolate-streaked napkin. *Damn, all gone.*

"So, Janine. I did speak with Scott. Tell me what happened?"

"Well, wait. What did he tell you?"

"Hmmm … he said that you were like hovering, waiting for people to put the clothes back down. You were ready to spring into action, but like, the shirt or pants were still in their hands.

Does that sound about right?" Jack studied her.

"Those people weren't going to buy those things. I simply wanted to fold everything back up for the next person. Do you know how stressful it is to have a ton of people messing up your perfectly arranged clothing displays? They pick a shirt up and wave it in the air like they have never seen a shirt before, and then they just drop it back down like it's trash. When a new person comes in, and they see the clothes balled up like that, do you think they want to buy them? Everybody wants to believe that they are the only person who has touched the shirt."

"I bet that was stressful. It must have been hard to be discreet but still get the job done."

"I know you are trying to be nice, but I'm feeling like such a loser right now." She picked at her drying frosting. "I love you and I don't know how you do it. You are confident, smart, and stylish. Wait, you are actually a genius! You make apps while I'm over here trying to remember to eat apples. You're a good person, you have a healthy relationship, and you volunteer. You are like a gay superhero. You put up with my bullshit and help me all the time. Aren't you busy? How do you have time for everything? How do you do it?"

"Maybe I *am* a superhero, and now I'm going to play matchmaker! We are getting you online!" Jack walked around the counter and plunked down on a barstool next to his sister.

"Uhhh … Jack, I don't know. I can't even fold clothes at the right time. Won't this mess up your friendship with Scott? I'm so sorry." Janine wiped her eyes with frosting on her fingers.

"Honey, no. Scott and I go way back. He just wanted to help. He understands that it's got to be the right thing for you, too. It sounded too hectic. I don't want you to have that much anxiety while you work." Jack raised a finger to her face and brushed away a bit of frosting.

"I'm not good at anything. I don't want to go anywhere."

"What are you going to do then—sit in here with all your plants?" Jack pointed to her walls.

"I guess so. I have no friends, except for my green babies. My little brother pays my rent. I can't keep a job. I have no real skills. I'm a loser!"

"It's okay to *feel* like a loser, for a time, but please know deep down you aren't one. Not at all. But it might be time for some transitions. You could meet people, get some community, put yourself out there."

"Ughhh," Janine groaned.

"Come on. Swiping with you will be fun."

"Meeting people won't be fun."

"Let's just start with a profile."

"Can you please do it?" Janine whined and put her head down on the counter.

"Gladly!" Jack reached for his bag and pulled out his tablet. Within seconds, it was on and open to a dating site.

"Jesus, Jack!"

"I'm always prepared. Now, what makes you happy, Janine?"

"Cupcakes!"

"Oh, love. We shouldn't start with the cupcakes, but I like where you are going. Can we use the word 'foodie' instead?" Jack began typing.

"I guess. But I don't care about other foods. I'm not a foodie—I just like cupcakes."

"I know, hun. But maybe that can be an endearing or fun fact that you share in person?"

Janine frowned.

"Please trust me. Let's get through this, and then we can go back and see about making changes. Alright? Now, what else are you passionate about?"

"Plants!"

"That's a good one, Janine, but I'm also going to add: 'Lover of nature and all things outdoors. Spontaneous, and always down for an adventure.'"

"I'm not spontaneous. And my little rows of succulents are a lot different than saying I love 'all things outdoors.'"

Jack nodded but kept typing. "Describe yourself, Janine."

"Female … ish, fake blonde hair, thin, tall."

"You don't need to say fake."

"I'm not going to shave for anyone. Put that in there."

"I'm glad you won't do something you aren't comfortable with, but if someone respectfully tells you their personal preference, or does something different with their body, that's okay too. Just as long as they aren't asking you to change yourself, right? It's about hearing each other with respect."

"Just put that I'm afraid of razors." Janine picked at her frosting napkin.

"No. We are going to say you are a beautiful, natural woman." He typed and nodded. "If you want to talk to me about anything, any fears, any past or current pain, stuff, anything, I'm here. But I got it: no razors, no shaving." He paused for a moment, looking at her tenderly. "What else?"

"I could have a picnic with somebody, or like you said, I'm adventurous and could go explore a park. I do love plants. Oh, and I love puppies! All the p words," Janine laughed nervously.

"Well, speaking of," Jack started slowly, "I did want to ask you, how do you identify right now? Last I remember, you identified as a lesbian. It's okay if you don't want to talk about it."

"I guess I'm a lesbian?" Janine shrugged and put her head down on the table.

"Oh, honey." Jack rubbed her back.

"I'm sorry. I don't know what I am, or who I am, but I know I have nothing to offer anyone. Put queer for now."

"Gotcha, queer! I love it!"

"How does this sound so far?" Jack cleared his throat. "Queer, early forties, foodie femme seeks outdoor adventures, friendship, spontaneous date nights, or something more serious."

"So many f words."

"That's right!" Jack winked at her. "I got it from here, don't you worry."

"Oh fuck. Can I tell you something?" she asked. "I can't say it out loud."

"Do you want to text me?"

"I don't know where my phone is."

"Well, we just got you that phone, and it was kind of an investment, so can we find it before I go?"

"Sure. I know it's here somewhere, Jack."

"Alright, grab a sticky note and tell me what's up."

Janine walked to the fridge and pulled the top sheet off her plant-shaped, magnetic notepad. She scribbled, groaned, and scribbled some more before folding the sheet as many times as she could. "I'm going to my bedroom for thirty seconds. Don't open it until I'm in there. Don't say anything to me about it, and don't look at me." She flicked the paper at him and hurried off.

Jack sighed. He unfolded it and saw the words he could have guessed. "Aww ... Janine," he whispered. "It will be alright. You can learn anything."

Janine left her bedroom and moved past Jack and into the living room, where the walls were almost covered by plants. She raised her hand and gently stroked the wide leaves of one of her aloe veras. "Hi, honey. How are you? Are you thirsty? I'll get you water very soon. I promise." She walked from wall to wall, checking on every plant. "Wow! You are growing, growing, growing! Oh, hi, little buddy. Aren't you cute? You don't need water but perhaps just need to be rotated a bit? There, that's better. Have a good day!" Janine smiled.

Jack reached for his phone and slowly turned his body to face her as he pretended to scroll. He clicked the photo button as she moved about the room, then put the phone down and smiled.

"Awww … Jack, why are you getting upset?"

"I'm not. You are wonderful, and I don't want you to be alone if you don't want to be alone."

"I'm never alone. I have my plants, and my year—"

"Don't even say it, Janine. Promise me, you will not show a first or second date your yearbooks. Maybe that will be something you keep to yourself for a while? But of course, you can talk about your plants, but do not talk *to* them in front of a first date. And please try to avoid cupcakes."

"Got it. I'll try to remember everything you've told me. Don't show those interests."

"Are you being sarcastic?"

"No." *I can't remember all this shit.*

After they found her phone and her brother left, Janine showered and wrapped a towel around her long, stringy, bleached-blonde hair. She looked at herself in the mirror. *Wow, my body is just as awkward as my hair.* Janine took a deep breath and looked down at the skin between her knees and her hips. She ran her fingers across the thin lines of scars covering each thigh. *Why are you all still here? Is there a cream out there I haven't tried? Are you all just going to be with me forever, popping out to say hello when I shower or pee?*

Several days later, Jack was pacing in his apartment. "Pick up, pick up, pick up! I know you are home, Janine! Pick up, pick up, pick up!"

"Hello?"

"My god, you take so long to answer!"

"I'm sorry, I was just—"

"You don't need to tell me what you were doing."

"I'm sorry, I was just—"

"Janine!"

"I'm sorry. What's going on, Jack? Are you okay?"

"You have a date!"

"A what?"

"Oh my god, Janine. A D-A-T-E!"

"Oh no!"

"What?"

"Oh no!"

"I'm coming up!"

"Up?"

"Yes, I'm here. Buzz me in! As soon as the date was confirmed, I ran over here!"

"You … ran?"

"Shut up. I rushed and got a Lyft!"

"Alright. Buzzing now."

Janine opened and stood at the door and felt for hangnails, but there was nothing left. *Come on. Come on.* Her thumbs frantically scanned her fingertips. *What am I going to do?*

"Janine!" Jack grabbed her hands and squeezed them.

"Oh … hi," she uttered.

"You did see me coming towards you down the hallway, right?" Jack peered into her eyes.

She nodded, and Jack calmly wrapped his arms around her.

"I don't think I can do this, Jack."

"That's alright. You don't have to. I'm so sorry for being so pushy. I just thought it would be fun for you to meet someone, even if it was nerve-wracking. I can easily call the whole thing off. Just let me know what you are comfortable with."

"Maybe I'm not scared, just very, very nervous? Wait, how

did you set a date up? I don't get it. What did you do?"

"You do sound a little bit excited. Let's go inside, and I will tell you everything."

Janine stepped back so he could go past her and into the apartment. She closed the door and leaned her head against it. Jack eyed her as he put his phone and bag down, and opened up her fridge. He closed the fridge and grabbed a cup from the cupboard and filled it from the sink.

"Oh my. We need to go shopping. And this water is disgusting. You need a Brita, too."

"Okay," she said slowly. "Okay."

"You ready?"

"Ready. I mean, wait, hold on." Janine stomped to the fridge and pulled out a giant plastic carton of cupcakes and sat down on the barstool. She roughly opened the carton, and Jack furrowed his brow at the loud cracking plastic.

"Sorry," Janine mumbled. "Can you hand me a spoon and paper towel?"

Jack shook his head and handed them to her before asking, "Are you ready now?"

Janine nodded and smeared frosting on her napkin. He cleared his throat and pulled out his phone. "You, my lovely sister, are going on a coffee date with River this Thursday."

"River?" Janine asked with her mouth full.

"You focus on your cupcake. Let me finish."

"River is thirty-eight, uses they/them pronouns, is five foot nine, has—oh my god, what am I doing? Here, I have the picture!" He held the phone up.

"I'm scared to look!"

"Jesus, Janine. Come on! This is exciting!"

Janine shoved some cupcake in her mouth and squinted as she studied the phone. In the picture, River sat at a table outside with colorful plates of food and drink in front of them, obviously having a *wonderful* time with friends. River was looking softly yet intently at the camera with their deep hazel eyes and smiling. Their stylish hair was buzzed on the sides, while long beautiful, deep red curls fell from the top of their head. River had a dark blue button-up shirt on with the sleeves rolled halfway up. They leaned forward and seemed engaged but still at ease, as though they were sitting perfectly content, and someone had called out their name. Click.

"Wow. They look like they are happy and live in the moment."

"I know, right? But so do you, honey. You are alive, and this is a moment. Don't be so hard on yourself." Jack could see his sister's face melting. "So cute, right? I did good!"

"Yeah, you did. I mean, wait, hold on. You said I have a date with them? You messaged River?"

"Yes, I told you that when I came in here," Jack huffed. "Pay at-ten-tion," he clapped with each syllable.

"Oh god, what? You pretended to be me? What?"

"Yes! I told you that! When we made your profile, I told you, 'I got it from here!' Of course, I was going to handle it! You don't even have the login info and would have lost it if I gave it to you. You left me with no choice."

"No, you didn't tell me you would message people pretending to be me. That's not right."

"Janine, you are anti-tech. I sent a total of four short messages and set up a casual date."

"But if I have seen River's picture, does that mean they have seen—? Oh no, you didn't take my picture! What picture did you use?" Her face dropped.

"You know, I *can* hear some excitement in your voice. Don't worry, I got a great pic of you when you weren't looking."

"Give me your phone! Now!" she gasped as her face reddened.

Jack held out his phone and crossed his arms.

Phone in hand, Janine realized she didn't know what to do, or how to find the pic he'd used. She stared frantically at the screen and began pushing buttons.

Jack shook his head. "Can I show you? Do you really think I would use a bad pic? I'm trying to help you here."

"I know, sorry. I can't do anything with this. Here. I'm a mess." She handed it back.

"No, you are excited! I took some pictures last time I was here when you were with your plants. Don't worry. You looked beautiful! Here, I'll show you." Jack pressed some buttons, nodded to himself in approval, and held the phone up. "See! I did great! You look lovely, Janine, and very in your element."

"Uh-huh," Janine studied the photo. "Fine. I don't look like a total disaster. Thank you. Wait, but oh my god, today is Tuesday! The date is this Thursday? What! What am I going to wear? You did this. You have to help me!" Janine popped two frosting-covered cupcake pieces in her mouth.

"Of course! Why do you think I'm here? But the number one rule is, no eating cupcakes."

"Why? Why not?"

"You can't do that on a first date. Promise me you will not eat cupcakes."

"Why not? What if it's *their* birthday?"

"If someone invites you on a first date, and it's their birthday, have as many cupcakes as you want, because that is weird."

"What if someone goes on a date on their birthday as a treat, as a way to feel special, to not be alone?"

"But on the first date?" Jack asked. "It seems awkward. Talk about extra pressure or feeling like you have to pay for *everything* to treat them! But if you're the guy, you might be doing that anyway."

"If I'm the guy? What the fuck are you talking about, Jack? What kind of gay are you?"

"The kind that is still trying to figure out lesbians," he winked.

"Are you the guy, Jack?" she asked, taking a huge bite of cupcake.

"When I feel like it!" Jack retorted in a girlish voice and curtsied and watched his sister chuckle. "All I'm saying is," he continued, "it might be hard to make a stranger feel special on their birthday."

"Well, I'd be down for it."

"But you are thinking about you, Janine, and your cupcake craving. What if it was your date's birthday, and they wanted steak?"

"Steak and cupcakes might go together." Janine smiled and scooped a bunch of frosting onto her knife and flicked it at her brother. A few small pieces hit his shirt and face.

"Hey! That's gross! What even is frosting? Sugar, lard, dye, what?" He brushed the frosting off.

"Don't even act like you don't remember how you used to eat all kinds of shit," she teased, but then her face fell. *Oh my god, why did I say that? Why did I say that?* She didn't want to look up but knew she had to. "I'm sorry. I didn't mean it."

Jack caught her eyes and took a breath. "As you know, we either ate shit or we ate nothing. I can't do either one ever again, Janine."

"I'm sorry."

"No, I'm sorry. I'm not trying to trash your favorite food. But that sweetness reminds me of something, something I'm not alright with. Like when we were kids and pocketed those pastries at gas stations just to have something to eat, those ones that *never* go bad. Or when we ate stolen candy for lunch. Obviously, I haven't worked through my sweetness aversion … I guess it's trauma." He shrugged and smiled. "Cupcakes aren't bad, Janine. They just don't taste good to me. Guess I can only drink my sweets."

"I understand, Jack. I really do." She nodded and put a piece of cupcake down to look at him.

"Oh, come here." Jack walked up to his sister and hugged her.

"We turned out alright, but you are a bit wacky, love," he teased, patting her back.

"Thank you! Now, what in the hell am I going to wear?"

"Your emerald dress! I have already thought this through. Your blonde hair, pop! Your green eyes, pop! Your green dress *and* your green eyes! Pop! Pop! Pop! It's going to be gorgeous! You're going to be gorgeous! Can we please try it on already?"

"Oh no, Jack. I wanted to wear pants. It's still early springtime."

"No, you are going to make it hot like summer with your green dress! Just try it on for me, and then we can shelve it if it doesn't work. Deal?"

"It was a really pretty dress you got me. I'm sorry I haven't worn it yet. It's just too nice."

"Janine, I don't want you to wear it because I got it for you. I am just thinking about the color, how it will pop on you! It's perfect for the season, too, and it's green like your plants."

"You said not to do anything I'm not comfortable with, and not to change for anybody."

"Fine, Janine! You are right. I'm being pushy. I'm sorry. I just thought I wouldn't be in the *anybody* category, seeing as how I set this date up! Whatever you wear will be great."

"Fine, Jack. I'll try it on."

Minutes later, she opened her bedroom door and slowly walked back to the kitchen. "Uhhh … Jack, I don't know." Janine looked down at herself.

"What are you talking about? The skirt, the sleeves, the color, the tie around the waist. Beautiful, it's beautiful! You're beautiful!"

"You mean it?" She scrunched up her face. "I don't wear skirts this short, Jack."

"Oh, I had no idea. It's at your knees, but that's not quite your style?"

"I don't know. I'm overwhelmed."

"Did you look at yourself before you came out here? I don't think you did. Go and look in your mirror! You will see what I see!"

Janine trudged back to her bedroom and stood in front of the full-length mirror tucked in the corner. She slowly scanned her body. *Wow, I actually do look alright. I can't believe I'm wearing this. Is that me?* Janine smiled and posed. *I feel like a giddy teenager. I feel like everyone I used to make fun of. Oh my god. I can't believe it. Oh shit, my scars!* She pushed down on the skirt and studied her legs as she took a few steps in each direction. *As long as this doesn't move, I think I will be okay. But what happens if it does move?* She gently reached for a bit of the fabric and pulled it up on her right leg. There it was. Two inches above her knee. The beginning of a thick band of scars. She lifted the fabric a bit more, studying her skin. *Why are you still here? Please disappear.*

"Janine! I have been calling your name. I brought you a congratulatory cupcake, straight from your fridge! Oh no, Janine! What happened?"

"Get out!" Janine screamed, dropping her skirt.

"I'm sorry! The door was open. I just wanted to bring you something to celebrate. I'm so sorry. I didn't mean to invade your privacy."

"Damnit, Jack!" She stomped her foot as hard as she could, and dropped her head.

"Janine, what happened to your leg?"

"Jack, please stop!" she cried.

"Alright. I will leave your cupcake on your dresser and go home."

"No, please don't go." Janine wiped her eyes but kept her head down.

"How about I just leave this here for you and I can go sit in the living room for a bit?"

Janine looked at the plate as he set it down. *He cut it up and scraped the frosting off.*

"Jack, I'm sorry. I didn't mean to yell. You scared me. I just need to get out of this dress."

"I understand. Take your time. I'll wait out there for you."

Twenty minutes later, Janine walked out of her bedroom and into the living room, where Jack sat on the couch. She had on gray sweatpants and a sweatshirt and fuzzy socks, and her eyes and face were puffy and tear-stained.

"Want to sit down?" Jack asked, reaching for her favorite blanket.

"Not yet. I'm going to tell you something, but I don't want you to ask me about it. I don't want to talk about it outside of this moment."

"I promise."

"OK." Janine swallowed. "I used to … cut myself, or I guess the proper … ummm … term is, self-harm," she looked up to the ceiling and blinked back tears. "It's been years since I did it. I won't ever do it again. I think you can guess why it happened, but please don't ask. The reasons are rotten. That's all I want to say about it right now." Janine looked at her brother. "I'm serious."

"I know. It just hurts to hear, and I'm sorry. I hate when you are in pain." He nodded and cleared his throat. "Thank you for telling me. I love you and I'm proud of you."

Janine wiped her eyes and took a few steps to sit next to her brother on the couch. She leaned against him, and he pulled the blanket over her before wrapping his arm around her. He kissed her head and closed his eyes, but tears came anyway. Jack struggled to keep his voice and breath and body as steady and even as possible.

"Janine, both of our birth roots are rotten. But we are different plants now, right? I love you."

ɔ

Two days later, Janine and Jack stood a couple blocks away from the coffee shop.

"Janine, I want you to remember that you putting yourself out there, being open, being vulnerable, being yourself, meeting people—that's the important part, that's what matters. Regardless of what unfolds, this is a huge step. I'm so proud of you, and you look wonderful!"

"So be myself, but don't eat cupcakes, don't talk about yearbooks, do talk about plants, but not *to* them if we see any?" She shrugged and put her palms up.

"Exactly! And don't worry—I will stay at the café until you are done."

"Got it. Thank you so much. Second date, I can go alone. I promise."

"No worries. This is exciting for me, too. How high are your hopes right now, Janine?"

"Well, you couldn't limbo underneath them."

"Ha! Okay, well, here we are. Oh wait, Janine!" Jack grabbed her arm as they approached the building.

"Jesus Christ! What?"

Jack pulled out his phone and pretended to text as he said, "River is right there. Look in the far window. We got here twenty minutes early, but they still beat us here!"

"What? No!" Janine flung her body against the brick wall. She scooted against the wall until she was at the edge where it met the windows and hunched down to try and peer around the corner.

"Nope, you are not doing that! I'll come in a minute after you!" Jack gently pushed her in front of the windows, so she had to keep walking.

Janine stood fully upright and shot Jack a look. He grinned and shooed her on. She turned back around and began moving her feet. *Am I walking weird? I'm sweating through this dress! Stay down, skirt! Oh my god, there they are! Oh fuck. Okay. Be cool. Which way does this door go? Push or pull? God, I hate these doors.* Janine stepped inside and made eye contact with River before lifting her hand to wave. *Is it still cool to wave? Put your hand down, Janine.* She weaved around two tables. *Made it.*

"Hi … Janine?" River raised their eyebrows and slowly motioned to stand up.

"Yes … River?" *Am I smiling?*

"Yes! Wonderful. It's great to meet you." River stood and held out their hand.

"Hi, River! It's so nice to meet you too." Janine pulled out the chair and tried to sit down as casually as possible right as she heard Jack come in behind her. River briefly glanced up before meeting Janine's eyes again.

"So, Janine, how are you today? Tell me a little about your-self?" River asked.

"Ummm … I'm Janine." *Oh my god, you idiot, keep talking.* "I'm forty-two, I'm queer. I have never lived anywhere else besides here. I like outdoor adventures, I'm a … foodie, I'm spontaneous."

"Yeah, that's right. That's what I remember from your pro-file," River nodded.

"I'm also very passionate about plants. I'm in between careers right now. I want to find the right fit for me. I worked in retail, but I decided I needed to make a change." *Oh no, I'm lying.*

"I admire that, I really do. Changing careers is hard, and it takes a lot of courage to leave something we are used to. I want to hear about your passion for plants, too. I love the outdoors, like you, but plant identification, natural habitat, all that stuff—I don't know anything about it. Maybe you can teach me?" River smiled.

"I'd love to," Janine gulped. *Holy shit. Who is this confident person?* "What about you, River?"

"I'm thirty-eight, they/them, which you know. Queer, which you also know. I grew up here and went to UW. I love numbers, and so I became an accountant, a CPA. I work for a co-op and infrequently do some freelance work for small businesses or entrepreneurs. I volunteer at the queer youth orgs and hangouts, and I like to mentor members of our community on how to make a budget, save, spend wisely, plan, set goals, and all that. And, I don't say that so you think I'm a good person— just so you can see that numbers are my life."

"I understand. But you are a good person. That's amazing. How do you even do that?"

"Do what?"

"All of it. Wow!"

"Umm … it's not that big of a deal. It's more just like me doing what I love, but other people happen to be there," River laughed. "Outside of work, I'm kind of a homebody, but I'm trying to get out more. I do like outdoor stuff. Movies. Although I can't remember the last time I went to a theater if I'm being honest. But I go *all out* for Pride. Haven't missed a march in twenty years."

"Oh wow! That's impressive." *Please don't ask me if I have gone recently.*

"Do you have any siblings, Janine?"

"Yes, actually a younger brother. We are five years apart, but he seems like the eldest. He is a developer, like one of those tech geniuses. Jack makes apps like people make dinner. I don't get that techy stuff. It's way over my head. He has the sweetest boyfriend and is just a really, really good person. Like you, smart and good." Janine smiled. *Was that too much? What should I do?*

"Let me guess: that cute gay guy that came in thirty seconds after you is your brother?"

"Who?" Janine tried to look confused. *Oh no! I ruined it!*

"The one fumbling by the coffee display." River tilted their head in the direction of Jack.

Janine didn't want to look but knew she had to. She slowly turned and glanced over. There stood Jack, on his toes, struggling to reach a bag on the highest shelf. He already had two in his arms.

"Did he set this whole thing up?" River asked, leaning in.

"Ughhh, I'm sorry! I'm so embarrassed! Please forgive me." Janine put her head in her hands.

"Hey, Janine. It's okay." River reached across the table to get her attention but was careful not to touch her. "Do you want to tell your brother that he doesn't need to pretend to shop anymore. It's a tad overpriced, and I truly doubt that boy makes his own coffee."

"Ha!" Janine's own loud laughter caught her off guard, and she looked up at River and smiled just as Jack had looked over in response. Janine met her brother's eyes. "I love him so much, but you are so right. He doesn't make his own coffee. He is changing the world, though!"

"I'll wave him over." River waved.

Even from across the café, Janine saw Jack's eyes get big. He held up a finger and waved a bag of beans in the air before nodding at the register.

"How did you get so observant?"

"Books," River said playfully.

"Ohhhhhh." *Oh crap, I don't read.*

"No, I'm kidding. I'm not a big reader, although I want to be. But being queer, it's like we have to be extra safe, extra observant, extra aware of every single thing. I don't walk in fear, but I watch everything. It's hard, and sometimes seems to be getting worse out here. You know?"

"Yeah," Janine exhaled, although she couldn't quite relate.

"Janine?"

"Yes, River?"

"Your brother is about here."

"He can just go home. It's fine. This is my fault. You don't need to meet him today."

"It's fine. I don't mind meeting family on the first date," River winked. "You must be Jack!"

"Sorry! Yes! Really nice to meet you, River!" Jack glanced at Janine, but she didn't look at him.

"Of course, you know who I am because you are the sweet sibling who set this up, right?"

"Oh boy!" Jack shrugged and adjusted his leather bag.

Janine felt for a hangnail under the table.

"Do you two go everywhere together?" River laughed.

"Not usually," Jack smiled and looked at River directly. "We just happened to be here today."

"Got it!" they nodded.

Jack met his sister's wide eyes.

"Well, Jack and Janine," River interrupted the siblings' eye contact, "do you two want to meet here in an hour and a half or so, so you can chat about how this date went?"

"Very funny. But yes, how does that sound, Janine? For the record, I just wanted to buy some coffee *and* ended up helping my sister on her very first date. I'm not usually hanging around her like this."

"I'll text you when I'm done, Jack. Let me ask you: Paul makes the coffee, right?" Janine asked.

"Yes! This is all for him! Why?"

"No reason." Janine smiled. And so did River.

"Alright, well it was so nice meeting you, River. And cheers, love!" Jack nodded to Janine.

"See you soon!" Janine huffed.

"Bye, Jack! Great to talk to you again!" River teased.

"Oh my god! So embarrassing and awkward! I'm so sorry. You probably think I'm a creep, or co-dependent, or both. I understand if you want to end this date," Janine groaned.

"Well …"

"Oh no!" Janine shook her head.

"I'm just playing. Sure, it's weird, but what's even weirder is 'cheers!' Haven't heard that in a long time."

"Yeah, I think he is watching a British show right now. This is what happens."

River laughed. "You are very funny. While it is kind of weird that he was running your dating profile, luckily the only messages exchanged were about setting this up. You … I guess he … said you were more of an in-person person. It would have been unacceptable if he went on and on. I do not recommend this for your dating future. It's not a good way to start."

"I'm so sorry."

"Hey, it's okay. Let's move on and not worry about it. You two are goofy and love each other a lot. He just wanted you to be supported and safe at this public café in the bright, early afternoon. It's cute. Any other family members for me to meet today, or is that the plan for the second date?"

"There isn't a soul left for you to meet," said Janine. "Oof. I didn't mean to sound that sad. But no, no one else to meet. Oh fuck, I'm blowing this." Janine couldn't believe her word choice and put her hand over her mouth.

"You're fine," River smiled. "I swear all the *fucking* time." They rattled their fingers on the table. "I'm going to go get us something to drink, and when I come back, let's start fresh, just me and you. How does that sound?"

"Okay."

"What can I get for you?"

"Ummm … I'll have what you are having."

"You sure? I don't even know what I'm having yet. I want you to have something you'll like."

"Yes! I'm feeling spontaneous. But can I have a cup—" she started but cut herself off.

"Yeah?"

"A cup of water."

"Yeah," River looked at her quizzically, "Sure, of course. Be right back."

"Thank you."

River walked toward the counter but realized they didn't know her dairy preferences. They looked back at Janine and saw her with her head down on the table.

"What a weird date," whispered River.

As they walked back to the table, they saw Janine eyeing other people's desserts.

"Why didn't you just say you wanted a dessert?" River asked, putting the drink tray down.

"I'm sorry. Is it your birthday?"

"No, why?" River shook their head. "Janine, please say what you want."

"Okay."

"What can I get you?"

"A cupcake."

"*Thank you*. I will be right back. I wanted to say, too, I love your dress. You look very beautiful."

The next day, a message from River popped up on Janine's phone:

"Hey Janine! I would like to see you again if you are interested. I'm out of town this weekend, but the following weekend works for me. Let me know what you think and if you are free."

Eight days later, River stood at Janine's door.

"How have you been, Janine? It's so good to see you. Can I give you a hug?"

"Of course!" Janine leaned in and opened her arms. *Is this what electricity feels like? They smell good. I feel sick. Say something.* "Wow! You look so handsome. I love your brown sweater."

"Thank you. Yeah, it's strange, but I tend to wear fall clothes almost year-round."

"What? Me too!"

"Really?" River asked while taking off their shoes.

"Yes, I tend to run cold, so it's perfect. I'm warm in the fall, only need a jacket in winter, warm in spring, and can easily adjust layers for summer. I have never met anyone like me."

"You're cute. I'm looking forward to learning what else we have in common. I love your place!"

"Oh, thank you so much. Yeah, I have been here forever. Come on in." *Be cool, Janine.*

"Your kitchen is yellow! Amazing! It's so bright and happy," said River.

"I'm glad you like it. Can I make you some coffee? I have a whole bag from you know who."

"Sure. Holy plant!" River exclaimed as they looked over into the living room. "You weren't kidding. You really do love plants."

"Yes." Janine furrowed her brow and scooped coffee into the machine. "They are my children."

"Well, I'd love to meet them."

"Really?" Janine dropped the bag but caught it mid-fall. She pushed the ON button and rushed over.

"Alright, so, these are my gentle ferns, those are my spider plants, those are my snake plants, and my beloved pothos. And here's anthurium, those rows are my succulents, and my dramatic jade, which is a type of succulent, my baby aloes and agaves, also in the adorable succulent family. These are my striking, happy, aglaonema. Up there are my air plants, and these terrariums have a little of everything. If you have questions, please ask. And this is my little ficus family, and my absolute favorite, dragon hearts. Two walls down—want to go to the other wall?"

"I'm totally lost, Janine. I think I got half of that. I'm sorry. They are all very beautiful."

"We don't need to know a plant's name to know what they need," Janine said.

"Seems like you do need to know their name."

"No, not really. See look, if we go over here, and I pick up my little water pitcher and lean it towards the cactus, you can see him put all of his fingers up. He is saying, 'No, no, go away.' Then I know it's not time. But if we go back to the first fern and listen to her, she is saying, 'I'm so thirsty, help me,' so she gets lots of water. Don't worry, honey, I'm here." Janine poured water into the white pot.

"Wow, I didn't know plants had such distinct voices and passionate personalities."

"Of course!" Janine put the water pitcher down. *Oh no, I*

did what he told me not to. Change the topic. Change the topic. Ummm … ummm … "River, what's your ACE score?"

"I don't know, Janine. I want to hear you, connect with you, and bond. But that doesn't mean we necessarily have to trauma bond. You know? How about we take our coffees and go for a walk. You can tell me more about plants and about your life. I'll answer any questions, too."

Janine nodded. "I'll go get our coffees ready." As she poured, she couldn't help but smile.

What is this feeling?

Five days later, River stood at Janine's door with a small bag in hand.

"Hi, Janine! Congratulations on the job! I'm so excited for you. When do you start? And I love your blue dress by the way. You look beautiful."

"Oh thanks. I start part-time next week. But I can hopefully get more hours if it works out."

"I'm so, so happy for you! And it's at a nursery, which is perfect! You will help both the plants and the people so much! I can't wait to hear everything about it."

"Jack got it for me. Gay guys and their connections, right?" *River truly does seem happy for me.*

"That doesn't matter. You are still going to be the one who is doing the work, and you will still need to prove yourself. Besides, so many opportunities are found because of connections. Sometimes it's not what you know, it's who you know, which is awful, but it's the truth. I actually got my job through a friend of a friend."

"Really?" Janine's mouth dropped.

"Oh yeah." River nodded and sat down on the barstool. They put the bag on the counter and their head in their hands. "I applied for so many jobs, and I always got first interviews and call backs for the second and third rounds. But there just aren't enough of us in higher-up positions yet. So, I ended up sitting across from a handful of corporate asshole white men. Sure, some of them are nice and respectful, but the others, they were looking at me and looking at me, and they couldn't figure out what I was. Forget pronouns! They seemed intimidated, confused, disgusted, and I know they would much rather be looking at someone else. I can't prove it, of course, but I have been around the block enough to know what's up. Especially when I'm more than qualified, have years and years of experience and great references. This town is progressive, but there are pockets of ignorance collecting obscene amounts of money in corner offices. Bigoted gatekeepers. Okay, soapbox over," River sighed. "I don't like to be like that, but it's the truth. The whole point of this is, if you have the knowledge, eagerness, and passion to do the job, use whatever connection you can. We have to look out for each other."

Janine wiped her eyes and took a few steps to sit down next to River. "You will do great at this job, and they are so lucky to have you. Jack and I have your back." Janine sniffled and wiped her eyes again. "I'm so sorry that happened to you, River. It makes me angry. I don't have people looking at me like that. I'm the one who can't figure me out."

"Thank you, but it's okay. I love where I'm at. It all worked out. Here, I got something for you." River pulled a small plant and a single plastic container holding a cupcake out of the bag.

"A new baby dragon heart! Oh, it's beautiful!" Janine exclaimed and lifted the tiny plant in the air. "And thank you so much for my cupcake! Vanilla with chocolate frosting, my favorite! We can have it together." Janine put the plant next to her cupcake and smiled.

"I'm glad you like it. And no, it's all yours. Hey, can I use your bathroom really quick?"

"Oh yeah. It's ummm … just around the corner." Janine pointed.

"Thank you. Be right back. What do you think about coming to see my home next time? Think about it. No pressure at all." River gently tapped the counter as they got up.

Janine nodded. *Oh no, they still haven't seen my room. How bad is it? I think I can check and make it back.* Janine listened for the door closing and got up and ran to her room. She pushed the door open and looked around. *Everything looks clean, but they are going to think I'm crazy.* Janine glanced at her bookshelves. *What can I cover these with? Quick, grab a blanket.*

"Janine?" River stood at the door. "What are you doing? Are you alright?"

"Nothing." Janine dropped the blanket in front of the two, waist-high bookcases.

"I like your room. Were you covering those with a blanket?"

"Oh … ummm …" Janine looked at the bookcases and the blanket on the floor.

"Janine, I totally respect privacy, but I also don't judge. I don't want you to worry about that."

"Jack told me my yearbooks would weird you out. But I can't get rid of them, not yet."

"I see, those are all yearbooks? High school yearbooks? Are you a collector or … ?"

"Yeah. I got them from my brother's friends, or I asked my neighbors. Sometimes I posted ads online. A surprising number of people aren't sentimental. I liked to look at them and study them."

"Study them? Tell me more."

"Yeah." *Here it goes. River is going to think I'm crazy.* "I don't do this anymore, I promise, but I used to. I'll show you." Janine grabbed a random black and red yearbook from 2000. She flipped through it until she landed on the senior photos. "Here,

I'll be … Rachel …" She pointed to a glamorous brunette posing against a tree in a park. "You can be Eric." Her finger landed on a handsome jock whose picture showed him mid-action in a field, smiling as he held a football.

"Oh, Eric, I can't believe we are graduating this year! My parents are throwing me the biggest party. They are so proud! It's so annoying how much they love me. I just got a car, too!"

"Ummmm …" River blinked and fumbled to play along. "Wow … Rachel … I can't wait to go to your party. But first I have to play my very important football game. Will you … watch and drive me home in your new car? Oh, Janine, I don't think I'm good at this game. I'm sorry."

"It's alright." Janine nodded and slammed the book shut. "I was just showing you."

"How does this game end, though? Do we just keep going backward through all these years?"

"Yes, until we are at the very beginning. And then we pretend that we get to be born again and be somebody else."

"I don't want to be anybody else, Janine."

"Why not?"

"I love my life. And I don't want you to be somebody else."

"Why not?"

"I have to tell you something. I don't keep secrets, and I feel bad not telling you," River sighed.

"What?" Janine put the yearbook on top of the bookcase.

"Well, I wanted to get in contact with Jack, and so I had no choice but to message your profile on the dating app. I wanted to ask him about any new plants you might like, or how I could surprise you. He answered my question but went on to tell me how you used to shield him when you were kids. He said you took the brunt of the abuse, and that your parents were drug addicts. Jack said you basically saved his life, and that you are his whole world. He is so protective of you because of how you protected him. He told me that he wouldn't let anything, or anyone, hurt you. I promised him I wouldn't hurt you. Janine, I didn't ask. He just sent this long message. I'm so sorry. I should have told you the moment I walked in here. I was just so excited about your job."

Janine wiped her eyes and looked away. *Breathe. Oh my god, Jack. I'm going to kill you. I can't believe it. Breathe. Ughhh. Thank you. I guess.* "Promise you won't hurt me?"

"I promise. I told Jack I had hoped you wouldn't need the dating app anymore. Do you want to be with me, Janine? I'm in love with you. I'm so sorry for what happened to you." River blinked a tear.

"What?" *What's happening? Breathe, Janine. Is this real?*

"I'll say it again—I'm in love with you."

Janine covered her face with her hands and whispered, "Can you see my heart through my skin?"

"No, but I can feel it. You have a dragon heart," River whispered back and took a step forward to gently place their hand on her heart.

Janine inhaled at the contact.

River paused.

"I want to be with you. Can you please touch me? Can you please kiss me?" Janine murmured.

River leaned in and kissed her collarbone.

"I'm terrified!"

"Oh, Janine. I'll stop. I'm so sorry." River took their hand off of her body and stood back.

"No, no. Please come back. I'm terrified, but I love you. I … I … I haven't done this before." Janine tightened the hands over her face and squeezed her closed eyelids even tighter.

"Thank you for telling me. We won't do anything you don't want to do. We don't have to do anything at all. We can look at yearbooks, walk around, get cupcakes, whatever you want."

"I don't want to do those things. I want to do this."

"Alright, but please talk to me every step of the way, and I will be checking in with you. Want to say cupcake when you want me to stop? You are safe, I'm safe, and we will go very, very slow."

"Please continue." She thought she felt River smile and squealed when their lips met her collarbone again. *Shit! That was so loud.* "I'm sorry," Janine whined.

"I love hearing you." River sighed and slowly kissed her neck.

"River, I should take my dress off. Can you do it?"

"Okay. Yes. How would you like me to do it?"

"Just, you know how. Just lift it up from the skirt. It's one piece and will go right over my head."

"Want to keep your eyes closed?"

"Yes, I will move my arms when I need to," Janine sighed.

River studied her face as they bent down and gently reached below her knees to take the bottom of her blue dress in their hands.

"River!"

"Yes?" They stopped and dropped the fabric completely.

"I used to do something. Something bad to myself."

"Oh, Janine. Do you want to stop and talk?"

"I don't want to talk about it, but I want you to know about it."

"What do you want me to know?"

"I used to cut myself, on my legs. Well, my thighs mostly. My scars won't fade. But that was a long time ago, in my teens and into my twenties. I haven't cut since then. I don't do that anymore. I don't need to. You don't need to be delicate with me. I'm ready."

"Thank you for trusting me and telling me. It takes a lot of courage."

"Ughhh! How did you get so perfect?" Janine whined.

"Thanks … I guess."

"I'm sorry, I just …"

"I know, it's alright. I think you are perfect, too."

"Please don't be scared. Please don't think I'm ugly." She ruffled her skirt. *Please keep going.*

"Not possible."

"River, ask me how this ends again," Janine stammered.

"How does this end, Janine?"

"It ends with you watering my plant!" Janine smiled bravely.

"Are you sure?"

"I love you. Water my plant!"

ACKNOWLEDGMENTS

I want to thank Eric Woodard and Jean LaBauve. Eric, your recognition of my papers in high school was the first time in my life that I felt truly seen and appreciated for my love of writing. Your high praise carried me through those extraordinarily difficult and dark years, and instilled a hope in me to keep going. Jean, you have been an angel to me. Your small notes, smiley faces, and thoughtful reflections moved me greatly. Thank you for your kindness and compassion, your wisdom, and for seeing me.

Thomas Parkin, there aren't enough words. Thank you for your years and years of friendship and closeness, and for understanding, celebrating, and encouraging me and my creativity. Thank you for loving my characters as much as I do. I wouldn't be here today without you.

To my husband, Dana. Thank you for your unwavering support, your love, your patience, and for always being a champion of me and my writing. Thank you for ensuring that there is always space for me to do what I love, and for being on this wild journey with me. We are doing it, and I'm so proud of us. I love you.

To my dad, Andrew Forsyth, thank you for being a lighthouse in my life, and for never giving up on me. Your love saved my life.

To Jenny and Todd Shaphren, thank you for your love, guidance, and for being such incredible supporters of me and Dana. Thank you for hearing us, holding us, and loving us.

To Jon Gosch and Kevin Breen, thank you for bringing *Aerate* to life. Jon, thank you for your commitment to *Aerate*, and for editing this book so it can be the very best possible version of itself. Our conversations about writing have challenged me, inspired me, and warmed my heart. Kevin, thank you for transforming this book into the third dimension, and for your incredible skills and expertise with formatting, graphics and design, and proofreading. Because of your work, *Aerate* has been unearthed!

A big thank you to my early readers, and to Bettie Stiritz and Percy Laird for their willingness to share their thoughts and impressions. Thank you from the bottom of my heart.

Everything I do is in honor and memory of Ethan Forsyth. Ethan, I carry you in my heart forever.